THE COMPLETE
FRENCH
GRAMMAR
COURSE

DYLANE MOREAU

Preface

·····················

The Complete French Grammar Course will help you navigate all the difficulties of French grammar. This book starts by analyzing a simple sentence made of the basic parts of speech: **subject + verb + article + noun**.

Each point will bring one more element to the sentence. Suddenly, you reach an advanced level without even thinking about it! How wonderful is that?

This book is written for French learners of all levels and has been inspired by French learners. It's the third book of the series after **The Complete French Pronunciation Course** and **The Complete French Conjugation Course**. Each book focuses on a specific part of the language and its exceptions, rules, and more. If you are starting French in school, learning by yourself as an adult, or just want to brush up on your French, this is the perfect tool for you. This book and the others are ideal for self-study or as additional practice.

Each chapter looks at a specific part of the sentence, starting with a simple sentence and moving into adjectives, prepositions, adverbs, and conjunctions, with one or more exercises to accompany the grammar points. Each chapter has a final review, and the last chapter has exercises to revise the entire book. The vocabulary used is simple and has been inspired by everyday French. The explanations are easy to understand without advanced grammatical jargon, so you can start learning French from the beginning.

Videos and audios

This books includes **7 chapters**, **200 exercises**, **all the rules explained**, an annex with the conjugation of a few verbs, and more than **45 video lessons** if you need a "teacher approach".

The video lessons can be found at www.theperfectfrench.com/french-grammar-course

To access the recordings, go to www.theperfectfrench.com/french-grammar-course-audios

The Complete French Grammar Course will guide you and help you remember all the how's and why's of French grammar.

A note from the author

Like **The Complete French Conjugation Course**, this book has been shaped by all my amazing students worldwide. All the difficulties I see you encounter daily inspired me. I hope to help you answer all your questions and reach an advanced level in no time!

Thanks again to all my wonderful students,

Dylane Moreau

Table of Content

....

Introduction 1

Glossary 3

Simple Sentence – La Phrase Simple **7**

Simple Sentence – La Phrase Simple **9**

Indefinite Articles – Les Articles Indéfinis **13**

Gender of Nouns – Le Genre des Noms **15**

    Masculine Nouns 16

    Feminine Nouns 18

    Professions & People 19

    Countries 21

    Nouns with Specific Gender 22

    Same Noun, Different Gender, Different Meanings 23

Plural of Nouns – Le Pluriel des Noms **25**

Subject Pronouns – Les Pronoms Sujets **31**

Definite Articles – Les Articles Définis **35**

    When and How to Use the Definite Articles? 35

    Le or L' with a Noun Starting with H? 38

Partitive Articles – Les Articles Partitifs **41**

Present Tense – Le Présent de l'Indicatif **43**

    Uses of the Present Tense 43

    Conjugation of Verbs 43

    Reflexive Verbs 51

    Impersonal Verbs 53

This is / These are – C'est / Ce sont **55**

    When to Use C'est and Ce sont 55

    What About Il est? 57

Demonstrative Adjectives – Les Adjectifs Démonstratifs **59**

Possessive Adjectives – Les Adjectifs Possessifs **63**

Count from 0 to 1000 and More – Compter de 0 à 1000 et Plus **67**

    0 to 100 67

    100 to 1000 69

    Ordinal Numbers 70

Negation – Négation...**73**

    Negation Followed by De...74

    Negation in Speech 75

    Negation with an Infinitive Verb...78

Perfect Tense – Le Passé Composé..**79**

    Uses of the Passé Composé 79

    Conjugation of Verbs 79

    Passé Composé with Avoir 81

    Passé Composé with Être 83

    Passé Composé of Reflexive Verbs..84

    Passé Composé and Negation 85

There is / There are – Il y a..**87**

Review **89**

Prepositions – Les Prépositions **95**

The Preposition à – La Préposition à **97**

    Uses of à 97

    Verbs Followed by the Préposition à..99

    Verbs Followed by à and an Infinitive Verb 101

    Être + Adjective + à 102

    Le seul à...103

    Ordinal Number + à 104

The Preposition de – La Préposition de **105**

    Uses of De...105

    Verbs Followed by the preposition De 107

    Verbs Followed by De and an Infinitive Verb 108

    Être + en train + De + Infinitive...110

    Être + sur le point + De + Infinitive 110

    Être + Adjective + De + Infinitive / Noun...111

    Il est + Adjective + De + Infinitive 112

    C'est + Adjective + De + Infinitive..113

The Preposition En – La Préposition En **115**

    Uses of En..115

    Common Expressions with Être and Ên..116

The Verb To go – Le Verbe Aller **117**

Prepositions of Place – Les Prépositions de Lieu **119**

    Simple Prepositions 119

    Prepositions Followed by De 120

Prepositions of Time – Les Prépositions de Temps **123**

    Simple Prepositions 123

    Jusqu'à – au - 124

    Durant – Pendant – Pour 125

Other Prepositions – Les Autres Prépositions **127**

    Par 127

    Pour 128

    Other Prepositions 129

When not to Use an Article – Quand ne pas Utiliser un Article **133**

Same Verb - Different Prepositions – Même Verbe – Prépositions Différentes **135**

The Recent Past – Le Passé Récent **139**

How to Ask a Question – Comment Poser une Question **141**

    Yes-no Questions 141

    Interrogative Adverbs 144

    Interrogative Pronouns 147

    The Interrogative Adjective – Quel 151

    The Interrogative Pronoun – Lequel 153

    Tag Questions 154

    How to Answer a Negative Question 155

    Review **156**

Adjectives – Les Adjectifs **159**

Adjectives – Les Adjectifs **161**

    Gender and Number 161

    Irregular Adjectives 164

    Adjectives with a Fifth Choice 165

    Tout 166

    Common Adjectives 166

    Adjectives and Brands 168

Where to Place the Adjective – Où Placer l'Adjectif **169**

    Before the Noun 169

    More than One Adjective 171

    Adjectives with 2 Different Meanings 172

The Imperfect Tense – L'Imparfait **173**
    Uses of the Imparfait 173
    Conjugation of Verbs 173

Comparatives & Superlatives – Comparatifs & Superlatifs **179**
    The Comparative 179
    The Superlative 181
    Irregular Comparatives & Superlatives.. 182

Indefinite Adjectives – Les Adjectifs Indéfinis **183**

The Future Tense – Le Futur Simple **185**
    Uses of the Futur Simple 185
    Conjugation of Verbs 185

The Near Future – Le Futur Proche **189**

Review... **191**

Direct & Indirect Pronouns – Les Pronoms Directs & Indirects........................ 193

Direct Object & Direct Object Pronoun – L'Objet Direct et Le Pronom Objet Direct........... **195**
    Direct Object.. 195
    Direct Object Pronouns 196
    Direct Object Pronouns and Negation 197
    Direct Object Pronouns with the Passé Composé 199

Indirect Object & Indirect Object Pronoun – L'Objet Indirect et Le Pronom Objet Indirect **202**
    Indirect Object... 202
    Indirect Object Pronouns 203
    Indirect Object Pronouns and Negation 204

The Pronouns Y & En – Les Pronoms Y & En **207**
    Y to Replace Places... 207
    Y to Replace Things... 207
    The Pronoun En 209

The Pronouns Together – Les Pronoms Ensemble **213**
    In What Order to Use Them?... 213

The Imperative – L'Impératif **216**
    Conjugation of Verbs 216
    The Imperative and Negation 218
    The Imperative and Object Pronouns.. 218

Review... **220**

Other Pronouns – Les Autres Pronoms 223

The emphatic Pronouns – Les Pronoms toniques 225
Uses of the Emphatic Pronouns 225
How to Use Soi 227
Myself, Yourself, Himself, ... .227

The Possessive Pronouns – Les Pronoms Possessifs 229

The Demonstrative Pronouns – Les Pronoms Démonstratifs 231

The Indefinite Demonstrative Pronouns – Les Pronoms Démonstratifs Indéfinis 231

The Indefinite Pronouns – Les Pronoms Indéfinis 237

The Relative Pronouns – Les Pronoms Relatifs 241
Qui 241
Que 242
Dont 244
Où 244
Lequel – Auquel – Duquel 245

Ce qui – Ce que – Ce dont - 247
Ce qui 247
Ce que 248
Ce dont 249
Ce ... quoi 250

The Present Conditional – Le Conditionnel Présent 253
Uses of the Conditionnel 253
Conjugation of Verbs 253

Review 257

Adverbs & Conjunctions – Les Adverbes et les Conjonctions 259

Adverbs – Les Adverbe 260
How to Form French Adverbs? 260
French Adverbs by Type 263

Where to Place the Adverbs – Où Placer les Adverbes 266

Bon vs Bien 270
Bon 270
Bien 271

Encore, Toujours & Déja, Jamais **276**
    Encore & Toujours 276
    Déjà & Jamais 277
The Present Subjunctive – Le Subjonctif Présent **278**
    Uses of the Subjonctif 278
    Conjugation of Verbs 278
Conjunctions – Les Conjonctions **284**
    Coordinating Conjunctions 284
    Subordinating Conjunctions 285
    Other Conjunctions 286

Review **289**

Annexe – 10 Main Verbs and Solutions **303**

Introduction

If you followed "The Complete French Conjugation Course", you can skip this part as you already know everything about it!

If you are new, before jumping into the grammar, here are a few things that you should know to avoid confusion as you navigate through the chapters:

The 3 Groups of Verbs

French verbs belong to 3 different groups:

- Regular verbs ending in **-er** are under the 1st group of verbs.
- Some have spelling changes with some conjugations, but they follow a general pattern most of the time. This group represents the majority of French verbs.
- Verbs ending in **-ir** are under the 2nd group of verbs.
- Verbs of the 3rd group are irregular verbs. They are the most used in the French language.

Tu and Vous

Tu and **Vous** both mean you in English.

In French, **tu** is a singular form and an informal way to address someone. It will be used with your friends, family members, colleagues, etc.

Vous, when used for one person, is formal. It will be used to address people you don't know or people that you must show respect to, like a stranger, your boss, the plumber, etc.

Vous in the plural form is used for more than one person.

Ils and Elles

In French, the distinction is made between masculine plural and feminine plural.
Ils refers to masculine plural, while **elles** refers to feminine plural, which is easy to understand.
However, if you are talking about a mix of men and women, use **ils**. Only use **elles** when the group is women only.

On and Nous

On and **nous** both mean we in French. **Nous** is used more in written French when **on** is used in spoken French.

The Neutral It

Neutral doesn't exist in French; everything is either masculine or feminine. *It* translates to *he* or *she*.

Abbreviations used in this book:

adj.	adjective
ex.	example or exercise
sing.	singular
f.	feminine (noun or subject)
f.pl	feminine plural noun
inf.	infinitive
m.	masculine (noun or subject)
m.pl.	masculine plural noun
p.	page
pl.	plural
qqch	quelque chose
qqn	quelqu'un
sb	somebody
sth	something

Glossary

Adjective
An adjective is a word that modifies a noun and gives additional information.

Adverb
An adverb is a word that helps describe other words, such as nouns, verbs, etc.

Agree
When a past participle or an adjective changes depending on if the subject is feminine, masculine, or plural.

Article
An article is a little word placed in front of a noun such as a, the, some, etc.

Auxiliary verb
The auxiliary verbs in French are **avoir** and **être**. They are used in compound tenses.

Clause
A clause is a group of words, including a verb.

Comparative
A comparative is an adjective or an adverb used to compare two things.

Compound tense
A tense composed by **avoir** or **être** conjugated and followed by the past participle.

Conjugation
A conjugation changes a verb depending on the action that has taken place.

Conjunction
Words that link two words or two sentences together, such as **et, mais,** and more.

Definite article
A definite article is the word the. It has multiple forms in French.

Demonstrative adjective
A demonstrative adjective is used to point out something or someone. It's the equivalent of this/that.

Demonstrative pronoun
A demonstrative pronoun is a demonstrative adjective turned into a pronoun as the subject of the sentence.

Direct object
A direct object is a person or a group of words answering the questions qui or quoi. It usually follows the verb.

Direct object pronoun
A direct object pronoun is a direct object in the form of a pronoun.

Elision
An elision happens when a word is used in its shorter version **j'**, **qu'**, etc.

Emphatic pronoun
Emphatic pronouns emphasize the person, such as us, him, me, etc...

Endings
The endings, or **terminaisons** in French, are the part of conjugation added to the stem to form conjugated verbs.

Feminine
Gender of a person, a noun, or an object.

Gender
Whether a noun or an object is feminine or masculine.

Indefinite adjective
An indefinite adjective is used to talk about people or things, specifying who or what.

Indefinite article
Indefinite articles are the words a and an.

Indefinite pronoun
Indefinite pronouns are similar to indefinite adjectives, but they are simply used as pronouns.

Infinitive
A verb without conjugation.

Impersonal verb
A verb that doesn't refer to a person but the weather, for example.

Indirect object
An indirect object is a person of a group of words answering the questions **à qui, à quoi, de qui, de quoi**. It usually follows the verb.

Indirect object pronoun
An indirect object pronoun is an indirect object in the form of a pronoun.

Inversion
The term used for questions when the verb is placed before the object.

Interrogative adjective
A question word used with a noun to ask what or which?

Interrogative pronoun
A question word used to find the subject, usually who, whom or what.

Irregular verb
A verb not following the rules of regular conjugation. Ex: **Faire**

Number
A number is used to count how many things or people.

Masculine
Gender of a person, a noun, or an object.

Ordinal number
Used to know where something or someone comes in order. Ex: The fifth.

Partitive article
A partitive article is used to talk about something, specifying how much or how many.

Plural
Used to refer to more than one person or object.

Possessive adjective
A possessive adjective is used with a noun to show what belongs to who, her, your, etc.

Possessive pronoun
A possessive pronoun replaces a possessive adjective and a noun and turns into a subject or an object, mine, yours, etc.

Question word
A word used in a question to have specific information. Ex: **Quand**.

Reflexive Pronoun
A pronoun included in a reflexive verb. In "se laver," the reflexive pronoun is se.

Reflexive verb
A reflexive verb is a verb when the action is being reflected on the subject. Ex: **Se changer**, to get changed.

Regular verb
A verb following the rules of regular conjugation. Ex: **Donner**

Relative pronoun
A word such as that or what. They are not always used in English but are in French.

Singular
Used to refer to one person or object.

Subject pronoun
A subject pronoun is used instead of a noun, usually placed before a verb. Ex: **Tu**

Tense
A tense is the conjugation of a verb that indicates if you refer to the future, the present or the past.

Verb
A verb is a word used to describe an action or a state. It gives context to the sentence and the conversation.

Past participle
The past participle is used to form compound tenses such as the **passé composé**, **plus-que-parfait** and more.

CHAPTER 1

Simple Sentence
La Phrase Simple

Simple Sentence – La Phrase Simple

In the first chapter, we are going to focus on simple sentences and learn the different components, the different articles, and simple conjugations.

Simple sentences are built the same way as in English, apart from the almost always present articles before nouns. They consist of a **subject**, a **conjugated verb**, an **article**, and a **noun**.

AUDIO 1.1 ◀)))

Je mange une pomme. *I am eating an apple.*
⇨ **Je** is the subject – I
   mange is the conjugated verb – am eating
   une is the article – an
   pomme is the noun – apple

> **S**ubject + **c**onjugated **v**erb + **a**rticle + **n**oun

A few other ones:

Tu regardes un film. *You are watching a movie.*
⇨ **Tu** is the subject – You
   regardes is the conjugated verb – are watching
   un is the article – a
   film is the noun – movie

Il boit un jus d'orange. *He is drinking orange juice.*
⇨ **Il** is the subject – He
   boit is the conjugated verb – is drinking
   un is the article – an
   jus d'orange is the noun – orange juice

Je suis une femme. *I am a woman.*
⇨ **Je** is the subject – I
   suis is the conjugated verb – am
   une is the article – a
   femme is the noun – woman

Tu es un homme. *You are a man.*
⇨ **Tu** is the subject – You
   es is the conjugated verb – are
   un is the article – a
   homme is the noun – man

Note:
Like in English, some nouns are made of more than one word, such as **jus d'orange** – orange juice.

EX. 1.1 *Trouvez le **sujet** (subject), le **verbe** (verb), l'**article** (the article) et le **nom** (the noun) dans chaque phrase.* AUDIO 1.2 ◀ﻼ)

1. Il regarde un film.

   Sujet : _____

   Verbe : _____

   Article : _____

   Nom : _____

2. Elle chante une chanson.

   Sujet : _____

   Verbe : _____

   Article : _____

   Nom : _____

3. Nous achetons une maison.

   Sujet : _____

   Verbe : _____

   Article : _____

   Nom : _____

4. Je conduis une voiture.

   Sujet : _____

   Verbe : _____

   Article : _____

   Nom : _____

5. Tu entends un oiseau.

   Sujet : _____

   Verbe : _____

   Article : _____

   Nom : _____

6. Ils font un vœu.

   Sujet : _____

   Verbe : _____

   Article : _____

   Nom : _____

EX. 1.2 *Remettez les phrases dans l'ordre.* AUDIO 1.3 ◀ﻼ)

1. rose / offre / une / elle

   _____

2. ai / un / rhume / j'

   _____

3. un / prends / tu / bain

   _____

4. apportons / nous / un / cadeau

   _____

5. vous / un / adoptez / chien

   _____

*Remember to **download the audio** of the lists and to **watch the videos** – see Preface*

6. un / elles / ont / enfant

    _____

7. tu / famille / une / photographies

    _____

8. série télé / regarde / je / une

    _____

9. accent / tu / as / un

    _____

10. achète / sac à main / elle / un

    _____

Notes :

Indefinite Articles – Les Articles Indéfinis

As mentioned in the introduction of this book, French nouns have genders.

They are either **masculine** or **feminine**. They are also influenced by numbers, which we will look into in the next chapter.

But before that, it's important to learn at least one type of article. I like to start with the indefinite articles for a very simple reason: **it's easy to see if a noun is masculine or feminine when preceded by an indefinite article.**

Indefinite articles change depending on if the noun is **masculine, feminine, singular,** or **plural.** We use them to talk about unspecified things or people. They translate to a, an, and some in English.

> We use indefinite articles to talk about **unspecified things** or **people.**

AUDIO 2.1 ◀⁓

	MASCULIN	FÉMININ
SINGULIER	**Un** – a, an **Un garçon** – a boy **Un appartement** – an apartment	**Une** – a, an **Une fille** – a girl **Une orange** – an orange
PLURIEL	**Des** – some / any **Des garçons** – some boys **Des appartements** – some apartment	**Des** – some / any **Des filles** – some girls **Des oranges** – some oranges

Note:
As you can see, the spelling of the article doesn't change if the noun starts with a vowel. When in English, a becomes an, in French, the article stays consistent. However, the pronunciation changes. We add a **liaison** between the article and the noun when the article ends with a consonant (**un** or **des**) and the noun starts with a vowel or a silent h:

Un appartement = un Nappartement – an apartment
Des appartements = des Zappartements – some apartments
Des oranges = des Zoranges – some oranges

Don't forget!
In French, we always have an article before a noun. Only in very rare cases can we omit it. We will come back on this later in this book.

What if there is more than one noun in the same sentence?

If we look again at our reference sentence and we add a pear:

Je mange une pomme et une poire. *I am eating an apple and a pear.*

Always add an article before a noun. There are only a few cases when we don't add an article.

What about des?

Des can be translated to some or any, but sometimes it will simply not be used in English.

J'ai des poux. *I have lice.*

Elle a des examens. *She has some exams.*

Gender of Nouns – Le Genre des Noms

But first, what is a noun?   AUDIO 3.1 🔊

Nouns represent the greatest part of the vocabulary used in a language. How many of them you know will determine your language level. They are used to name everything you see or think about. It can be:

- An object: **un téléphone** – a phone
- A person: **un homme** – a man
- An animal: **un chien** – a dog
- A place: **une ville** – a city
- And more!

In French, every noun is assigned a gender. Unlike in English, articles in front of the noun don't change depending on the person they refer to but depending on the gender of the noun. Another difference is that there is no neutral. Everything is either **masculin** or **féminin**.

> Every noun is either **masculin** or **féminin**.
> Neutral doesn't exist in French.

The obvious gender: AUDIO 3.2 🔊

For some nouns, finding the gender is obvious, especially when we talk about people:

MASCULIN	FÉMININ
Un garçon – a boy	**Une fille** – a girl
Un homme – a man	**Une femme** – a woman
Un oncle – an uncle	**Une tante** – an aunt
Un grand-père – a grandfather	**Une grand-mère** – a grandmother
Un frère – a brother	**Une sœur** – a sister

But not all nouns are as simple as that. For most of them, you will have to know the gender by heart. To make it easier, always study nouns with their articles, especially indefinite articles "**un – une – des**" that we saw before.

Why?

Because "**un – une – des**" don't change if the noun starts with a vowel or a silent h, unlike "**le – la** (the)", which will change to "**l'**" when the noun starts with a vowel or a silent h, making it impossible to know if a noun is **masculin** or **féminin** by looking at the gender since "**l'**" can be **masculin** or **féminin**. More on this in the next point.

Because of this, always study nouns preceded by the articles "**un – une**". It will be easier to remember the gender this way.

The 90% Rule   AUDIO 3.3 ◀))

The 90% rule is what I usually advise students to use when they start learning French.

French nouns can end with almost any letter. But it appears that **90% of the nouns ending with E are feminine.** It's an important rule of thumb.

> **Une plante** – a plant
> **Une fenêtre** – a window
> **Une couverture** – a blanket

Some masculine nouns ending with a letter other than E:

> **Un fauteuil** – an armchair
> **Un tabouret** – a stool
> **Un rideau** – a curtain

Easy, isn't it? Well, not too fast. As I said, I only advise using this rule at the beginning because there is more to it than that. Let's see all the different categories, shall we?

Masculine Nouns

Some specific endings are masculine: AUDIO 3.4 ◀))

ACLE

Un obstacle – an obstacle
Un miracle – a miracle
Un oracle – an oracle

AGE

Un paysage – a landscape
Un coloriage – a coloring
Un âge – an age
*ex: une page – a page
   une plage – a beach

AL

Un cheval – a horse
Un canal – a canal
Un journal – a newspaper

EAU

Un morceau – a piece
Un château – a castle
Un gâteau – a cake
*ex: une eau – a water
   une peau – a skin

EU

Un cheveu – a hair
Un neveu – a nephew
Un bleu – a bruise

ET

Un tabouret – a stool
Un fouet – a whip
Un ticket – a receipt

*Remember to **download the audio** of the lists and to **watch the videos** – see Preface*

IER

Un pommier – an apple tree
Un papier – a paper
Un chantier – a construction site

IN

Un vin – a wine
Un voisin – a neighbor
Un raisin – a grape

ISME

Un organisme – an organization
Un prisme – a prism

MENT

Un changement – a change
Un argument – an argument
Un jugement – a judgment

OIR

Un rasoir – a razor
Un bavoir – a bib
Un devoir – a homework (task)

OU

Un trou – a hole
Un clou – a nail
Un hibou – an owl

ON

Un avion – a plane
Un garçon – a boy
Un crayon – a pencil
***ex: une prison** – a jail

Some topics are masculine only: AUDIO 3.5 ◄ﭠ)

Days of the week are always masculine:

Le lundi – Monday
Le mardi – Tuesday
Le mercredi – Wednesday

Seasons are always masculine:

Un été – summer
Un hiver – winter
Un printemps – spring
Un automne – fall

Languages are always masculine:

Le français – French
Le russe – Russian
Le grecque – Greek

Weights and metrics are always masculine:

Un kilomètre – a kilometer
Un litre – a liter
Un gramme – a gram

English words used in French:

Un week-end – a weekend
Un email – an email
Un parking – a parking lot

Feminine Nouns

Some specific endings are feminine: AUDIO 3.6 ◀))

ADE

Une balade – a walk
Une pommade – an ointment

ALE

Une rivale – a rival
Une chorale – a choir
Une finale – a final

ANCE

Une chance – a chance
Une nuance – a nuance
Une balance – a scale

ENCE

Une exigence – a requirement
Une agence – an agency
Une urgence – an emergency

ETTE

Une vedette – a star
Une sucette – a lollipop
Une vignette – a thumbnail

IE

Une galaxie – a galaxy
Une colonie – a colony
Une calorie – a calorie

IQUE

Une brique – a brick
Une manique – a pot holder
Une crique – a creek

OIRE

Une victoire – a victory
Une poire – a pear
Une foire – a fair

SION

Une télévision – a television
Une révision – a revision
Une passion – a passion

TÉ - TIÉ

Une société – a society
Une moitié – a half
Une amitié – a friendship
*ex: un été – a summer

TION

Une partition – a partition
Une fraction – a fraction
Une lotion – a lotion

URE

Une aventure – an adventure
Une rayure – a stripe
Une voiture – a car

EX. 1.3 *Donnez le genre des noms ci-dessous.* **M** = *masculin* / **F** = *féminin*   AUDIO 3.7 ◀))

1. Rasoir _____
2. Printemps _____
3. Voiture _____
4. Mètre _____

5. Couteau _____
6. Histoire _____
7. Raison _____
8. Chinois _____

*Remember to **download the audio** of the lists and to **watch the videos** – see Preface*

9. Été _____

10. Limonade _____

11. Chapeau _____

12. Devoir _____

13. Couverture _____

14. Télévision _____

15. Chance _____

16. Mercredi _____

17. Skateboard _____

18. Hibou _____

19. Bleu _____

20. Crayon _____

EX. 1.4 *Parmi ces noms, lesquels sont **masculins** et lesquels sont **féminins** ?* **AUDIO 3.8 ◄ϑ)**

tante – fauteuil – ordinateur – t-shirt – eau – souris – film – livre – tasse – orange – bureau – carte – ligne – micro – crème – ananas – baignoire – tiroir – lampe - chaussure

Masculin : _____

_____

_____

Féminin : _____

_____

_____

Professions & People

Nouns where only the article changes:

Some nouns referring to a person and ending with E (or T for one of them) can be either masculine or feminine. The only difference is the article in front.

AUDIO 3.9 ◄ϑ)

MASCULIN	FÉMININ
Un architecte – an architect	**Une architecte** – an architect
Un collègue – a colleague	**Une collègue** – a colleague
Un élève – a student	**Une élève** – a student
Un enfant – a child	**Une enfant** – a child
Un malade – a sick person	**Une malade** – a sick person
Un secrétaire – a secretary	**Une secrétaire** – a secretary
Un touriste – a tourist	**Une touriste** – a tourist
Un guide – a tour guide	**Une guide** – a tour guide

Genders of professions and people:

If a noun ends with a vowel such as I or É, the feminine will take an E:

MASCULIN	FÉMININ
Un apprenti – an apprentice	**Une apprentie** – an apprentice
Un ami – a friend	**Une amie** – a friend
Un associé – an associate	**Une associée** – an associate

Add an E after a consonant:

MASCULIN	FÉMININ
Un avocat – a lawyer	**Une avocate** – a lawyer
Un étudiant – a student	**Une étudiante** – a student
Un client – a customer	**Une cliente** – a customer
Un enseignant – a teacher	**Une enseignante** – a teacher
Un cousin – a cousin	**Une cousine** – a cousin
Un voisin – a neighbor	**Une voisine** – a neighbor
Un Américain – an American	**Une Américaine** – an American
Un Anglais – an English person	**Une Anglaise** – an English person
Un Français – a French person	**Une Française** – a French person

Specific feminine endings for professions and people:

Sometimes adding an E at the end isn't enough; the spelling of the ending will slightly change.

MASCULIN – **ER**	FÉMININ – **ÈRE**
Un infirmier – a nurse	**Une infirmière** – a nurse
Un boulanger – a baker	**Une boulangère** – a baker

MASCULIN – **EUR**	FÉMININ – **EUSE**
Un coiffeur – a hairdresser	**Une coiffeuse** – a hairdresser
Un chanteur – a singer	**Une chanteuse** – a singer

MASCULIN – **IEN**	FÉMININ – **IENNE**
Un pharmacien – a pharmacist	**Une pharmacienne** – a pharmacist
Un diététicien – a dietician	**Une diététicienne** – a dietician

MASCULIN – **ON**	FÉMININ – **ONNE**
Un patron – a boss	**Une patronne** – a boss
Un baron – a baron	**Une baronne** – a baron

MASCULIN – **TEUR**	FÉMININ – **TRICE**
Un acteur – an actor	**Une actrice** – an actress
Un explorateur – an explorer	**Une exploratrice** – an explorer

*Remember to **download the audio** of the lists and to **watch the videos** – see Preface*

MASCULIN – **F**	FÉMININ – **VE**
Un veuf – a widower	**Une veuve** – a widow
MASCULIN – **X**	FÉMININ – **SE**
Un époux – a spouse	**Une épouse** – a spouse

EX. 1.5 *Transformez le nom masculin en nom féminin.*   **AUDIO 3.10** 🔊

1. Un acteur – Une _____
2. Un ami – Une _____
3. Un cousin – Une _____
4. Un coiffeur – Une _____
5. Un veuf – Une _____
6. Un Australien – Une _____
7. Un infirmier – Une _____
8. Un étudiant – Une _____
9. Un Américain – Une _____
10. Un patron – Une _____

Countries

Countries also have genders in French. Most of the time if a country ends with an E, it's a feminine country, besides **Le Mexique**. A few are also always plural.

Nationalities change for men and women, except when the nationality ends with an E.
Let's see a short list of countries and their nationalities.
Le = masculin   **La = féminin**   **Les = pluriel**

AUDIO 3.11 🔊

PAYS	NATIONALITÉ – M	NATIONALITÉ – F
L'Algérie (f) – Algeria	**Un Algérien**	**Une Algérienne**
L'Allemagne (f) – Germany	**Un Allemand**	**Une Allemande**
L'Angleterre (f) – England	**Un Anglais**	**Une Anglaise**
L'Australie (f) – Australia	**Un Australien**	**Une Australienne**
La Belgique – Belgium	**Un Belge**	**Une Belge**
Le Brésil – Brazil	**Un Brésilien**	**Une Brésilienne**
Le Canada – Canada	**Un Canadien**	**Une Canadienne**
La Chine – China	**Un Chinois**	**Une Chinoise**

L'Espagne (f) – Spain	Un Espagnol	Une Espagnole
Les États-Unis – United States	Un Américain	Une Américaine
La France (f) – France	Un Français	Une Française
L'Inde (f) – India	Un Indien	Une Indienne
L'Indonésie (f) – Indonesia	Un Indonésien	Une Indonésienne
L'Irlande (f) – Ireland	Un Irlandais	Une Irlandaise
L'Italie (f) – Italy	Un Italien	Une Italienne
Le Japon – Japan	Un Japonais	Une Japonaise
Le Maroc – Morocco	Un Marocain	Une Marocaine
Le Mexique – Mexico	Un Mexicain	Une Mexicaine
La Nouvelle-Zélande – New Zealand	Un Néo-Zélandais	Une Néo-Zélandaise
Les Pays-Bas – Netherlands	Un Néerlandais	Une Néerlandaise
Les Philippines – Philippines	Un Philippin	Une Philippine
La Pologne – Poland	Un Polonais	Une Polonaise
La Russie – Russia	Un Russe	Une Russe
La Suisse – Switzerland	Un Suisse	Une Suisse
Le Vietnam – Vietnam	Un Vietnamien	Une Vietnamienne

EX. 1.6 *Est-ce que ces pays sont masculins ou féminins ? **M** = masculin / **F** = féminin*   AUDIO 3.12 ◀))

1. Inde _____
2. Algérie _____
3. Danemark _____
4. Japon _____
5. Canada _____

6. Vietnam _____
7. Portugal _____
8. Bénin _____
9. Italie _____
10. France _____

Nouns with Specific Gender

A few nouns referring to people won't change depending on the person. The same gender is used for both men and women.

AUDIO 3.13 ◀))

Un bébé – a baby
Un mannequin – a model
Une connaissance – an acquaintance

Une star – a star
Une vedette – a star
Une victime – a victim

*Remember to **download the audio** of the lists and to **watch the videos** – see Preface*

Same Noun, Different Gender, Different Meanings

A very short list of nouns in French have a different meaning depending on their gender.

AUDIO 3.14 ◀))

Champagne

    Le champagne – champagne
    La Champagne – Champagne (region)

Chèvre

    Le chèvre – goat cheese
    La chèvre – goat

Livre

    Le livre – book
    La livre – pound

Manœuvre

    Le manœuvre – laborer
    La manœuvre – operation

Mort

    Le mort – dead person
    La mort – death

Mémoire

    Le mémoire – memoir
    La mémoire – memory

Mode

    Le mode – method
    La mode – fashion

Moule

    Le moule – mold
    La moule – mussel

Poêle

    Le poêle – stove
    La poêle – pan

Poste

    Le poste – job
    La poste – post office

Rose

    Le rose – pink (color)
    La rose – rose (flower)

Tour

    Le tour – turn
    La tour – tower

Vase

    Le vase – vase
    La vase – mud

Voile

    Le voile – veil
    La voile – sail

Notes :

Plural of Nouns – Le Pluriel des Noms

Now that we have seen the differences between feminine and masculine, let's look at the **plural of nouns**.

Like in English, the noun is plural when there is more than one person, object, place, idea, etc.

Note:
Plural articles **"des – les"** don't show you the gender of the noun. All we know is that the noun is plural.
The ending S and X of plural nouns are always silent unless the ending changes to a different pronunciation.

Nouns ending with E:

Nouns ending with E will simply take an S when plural: **AUDIO 4.1** 🔊

SINGULIER	PLURIEL
Une plante – a plant	**Des plantes** – plants
Un téléphone – a phone	**Des téléphones** – phones
Une lampe – a lamp	**Des lampes** – lamps

EX. 1.7 *Changez ces noms du **singulier** au **pluriel** :*   **AUDIO 4.2** 🔊

1. Une année – Des _____
2. Une personne – Des _____
3. Un insecte – Des _____
4. Une ligne – Des _____
5. Une image – Des _____
6. Une femme – Des _____
7. Une robe – Des _____
8. Un frère – Des _____
9. Un élève – Des _____
10. Une chemise – Des _____

11. Une faute – Des _____
12. Un verre – Des _____
13. Un rhume – Des _____
14. Une ville – Des _____
15. Une peinture – Des _____
16. Une balle – Des _____
17. Une histoire – Des _____
18. Une brosse – Des _____
19. Une jambe – Des _____
20. Une fille – Des _____

Nouns ending with S, X, or Z:

When a noun ends with S, X or Z, the ending doesn't change. AUDIO 4.3 ◀))

SINGULIER

Un bras – an arm
Un corps – a body
Un bus – a bus
Un campus – a campus
Un pays – a country
Un repas – a meal
Une croix – a cross
Un choix – a choice
Un prix – a price
Un époux – a spouse
Un nez – a nose

PLURIEL

Des bras – arms
Des corps – bodies
Des bus – bus
Des campus – campus
Des pays – countries
Des repas – meals
Des croix – crosses
Des choix – choices
Des prix – prices
Des époux – spouses
Des nez – noses

EX. 1.8 *Changez ces noms du singulier au pluriel :* AUDIO 4.4 ◀))

1. Une souris – Des _____

2. Un bus – Des _____

3. Une croix – Des _____

4. Un bras – Des _____

5. Un tapis – Des _____

6. Un gaz – Des _____

7. Une noix – Des _____

8. Un choix – Des _____

9. Un pays – Des _____

10. Un repas – Des _____

Nouns ending with EAU, AU, or EU: AUDIO 4.5 ◀))

When a noun ends with EAU, AU, or EU, the ending will simply take an X = **EAUX – AUX – EUX.**

SINGULIER

Un oiseau – a bird
Un agneau – a lamb
Un bateau – a boat
Un chapeau – a hat
Un château – a castle
Un drapeau – a flag
Un rideau – a curtain

Un noyau – a pit
Un tuyau – a pipe
  *Except: un landau – des landaus – a baby carriage**

Un cheveu – a hair
Un neveu – a nephew
Un feu – a fire
  *Except: un bleu – des bleus – a bruise**

PLURIEL

Des oiseaux – birds
Des agneaux – lambs
Des bateaux – boats
Des chapeaux – hats
Des châteaux – castles
Des drapeaux – flags
Des rideaux – curtains

Des noyaux – pits
Des tuyaux – pipes

Des cheveux – hair
Des neveux – nephews
Des feux – fires

---

*Remember to **download the audio** of the lists and to **watch the videos** – see Preface*

Nouns ending in OU: AUDIO 4.6 ◀»

Nouns ending in **OU** take an **S** but have quite a few exceptions that will take an X.

The ones you will use the most will be the ones taking an X. Remember the rule that works best for you; either the S is the exception, or the X is the exception.

SINGULIER	PLURIEL
Un bisou – a kiss	**Des bisous** – kisses
Un clou – a nail	**Des clous** – nails
Un fou – a lunatic	**Des fous** – lunatics
Un verrou – a lock	**Des verrous** – locks
Un voyou – a thug	**Des voyous** – thugs

Here are the exceptions:

SINGULIER	PLURIEL
Un bijou – a jewel	**Des bijoux** – jewelry
Un caillou – a rock	**Des cailloux** – rocks
Un chou – a cabbage	**Des choux** – cabbages
Un genou – a knee	**Des genoux** – knees
Un hibou – an owl	**Des hiboux** – owls
Un joujou – a toy	**Des joujoux** – toys
Un pou – a louse	**Des poux** – lice

Remember it this way:
Viens mon **chou**, mon **bijou**, mon **joujou**, sur mes **genoux**, et jette des **cailloux** à ce **hibou** plein de **poux**.

EX. 1.9 *Changez ces noms du **singulier** au **pluriel** :* AUDIO 4.7 ◀»

1. Un cheveu – Des _____
2. Un voyou – Des _____
3. Un feu – Des _____
4. Un chou – Des _____
5. Un tuyau – Des _____
6. Un bateau – Des _____
7. Un genou – Des _____
8. Un bleu – Des _____
9. Un pou – Des _____
10. Un caillou – Des _____

Nouns ending in AL: AUDIO 4.8 ◄))

Nouns ending in AL change into AUX; exceptions will only take an S.

SINGULIER	PLURIEL
Un animal – an animal	**Des animaux** – animals
Un bocal – a jar	**Des bocaux** – jars
Un canal – a canal	**Des canaux** – canals
Un cristal – a crystal	**Des cristaux** – crystals
Un hôpital – a hospital	**Des hôpitaux** – hospitals
Un journal – a newspaper	**Des journaux** – newspapers
Un métal – a metal	**Des métaux** – metals
Un rival – a rival	**Des rivaux** – rivals
Un signal – a signal	**Des signaux** – signals
Un total – a total	**Des totaux** – totals
Un tribunal – a tribunal	**Des tribunaux** – tribunals

Except:

Un bal – a ball	**Des bals** – balls
Un carnaval – a carnival	**Des carnavals** – carnivals
Un festival – a festival	**Des festivals** – festivals
Un récital – a recital	**Des récitals** – recitals

Nouns ending in AIL: AUDIO 4.9 ◄))

Nouns ending in **AIL** will only take an **S**, but the exceptions will change for **AUX**.

SINGULIER	PLURIEL
Un chandail – a sweater	**Des chandails** – sweaters
Un détail – a detail	**Des détails** – details
Un épouvantail – a scarecrow	**Des épouvantails** – scarecrows
Un éventail – a fan	**Des éventails** – fans
Un portail – a gate	**Des portails** – gates
Un rail – a track	**Des rails** – tracks

Except:

SINGULIER	PLURIEL
Un bail – a lease	**Des baux** – leases
Un corail – a coral	**Des coraux** – corals
Un émail – an enamel	**Des émaux** – enamels
Un soupirail – a window	**Des soupiraux** – windows
Un travail – a work	**Des travaux** – works
Un vitrail – a stained glass	**Des vitraux** – stained glasses

EX. 1.10 *Changez ces noms du **singulier** au **pluriel** :*   AUDIO 4.10 🔊

1. Un journal – Des _____
2. Un rail – Des _____
3. Un détail – Des _____
4. Un total – Des _____
5. Un vitrail – Des _____

6. Un travail – Des _____
7. Un récital – Des _____
8. Un hôpital – Des _____
9. Un bal – Des _____
10. Un bocal – Des _____

Nouns ending with a consonant: AUDIO 4.11 🔊

Nouns ending with **a consonant** will take an **S** when plural.

SINGULIER - **R**	PLURIEL - **RS**
Une fleur – a flower	**Des fleurs** – flowers
Un cœur – a heart	**Des cœurs** – hearts
SINGULIER - **T**	PLURIEL - **TS**
Un rat – a rat	**Des rats** – rats
Un étudiant – a student	**Des étudiants** – students
SINGULIER - **L**	PLURIEL - **LS**
Un outil – a tool	**Des outils** – tools
Un fusil – a rifle	**Des fusils** – rifles

Nouns ending with ON, AN, IN, UM: AUDIO 4.12 🔊

Nouns ending with a nasal vowel such as **ON, AN, IN, UM**, will take an **S** when plural.

SINGULIER - **ON**	PLURIEL - **ONS**
Un crayon – a pencil	**Des crayons** – pencils
Un pantalon – a pair of trousers	**Des pantalons** – pairs of trousers
SINGULIER - **AN**	PLURIEL - **ANS**
Un ruban – a ribbon	**Des rubans** – ribbons
Un roman – a novel	**Des romans** – novels
SINGULIER - **IN**	PLURIEL - **INS**
Un sapin – a pine tree	**Des sapins** – pine trees
Un brin – a strand	**Des brins** – strands
SINGULIER - **UM**	PLURIEL - **UMS**
Un parfum – a perfume	**Des parfums** – perfumes

Irregular plurals: AUDIO 4.13 ◀⟩

SINGULIER	PLURIEL
Un œil – an eye	**Des yeux** – eyes
Madame – Madam	**Mesdames** – Madams
Monsieur – Sir	**Messieurs** – Sirs

Including 2 irregulars where the spelling stays consistent, but the pronunciation differs:

SINGULIER	PLURIEL
Un œuf – an egg	**Des œufs** – eggs
Un bœuf – a beef	**Des bœufs** – beefs

EX. 1.11 *Changez ces noms du **singulier** au **pluriel** :* AUDIO 4.14 ◀⟩

1. Une sœur – Des _____
2. Un aéroport – Des _____
3. Un œil – Des _____
4. Un coussin – Des _____
5. Un éclair – Des _____
6. Un lit – Des _____
7. Un toit – Des _____
8. Un parfum – Des _____
9. Un chat – Des _____
10. Madame – _____

11. Un citron – Des _____
12. Un écran – Des _____
13. Un escalier – Des _____
14. Un avocat – Des _____
15. Un fil – Des _____
16. Un professeur – Des _____
17. Un écouteur – Des _____
18. Un bain – Des _____
19. Un habit – Des _____
20. Monsieur – _____

Some nous are always plural: AUDIO 4.15 ◀⟩

Les vacances – a vacation
Les mathématiques – math
Les lunettes – glasses
Les gens – people
Les ciseaux – scissors

Les fiançailles – engagement
Les ordures – garbage
Les pâtes – pasta
Les sciences – science
Les épinards – spinach

A few nouns are singular but refer to a group of people:

Le public – the public
La foule – the crowd

La famille – the family
Le groupe – the group

*Remember to **download the audio** of the lists and to **watch the videos** – see Preface*

Subject Pronouns – Les Pronoms Sujets

A **subject pronoun** is a word used to replace the subject of the sentence. Using pronouns helps you to avoid repetition.

> In simple sentences, subject pronouns are followed by a conjugated verb.

AUDIO 5.1 🔊

SINGULIER

Je / J' – I
Tu – you
Il – he / it
Elle – she / it
On – we

PLURIEL

Nous – we
Vous – you
Ils – they
Elles – they

AUDIO 5.2 🔊

JE / J'

Je becomes **j'** when followed by a verb starting with a vowel or a silent h.

Je viens – I am coming / I come
J'arrive – I am arriving / I arrive
J'habite – I am living / I live

TU

In French, YOU has 2 different translations. **tu** and **vous. Tu** is used to address a single person you are familiar with, a family member, a friend, a colleague, etc.

Tu es un génie. *You are a genius.*

IL

Il is only used for a masculine person or a masculine thing.

L'avion atterrit = **Il** atterrit – *The plane is landing = It's landing*
L'homme cuisine = **Il** cuisine – *The man is cooking = He is cooking*

ELLE

Elle is only used for a feminine person or a feminine thing.

La fleur pousse = **Elle** pousse – *The flower is growing = It's growing*
La dame parle = **Elle** parle – *The lady is speaking = She is speaking*

ON

On is often used to replace **nous**. It's a more casual way to speak. **On** is conjugated as if it was a singular subject.

> **On** a un chien. *We have a dog.*

On can also be used as one when talking about general facts.

> **On** peut admirer l'architecture. *One can admire the architecture.*

NOUS

Nous is used to talk about a group of people, including the person speaking.

> **Nous** allons au magasin. *We are going to the store.*
> **Nous** sommes étudiants. *We are students.*

VOUS

Vous has two different uses in French:

The first and most obvious is when you talk to a group of people, no matter the gender. If there is more than one person, you should use **vous**.

The second one is to address one person only. This is the formal use of **vous**. Use **vous** to address people you don't know or must show respect to: a cashier, your teacher, your boss, etc.

> **Vous** mangez une pomme. *You are eating an apple.*
> **Vous** aimez les bananes. *You like bananas.*

ILS

Ils refers to a group of men or masculine things. But it can also refer to a group of mixed genders, as long as there is a man or a masculine thing in the group, we will use **ils**.

Steve and Jeff arrive – They arrive = **Ils** arrivent	M + M = Masculine
Steve, Jeff, and Luna arrive – They arrive = **Ils** arrivent	M + M + F = Masculine

ELLES

Unlike **ils**, **elles** only refers to a group of women or feminine things.

Luna and Maria arrive – They arrive = **Elles** arrivent	F + F

> **Les oranges** sont sur la table. *The oranges are on the table.*
> **Elles** sont sur la table. *They are on the table.*

EX. 1.12 *Traduisez les pronoms sujets en français.* AUDIO 5.3 ◀))

1. They (f) _____
2. We _____
3. I _____
4. You (pl) _____
5. He _____

6. We (casual) _____
7. You (sing) _____
8. She _____
9. They (m) _____

EX. 1.13 *Changez le groupe de mots par **il** ou par **elle**.* AUDIO 5.4 ◀))

1. Une tasse _____
2. Un rêve _____
3. Une femme _____
4. Un gâteau _____
5. Une histoire _____
6. Un sandwich _____
7. Une glace _____
8. Un détail _____
9. Une ampoule _____
10. Un voisin _____

11. Une dent _____
12. Un café _____
13. Une nièce _____
14. Un documentaire _____
15. Un roman _____
16. Un bol _____
17. Une chemise _____
18. Un crayon _____
19. Une couverture _____
20. Un jardin _____

EX. 1.14 *Changez le groupe de mots par **ils** ou par **elles**.* AUDIO 5.5 ◀))

1. Des voyages _____
2. Des tortues _____
3. Des claviers _____
4. Des voitures _____
5. Des chaussures _____
6. Des champs _____
7. Des vacances _____
8. Des devoirs _____
9. Des idées _____
10. Des pièces _____

11. Des réunions _____
12. Des festivals _____
13. Des invitations _____
14. Des rues _____
15. Des enfants _____
16. Des fleuves _____
17. Des dentistes _____
18. Des entreprises _____
19. Des époques _____
20. Des affaires _____

EX. 1.15 *Récrivez les phrases avec le bon pronom sujet.* AUDIO 5.6 ◄))

1. **Les singes** aiment voler des bananes.

   _____

2. **L'herbe** est brûlée par le soleil.

   _____

3. **L'étagère** n'est pas droite.

   _____

4. **Paul et Myles** sont en retard.

   _____

5. **Charlotte et les enfants** vont au parc.

   _____

6. **Le chat** dort sur le lit.

   _____

7. **Les restaurants** sont fermés aujourd'hui.

   _____

8. **Cette fille** s'intéresse à la peinture.

   _____

9. **Les avocats** discutent du meurtre.

   _____

10. **La lettre** est arrivée ce matin.

    _____

*Remember to **download the audio** of the lists and to **watch the videos** – see Preface*

Definite Articles – Les Articles Définis

Definite articles change depending on if the noun is **masculine, feminine, singular**, or **plural**. We use them to talk about specific things or people. They translate to the in English.

> We use definite articles to talk about **specific things** or **people**.

When a word starts with a vowel or a silent h, **LE** and **LA** become **L'**. As stated before, when the article is L', it's impossible to know if the noun is masculine or feminine. Make sure to use "un – une" as much as possible when studying vocabulary.

AUDIO 6.1 🔊

	MASCULIN	FÉMININ
SINGULIER	**Le / L'** – the **Le café** – the coffee **L'homme** – the man	**La / L'** – the **La limonade** – the lemonade **L'eau** – the water
PLURIEL	**Les** – the **Les cafés** – the coffees **Les hommes** – the men	**Les** – the **Les limonades** – the lemonades **Les eaux** – the waters

Note:
When preceded by **à** or **de**, the articles change to **au, aux, du, des, à la, de la**, etc. We will look at this in more detail in the next point.

When and How to Use the Definite Articles?

AUDIO 6.2 🔊

French definite articles are used mostly the same way as in English:

L'école ouvre à 10 heures. *The school opens at 10 a.m.*
Elle connait **la** chanson par cœur. *She knows the song by heart.*

But sometimes they are used differently:

With abstracts nouns for things that you can't touch:

Les sciences sont importantes. *Science is important.*
Le temps passe vite. *Time flies. (Literally, time passes fast)*
Il a **le** cancer. *He has cancer.*

With concrete nouns (things that you can touch) when talking about them in a general way:

Le café contient de la caféine. *Coffee contains caffeine.*
Les chiens aiment jouer à la balle. *Dogs love to play with balls.*
Les voitures sont un luxe. *Cars are a luxury.*

With languages and school subjects:

Les maths sont difficiles. *Math is difficult.*
On étudie **le** français. *We study French.*
La biologie est sa matière préférée. *Biology is her favorite subject.*

With continents, countries, and provinces:

L'Afrique est un continent. *Africa is a continent.*
La France est magnifique. *France is beautiful.*
La Colombie Britannique est une province du Canada. *British Columbia is a province of Canada.*

With quantities and prices:

50 kilomètres à **l'**heure. *50 kilometers per hour.*
2 euros **la** pièce. *2 euros each.*
Cela coûte 10 dollars **le** kilo. *It costs 10 dollars per kilo.*

With dates and days of the week. For days of the week, we only use it to talk about something that you do regularly:

Je travaille depuis **le** 5 mai. *I have been working since May 5th.*
Noël est **le** 25 décembre. *Christmas is on December 25th.*
Elle travaille **le** lundi. *She works on Mondays.*

With parts of the body:

Je me brosse **les** cheveux. *I am brushing my hair.*
Il s'est cassé **le** bras. *He broke his arm.*
J'ai mal à **la** gorge. *I have a sore throat.*

---

*Remember to **download the audio** of the lists and to **watch the videos** – see Preface*

EX. 1.16 *Ajoutez le bon article défini devant le nom.*   AUDIO 6.3 🔊

1. _____ anglais
2. _____ photo
3. _____ mère
4. _____ pays
5. _____ sang
6. _____ bague
7. _____ téléphone
8. _____ travail
9. _____ erreur
10. _____ soupe

11. _____ carotte
12. _____ moulin
13. _____ donnée
14. _____ tâche
15. _____ guerre
16. _____ contenu
17. _____ muscle
18. _____ bruit
19. _____ table
20. _____ chance

EX. 1.17 *Ajoutez le bon article défini dans la phrase.*   AUDIO 6.4 🔊

1. _____ incendie a brûlé la maison.
2. _____ Nouvelle-Zélande est divisée en deux îles.
3. Il a réservé _____ chambres d'hôtel.
4. Mes parents font _____ cuisine à tour de rôle.
5. Tu as reçu _____ carte que je t'ai envoyée ?
6. J'ai imprimé _____ document pour toi.
7. _____ plafond est peint en blanc.
8. Ils rénovent _____ cuisine cet été.
9. _____ courses sont livrées tous les samedis.
10. _____ soupe est trop chaude.

Parler le?   AUDIO 6.5 🔊

After the verb **parler**, and before a language, we can either have **le** or **nothing**:

Je parle l'anglais. *I speak English.*
Tu parles espagnol. *You speak Spanish.*

Le or L' with a Noun Starting with H?

French has two types of h, **silent h** and **aspirated h**.

When h is **silent** it acts as a **vowel**. Therefore, we use **L'**. Make sure to study the gender of the noun because it's impossible to tell with the article L'. Here are the most frequent nouns starting with a silent h:

L'habit (m) – the piece of clothing
L'habitude (f) – the habit
L'haleine (f) – the breath
L'harmonica (m) – the harmonica
L'hélicoptère (m) – the helicopter
L'herbe (f) – the grass
L'héroïne (f) – the heroine
L'heure (f) – the hour / the time
L'hexagone (m) – the hexagon
L'hippopotame (m) – the hippopotamus
L'hirondelle (f) – the swallow
L'histoire (f) – the story
L'hiver (m) – the winter
L'homicide (m) – the homicide
L'hommage (m) – the tribute

L'honneur (m) – the honor
L'hôpital (m) – the hospital
L'horaire (m) – the schedule
L'horizon (m) – the horizon
L'horloge (f) – the clock
L'horoscope (m) – the horoscope
L'horreur (f) – the horror
L'hospitalité (f) – the hospitality
L'hôte (m) – the host
L'huile (f) – the oil
L'huître (f) – the oyster
L'humain (m) – the human
L'humeur (f) – the humor
L'hygiène (f) – the hygiene

When h is **aspirated**, it acts as a **consonant**. In this case, we use **Le** or **La**. Here are the most frequent nouns starting with an aspirated h:

La hache – the axe
La haie – the edge
La haine – the hate
Le hall – the hall
Le hamac – the hammock
Le hamburger – the hamburger
Le hamster – the hamster
La hanche – the hip
Le handicap – the handicap
Le hangar – the hangar
Le hareng – the herring
Le haricot – the bean
La harpe – the harp

Le hasard – the luck
La hâte – the haste
La hauteur – the height
Le hérisson – the hedgehog
Le héros – the hero
Le hibou – the owl
Le hobby – the hobby
La Hollande – Holland
Le homard – the lobster
La Hongrie – Hungary
La honte – the shame
Le hoquet – the hiccup
La housse – the cover

EX. 1.18 *Ajoutez **le** / **la** ou **l'** devant ces noms commençant par **h**.*   AUDIO 6.7 ◄))

1. _____ hauteur

2. _____ habit

3. _____ haricot

4. _____ histoire

5. _____ horreur

6. _____ héros

7. _____ hérisson

8. _____ Hongrie

9. _____ herbe

10. _____ humain

11. _____ hiver

12. _____ horloge

13. _____ haine

14. _____ hôpital

15. _____ haleine

16. _____ hasard

17. _____ hélicoptère

18. _____ horoscope

19. _____ hibou

20. _____ hamburger

Notes :

Partitive Articles – Les Articles Partitifs

Partitive articles are used to talk about something without specifying the quantity. We just understand that the quantity is unknown. They can be mistaken by the preposition "de", which we will see later in this chapter.

> We use partitive articles to talk about something without specifying the quantity.

When a word starts with a vowel or a silent h, LE and LA become L'. As stated before, when the article is L', it's impossible to know if the noun is masculine or feminine. Make sure to use "un – une" as much as possible when studying vocabulary.

AUDIO 7.1 🔊

MASCULIN – SINGULIER

Du (de + le) + masculine noun starting with a consonant

Du fromage – some cheese
Du pain – some bread

FÉMININ – SINGULIER

De la + feminine noun starting with a consonant

De la farine – some flour
De la limonade – some lemonade

MASCULIN & FÉMININ – SINGULIER

De l' + masculine or feminine noun starting with a vowel or a silent h

De l'eau (f) – some water
De l'ail (m) – some garlic

PLURIEL

Des (de + les) + masculine or feminine noun but plural

Des cerises (f) – some cherries
Des chiens (m) – some dogs

Note:
Partitive articles become **de** in negative sentences.

EX. 1.19 *Ajoutez **du, de la, de l'** ou **des** devant ces noms.* AUDIO 7.2 ◀))

1. _____ chance
2. _____ temps
3. _____ bébés
4. _____ énergie
5. _____ lait
6. _____ abricot
7. _____ cannelle
8. _____ courage
9. _____ chips
10. _____ vie

11. _____ crème
12. _____ espoir
13. _____ yaourt
14. _____ vacances
15. _____ shampoing
16. _____ graisse
17. _____ vin
18. _____ inspiration
19. _____ nouvelles
20. _____ pain

EX. 1.20 *Remettez les phrases dans l'ordre ajoutez l'article partitif.* AUDIO 7.3 ◀))

1. chocolat / les / mangent / Belges

   _____

2. je / salade / fromage / et / vais prendre

   _____

3. a fait pousser / elle / tomates

   _____

4. tous les dimanches / mangeons / pâtisseries / nous

   _____

5. glace / achète / j'

   _____

6. frites / prendra / avec / hamburger / elle / le

   _____

7. il / chiens / chats / a / et

   _____

8. a volé / elle / argent

   _____

9. ma / ajoute / grand-mère / farine

   _____

10. mange / mari / tous les matins / mon / flocons d'avoine

   _____

*Remember to **download the audio** of the lists and to **watch the videos** – see Preface*

Present Tense – Le Présent de l'Indicatif

> This is a review of "*The Complete French Conjugation Course*". This review includes only a part of what is taught in the conjugation course.

The **present tense**, called **présent de l'indicatif**, replaces 3 tenses in English: the **simple present** (he reads) – the **continuous present** (he's reading) – the **emphatic present** (he does read) = **Il lit**

Uses of the Present Tense

We use the present tense to talk about: AUDIO 7.1.1 ◀))

- Things that are happening now:
  Je regarde la télévision. *I am watching TV.*

- Things that happen all the time or some habits that you have:
  Il dort toujours avec la fenêtre ouverte. *He always sleeps with the window open.*

- General actions or states:
  Il est deux heures. *It's two o'clock.*

- To express the future in some cases:
  On part demain matin. *We are leaving tomorrow morning.*

- With the word "depuis":
  Elle travaille ici depuis février. *She has been working here since February.*

Conjugation of Verbs

Verbs of the 1st group – regular verbs ending in -er: AUDIO 7.1.2 ◀))

The stem of the verb **regarder** is **regard-**
To conjugate the verb, add the endings to the stem: **-e -es -e -ons -ez -ent**

Regarder To look / To watch

Je **regarde**
Tu **regardes**
Il-Elle-On **regarde**
Nous **regardons**
Vous **regardez**
Ils-Elles **regardent**

Irregular verbs from the 1st group:

Verbs ending in **-cer** and **-ger**:

Annoncer To announce	J'annonce	Nous annonçons
Ranger To tidy	Je range	Nous rangeons

Verbs ending in **-yer**:

Essayer To try	J'essaye / J'essaie	Nous essayons
Employer To employ	J'emploie	Nous employons
Appuyer To push	J'appuie	Nous appuyons

Verbs ending in **-eler** and **-eter**, double consonants:

Appeler To call	J'appelle	Nous appelons
Jeter To throw	Je jette	Nous jetons

Verbs ending in **-eler**, **-ener**, **-eser**, **-eter**, **-ever**, **E** becomes **É**:

Geler To freeze	Je gèle	Nous gelons
Mener To lead	Je mène	Nous menons
Peser To weigh	Je pèse	Nous pesons
Acheter To buy	J'achète	Nous achetons
Enlever To remove	J'enlève	Nous enlevons

Verbs ending in **-éder**, **-érer**, **-éter**, **-ébrer**, **É** becomes **È**:

Posséder To possess	Je possède	Nous possédons
Espérer To hope	J'espère	Nous espérons
Répéter To repeat	Je répète	Nous répétons
Célébrer To celebrate	Je célèbre	Nous célébrons

Verbs of the 2nd group – regular verbs ending in -ir: AUDIO 7.1.3 ◄))

The stem of the verb **finir** is **fin-**
To conjugate the verb, add the endings to the stem: **-is -is -it -issons -issez -issent**

Finir To finish
___
Je **finis**
Tu **finis**
Il-Elle-On **finit**
Nous **finissons**
Vous **finissez**
Ils-Elles **finissent**
___

Verbs of the 3rd group – regular verbs ending in -re: AUDIO **7.1.4** 🔊

The stem of the verb **attendre** is **attend-**
To conjugate the verb, add the endings to the stem: **-s -s -/ -ons -ez -ent**

Attendre To wait

J'**attends**
Tu **attends**
Il-Elle-On **attend**
Nous **attendons**
Vous **attendez**
Ils-Elles **attendent**

EX. 1.21 *Conjuguez les verbes suivants au **présent de l'indicatif**.*   AUDIO **7.1.5** 🔊

1. **Chanter**

   Je _____

   Tu _____

   On _____

   Nous _____

   Vous _____

   Elles _____

2. **Grandir**

   Je _____

   Tu _____

   Il _____

   Nous _____

   Vous _____

   Ils _____

3. **Pendre**

   Je _____

   Tu _____

   Il _____

   Nous _____

   Vous _____

   Ils _____

EX. 1.22 *Choisissez un verbe dans la liste et conjuguez-le au **présent de l'indicatif.*** AUDIO **7.1.6** ◄⑴

défendre – bâtir – porter – finir – vendre – chercher – marcher – entendre – vérifier – vieillir

1. Le banquier _____ le numéro de compte.
2. L'entreprise _____ de construire la maison.
3. J' _____ les oiseaux depuis le balcon.
4. Nous _____ dans la forêt.
5. L'enfant _____ son jouet.
6. Les hommes _____ moins vite que les femmes.
7. L'armée _____ le pays.
8. Le magasin _____ du vin d'Espagne.
9. L'entreprise _____ les appartements.
10. Il _____ des lunettes.

Être and avoir: AUDIO **7.1.7** ◄⑴

Être and **avoir** are the 2 most used verbs in French. They are both verbs and auxiliaries and can also be impersonal verbs.

Être To be
Je **suis**
Tu **es**
Il-Elle-On **est**
Nous **sommes**
Vous **êtes**
Ils-Elles **sont**

Être is used in a lot of everyday expressions, here are a few:

Être + nationality – To be + nationality
Être **de** – To be from
Être à (qqn) – To belong to sb
Être à l'heure – To be on time
Être au courant – To be informed

Être d'accord – To agree
Être de bonne humeur – To be in a good mood
Être de retour – To be back

*Remember to **download the audio** of the lists and to **watch the videos** – see Preface*

Être en avance – To be early
Être en retard – To be late
Être en colère – To be angry
Être en train de (+ inf) – To be in the process of (doing)
Être en bonne santé – To be healthy

Être sur le point de (+ inf) – To be about to (do)

Avoir To have
_____

J'**ai**
Tu **as**
Il-Elle-On **a**
Nous **avons**
Vous **avez**
Ils-Elles **ont**

Expressions and idioms with Avoir:

Expressions with **avoir** are even more important than the ones with **être**. And this is where it gets confusing for a lot of French learners. In English, the most common expressions are used with the verb To be (être). The same expressions are used with the verb **avoir** (to have) in French.

Avoir _____ ans – To be _____ years old
Avoir faim – To be hungry
Avoir soif – To be thirsty
Avoir chaud – To be hot
Avoir froid – To be cold
Avoir sommeil – To be sleepy
Avoir peur (de) – To be afraid (of)
Avoir de la chance – To be lucky

Avoir besoin de – To need
Avoir envie de – To want

Avoir mal à + body part – To have a(n) _____ ache
Avoir mal à la tête – To have a headache
Avoir mal à la gorge – To have a sore throat
Avoir mal au ventre – To have a stomachache
Avoir mal au dos – To have back pain
Avoir mal aux dents – To have a toothache

Aller - the only fully irregular verb ending in ER:

Aller To go

Je **vais**	Nous **allons**
Tu **vas**	Vous **allez**
Il-Elle-On **va**	Ils-Elles **vont**

The common question "How are you?" in French uses the verb **aller**, not être:

Comment allez-vous ? How are you? (form.)
Comment ça va ? How are you? (inform.)

Other expressions and idioms with Aller:

Aller + inf. – To be going + inf.
Aller à pied – To go on foot
Aller à quelqu'un – To suit someone
Allez (filler word) – Come on – Let's go

Note:
Aller is of course used as a verb of motion, To go somewhere. It's always followed by a preposition.
Aller is also used to form the tense called "futur proche".

The verb **faire** is probably the most versatile verb in French. We use it to talk about what we do, make, play, bake, to talk about the weather, and more! **Faire** is also used as an impersonal verb.

Faire To do – To make

Je **fais**	Nous **faisons**
Tu **fais**	Vous **faites**
Il-Elle-On **fait**	Ils-Elles **font**

Expressions with faire – À la maison:

Faire la cuisine – To cook
Faire la lessive – To do the laundry
Faire la vaisselle – To do the dishes
Faire son lit – To make one's bed

Expressions with faire – À l'école:

Faire ses devoirs – To do one's homework
Faire des progrès – To make progress
Faire des fautes – To make mistakes

Expressions with faire – Du sport:

Faire du sport – To exercise
Faire du vélo – To bike
Faire du football – To play soccer
Faire de la natation – To swim

Expressions with faire – Les loisirs:

Faire une promenade – To take a walk
Faire un voyage – To take a trip

Expressions with faire – Le temps:

Quel temps fait-il ? – How is the weather?
Il fait chaud – It's warm
Il fait froid – It's cold
Il fait bon – It's nice

Other expressions with faire:

Faire attention – To pay attention
Faire la tête – To be moody
Faire peur (à) – To scare
Faire croire – To make someone believe

EX. 1.23 *Choisissez entre **être – avoir – aller - faire** et conjuguez le verbe au **présent de l'indicatif.***

AUDIO 7.1.8 ◄))

1. Il _____ chaud aujourd'hui.

2. Elle _____ peur des araignées.

3. Ce sac _____ à ma mère.

4. Mes parents _____ au magasin à pied.

5. J' _____ de la chance.

6. La tempête _____ de retour.

7. Tu _____ des progrès à l'école ?

8. Nous _____ du vélo ensemble.

9. Comment ça _____ ?

10. L'ouvrier _____ mal au dos.

Other irregular verbs to know in all tenses: AUDIO **7.1.9** ◄))

Prendre To take

Je **prends**	Nous **prenons**
Tu **prends**	Vous **prenez**
Il-Elle-On **prend**	Ils-Elles **prennent**

Mettre To put

Je **mets**	Nous **mettons**
Tu **mets**	Vous **mettez**
Il-Elle-On **met**	Ils-Elles **mettent**

Venir To come

Je **viens**	Nous **venons**
Tu **viens**	Vous **venez**
Il-Elle-On **vient**	Ils-Elles **viennent**

Venir is also used to form the tense called "passé récent".
Venir de + location translates to To be from.

Tenir To hold

Je **tiens**	Nous **tenons**
Tu **tiens**	Vous **tenez**
Il-Elle-On **tient**	Ils-Elles **tiennent**

Savoir To know

Je **sais**	Nous **savons**
Tu **sais**	Vous **savez**
Il-Elle-On **sait**	Ils-Elles **savent**

Connaître To know

Je **connais**	Nous **connaissons**
Tu **connais**	Vous **connaissez**
Il-Elle-On **connaît**	Ils-Elles **connaissent**

Devoir To owe – Must – To have to

Je **dois**	Nous **devons**
Tu **dois**	Vous **devez**
Il-Elle-On **doit**	Ils-Elles **doivent**

Vouloir To want

Je **veux**	Nous **voulons**
Tu **veux**	Vous **voulez**
Il-Elle-On **veut**	Ils-Elles **veulent**

Pouvoir To be able to - Can

Je **peux**	Nous **pouvons**
Tu **peux**	Vous **pouvez**
Il-Elle-On **peut**	Ils-Elles **peuvent**

Dire To tell - To say

Je **dis**	Nous **disons**
Tu **dis**	Vous **dites**
Il-Elle-On **dit**	Ils-Elles **disent**

Reflexive Verbs

What is a reflexive verb?

In French, a reflexive verb is a verb indicating that the action is being performed on the subject. There are similar verbs in English, such as *To burn oneself.*

In French, a reflexive verb is called **un verbe pronominal** because it includes a pronoun (pronom).
The infinitive of a reflexive verb is always **SE + verb**, or **S' + verb** if the verb starts with a vowel or a silent h.
SE is the pronoun.

AUDIO 7.1.10 🔊

Differences between a regular and a reflexive verb:

Regular verb: **Préparer** – To prepare
Il **prépare** le projet. *He is preparing the project.*

Reflexive verb: **Se préparer** – To get ready
Il **se prépare** dans la salle de bain. *He is getting ready in the bathroom.*

Many reflexive verbs and regular verbs have the same meaning, just that the reflexive verb refers to the person or the object.

How to conjugate a reflexive verb?

When a reflexive verb is conjugated, it's a mix of a simple verb with a direct object pronoun. The direct object pronoun is always placed before the verb.

The verb part is conjugated the same way as the regular verb, with the pronoun before the verb.

The pronouns are:

Subject pronouns	Reflexive pronouns
Je	**me - m'**
Tu	**te - t'**
Il-Elle-On	**se - s'**
Nous	**nous**
Vous	**vous**
Ils-Elles	**se - s'**

Remember that in the case of **me**, **te** and **se**, if the verb starts with a vowel or a silent h, we use **m'**, **t'**, **s'**.

And here is the complete conjugation:

Regular verb:

Préparer To prepare

Je **prépare**	Nous **préparons**
Tu **prépares**	Vous **préparez**
Il-Elle-On **prépare**	Ils-Elles **préparent**

Reflexive verb:

Se préparer To get ready

Je **me prépare**	Nous **nous préparons**
Tu **te prépares**	Vous **vous préparez**
Il-Elle-On **se prépare**	Ils-Elles **se préparent**

A few reflexive verbs:

S'adresser (à) To address / To speak to
S'amuser To have fun
S'énerver To get mad
S'épiler To pluck / To wax
S'excuser To apologize
S'habiller To get dressed
Se brosser To brush (one's hair/one's teeth)
Se cacher To hide
Se coucher To go to bed / To lay down
Se demander To wonder

Se doucher To take a shower
Se laver To wash oneself
Se maquiller To put on makeup
Se passer To happen
Se perdre To get lost
Se raser To shave
Se rendre compte (de) To realize
Se réveiller To wake up
Se terminer To come to an end

EX. 1.24 *Conjuguez le verbe entre parenthèses au **présent**. N'oubliez pas de changer le pronom réflexif.*   **AUDIO 7.1.11** ◀))

1. **(Se raser)** Les hommes _____ le matin.
2. **(Se demander)** Je _____ si je vais y arriver.
3. **(S'habiller)** Le garçon _____ tout seul.
4. **(Se passer)** Il _____ beaucoup de choses.
5. **(S'excuser)** Je _____ , je suis en retard.

Impersonal Verbs

Impersonal verbs are verbs that refer to no one or things in particular. As impersonal verbs, they are all conjugated with **il**, sometimes **ça – c'**.

Impersonal verbs are used to talk about general subjects: **AUDIO 7.1.12** ◀))

Avoir	**Il y a** There is - There are
Être + time	**Il est deux heures** It's two o'clock
Être	**Il est temps** It's time
Être	**C'est** It is - This is
Faire	**Il fait jour** It's daylight
Falloir	**Il faut** We have to
Manquer	**Il manque** There is - There are … missing
Paraître	**Il paraît que** It appears that
Rester	**Il reste** There is … left
Sembler	**Il semble** It seems that
Valoir	**Il vaut mieux** It's better that

Impersonal verbs used to talk about the weather:

Faire	**Il fait chaud** It's hot
Geler	**Il gèle** It's freezing
Neiger	**Il neige** It's snowing
Pleuvoir	**Il pleut** It's raining

Il **fait** bon. *It's nice out.*
Il **manque** de l'argent. *Some money is missing*
Il **est** l'heure. *It's time.*

EX. 1.25 *Choisissez un verbe impersonnel dans la liste ci-dessus et conjuguez-le au* **présent**.

1. Il _____ du café.

2. Il _____ 3 degrés.

3. Il y _____ des chats sur la table.

4. Il _____ midi.

5. Il _____ temps de partir.

6. Il _____ se décider.

7. Il _____ depuis ce matin.

8. Il _____ , les routes sont glissantes.

9. Il _____ trop de personnes ici.

10. Il _____ triste.

This is / These are – C'est / Ce sont

C'est and ce sont are part of what we call **demonstrative pronouns** simply because we use them to demonstrate what we are talking about.

In the last chapter, we saw the conjugation of the verb **être**:　　AUDIO 8.1 ◀))

Être To be

Je **suis**
Tu **es**
Il-Elle-On **est**
Nous **sommes**
Vous **êtes**
Ils-Elles **sont**

Only **est** and **sont** will be needed in this lesson, and we will pair them with the pronoun **ce** (the demonstrative pronoun). **Ce** will be contracted to **c'** when followed by **est** = **c' + est**.

SINGULIER
C'est – This is / It is / That is

PLURIEL
Ce sont – These are / They are

C'est and **ce sont** agree in number but never in gender.

When to Use C'est and Ce sont

For persons, things, nationalities and jobs:

C'est / ce sont + article + masculine noun
C'est / ce sont + article + feminine noun
*With or without an adjective

For opinions:

C'est + adjective / adverb

AUDIO 8.2 ◀))

For persons, things, nationalities, and jobs:

Masculin:

C'est un homme. *This is a man.*
Ce sont des garçons. *They are boys.*

C'est un téléphone. *This is a phone.*
Ce sont des crayons. *These are pencils.*

C'est un Français. *It's a French man.*
Ce sont des Anglais. *They are English.*

C'est un avocat. *This is a lawyer.*
Ce sont des ingénieurs. *They are engineers.*

Féminin:

C'est une dame. *This is a lady.*
Ce sont des filles. *They are girls.*

C'est une tasse. *This is a cup.*
Ce sont des fourchettes. *These are forks.*

C'est une Canadienne. *It's a Canadian.*
Ce sont des Canadiennes. *They are Canadians.*

C'est une avocate. *This is a lawyer.*
Ce sont des avocates. *They are lawyers.*

For opinions:

When **c'est** is followed by an adjective or an adverb, we never use **ce sont**. It always stays singular. As a result, the adjective is only masculine and singular as well.

C'est beau. *It's beautiful.*
C'est bien. *It's good.*
C'est bon. *It's good.*
C'est super. *It's great.*
C'est magnifique. *It's wonderful.*
C'est incroyable. *It's incredible.*

Note:

Ce sont is quite formal. In spoken French, you will more often find **c'est,** even before a plural:

Ce sont les fêtes ! *It's the Holiday season!*
C'est les fêtes ! *It's the Holiday season!*

Ce sont mes affaires. *This is my stuff.*
C'est mes affaires. *This is my stuff.*

EX. 1.26 *Choisissez entre **c'est** and **ce sont**.* AUDIO 8.3 ◄))

1. _____ des ours.
2. _____ bon.
3. _____ un verre d'eau.
4. _____ une pilote.
5. _____ génial.

6. _____ des Américaines.

7. _____ Pâques.

8. _____ super.

9. _____ des bonnes idées.

10. _____ un Canadien.

What About Il est?

Il est is the masculine of **elle est** = she is. But it can also be used as an impersonal verb. **Il est** is always masculine.

Il est is used for:

Descriptions:
Il est + adjective / adverb

Time:
Il est + time

For jobs:
Il est + masculine noun

For nationalities:
Il est + adjective

AUDIO 8.4 ◄))

For descriptions:

Il est beau. *It's beautiful / He is beautiful.*
Il est tard. *It's late.*
Il est ennuyant. *He is annoying.*

For time:

Il est deux heures. *It's two o'clock.*
Il est minuit. *It's midnight.*
Il est 21 heures. *It's 9 p.m.*

For jobs:

When talking about jobs with **il est**, we don't add an article between il est and the occupation.

Il est caissier. *He is a cashier.*
Il est fermier. *He is a farmer.*
Il est vendeur. *He is a salesman.*

For nationalities:

When talking about nationalities with **il est**, just like jobs, we don't add an article between il est and nationality.

Il est suisse. *He is Swiss.*
Il est mexicain. *He is Mexican.*
Il est islandais. *He is Icelandic.*

EX. 1.27 *Traduisez les phrases suivantes et choisissez entre **c'est, ce sont** and **il est**.* AUDIO 8.5 ◀))

1. He is beautiful.

   _____

2. He is French.

   _____

3. It's great!

   _____

4. This is a book.

   _____

5. It's noon.

   _____

6. This is a surprise.

   _____

7. This is a teacher.

   _____

8. This is lady.

   _____

9. These are pictures.

   _____

10. It's late.

   _____

Demonstrative Adjectives
Les Adjectifs Démonstratifs

Demonstrative adjectives are the equivalent of this / that and these / those in English. They are placed before a noun or sometimes before an adjective.

2 simple rules to remember:

1. French demonstrative adjectives agree with what they describe and therefore take the gender and number of the following noun.
2. When a masculine, singular noun or adjective starts with a vowel or a silent h, we will use **cet** and not **ce**.

AUDIO 9.1 🔊

	MASCULIN	FÉMININ
SINGULIER	**Ce** – this / that	**Cette** – this / that
	Ce bonbon – this candy **Ce film** – this movie	**Cette couverture** – this blanket **Cette voiture** – this car
	Cet – this / that Only when followed by a masculine noun or an adjective starting with a vowel or a silent h.	
	Cet homme – this man **Cet arbre** – this tree	
PLURIEL	**Ces** – these / those	**Ces** – these / those
	Ces bonbons – these candies **Ces verres** – these glasses	**Ces chaussettes** – these socks **Ces bouteilles** – these bottles

AUDIO 9.2 🔊

Ce = masculine singular:

J'adore **ce** chanteur. *I love this singer.*
Ce film est triste. *This movie is sad.*
Ce manteau est trop petit. *This coat is too small.*

Cet = masculine singular, vowel or silent h:

Cet arbre est vieux. *This tree is old.*
Cet hôtel est somptueux. *This hotel is sumptuous.*
Cet arrosoir a un trou. *This watering can has a hole.*

---

*Remember to **download the audio** of the lists and to **watch the videos** – see Preface*

Cette = feminine singular:

Cette plante a besoin d'eau. *This plant needs water.*
Cette voiture est à vendre. *This car is for sale.*
Comment s'appelle **cette** ville ? *What is the name of this city?*

Ces = masculine plural:

Ces coussins sont confortables. *These pillows are comfortable.*
Ces avocats sont délicieux. *These avocados are delicious.*
Ces employés travaillent dur. *These employees work hard.*

Ces = feminine plural:

Ces chaises sont cassées. *These chairs are broken.*
Ces couleurs sont belles. *These colors are beautiful.*
Ces livraisons arrivent bientôt. *These deliveries arrive soon.*

EX. 1.28 *Ajoutez ce, cet, cette ou ces devant ces noms.* AUDIO 9.3 ◀))

1. _____ magasin		11. _____ laine
2. _____ coiffeuse		12. _____ chemin
3. _____ avion		13. _____ singe
4. _____ olives		14. _____ exemple
5. _____ vue		15. _____ aéroport
6. _____ haricots		16. _____ idée
7. _____ héros		17. _____ buisson
8. _____ enquêteurs		18. _____ table
9. _____ lit		19. _____ envies
10. _____ fauteuils		20. _____ maison

EX. 1.29 *Remettez les phrases suivantes dans le bon ordre et ajoutez l'adjectif démonstratif approprié **ce – cet – cette – ces**.* AUDIO 9.4 ◀))

1. acteur / aime / j'

   _____

2. veulent / parents / télévision / mes

   _____

3. oncle / est / homme / mon

   _____

4. est / bureau / bureau / son

_____

5. couleur de / tableau / magnifique / la / est

_____

6. des / a / elle / semaines / idée / depuis

_____

7. est cassé / ordinateur

_____

8. leur / font / nid / oiseaux

_____

9. est perdu / petit chat

_____

10. sombre / est / forêt

_____

Notes :

Possessive Adjectives
Les Adjectifs Possessifs

French **possessive adjectives** give us a lot of information about the noun they modify, especially whom or what the noun belongs to. They are used the same way as in English. They can be followed by a noun or an adjective.

3 simple rules to remember:

1. French possessive adjectives agree in gender and number with the noun.
2. Remember that we have formal speech and informal speech. **Tu** and **vous** in French both mean you.
3. When a feminine noun starts with a vowel or a silent h, we use "**mon – ton – son** ".

AUDIO 10.1 🔊	Masc. Sing Or fem. starting with a vowel or a silent h	Fem. Sing.	Plural
My	**mon**	**ma**	**mes**
Your	**ton**	**ta**	**tes**
His / Her / Its	**son**	**sa**	**ses**
Our	**notre**	**notre**	**nos**
Your	**votre**	**votre**	**vos**
Their	**leur**	**leur**	**leurs**

Remember them:

To remember them, use the conjugation of a reflexive verb. Reflexive pronouns are very similar.

AUDIO 10.2 🔊	Masc. Sing Or fem. starting with a vowel or a silent h	Fem. Sing.	Plural
Je **me** prépare	**m**on	**m**a	**m**es
Tu **te** prépares	**t**on	**t**a	**t**es
Il / Elle / On **se** prépare	**s**on	**s**a	**s**es
Nous **n**ous préparons	**n**otre	**n**otre	**n**os
Vous **v**ous préparez	**v**otre	**v**otre	**v**os
Ils **se** préparent	**l**eur	**l**eur	**l**eurs

It doesn't work that well for **leur,** but at least we have a common "e".

MON – MA – MES = My

Mon verre est cassé. *My glass is broken.*
Ma tasse est cassée. *My cup is broken.*
Mon ordinateur est cassé. *My computer is broken.*
Mes écouteurs sont cassés. *My headphones are broken.*

TON – TA – TES = Your

Ton frère est là. *Your brother is here.*
Ta sœur est là. *Your sister is here.*
Ton amie (f) est là. *Your friend is here.*
Tes cousins sont là. *Your cousins are here.*

SON – SA – SES = His, Her, Its

Son pull est sale. *His / Her sweater is dirty.*
Sa veste est sale. *His / Her jacket is dirty.*
Son imperméable est sale. *His / Her rain jacket is dirty.*
Ses chaussures sont sales. *His / Her shoes are dirty.*

NOTRE – NOTRE – NOS = Our

Notre rendez-vous est annulé. *Our appointment is canceled.*
Notre inscription est annulée. *Our subscription is canceled.*
Nos rendez-vous sont annulés. *Our appointments are canceled.*

VOTRE – VOTRE – VOS = Your

Votre père est vieux. *Your father is old.*
Votre mère est vieille. *Your mother is old.*
Vos parents sont vieux. *Your parents are old.*

LEUR – LEUR – LEURS = Their

Leur tableau est vendu. *Their painting is sold.*
Leur voiture est vendue. *Their car is sold.*
Leurs appartements sont vendus. *Their apartments are sold.*

EX. 1.30 *Ajoutez le bon **adjectif possessif** dans la phrase.*   **AUDIO 10.4** 🔊

1. Elle répète _____ (her) discours.

2. C'est _____ (their) maison.

3. _____ (their) commandes sont arrivées.

4. C'est _____ (your - inf) tour.

---

5. _____ (my) idée n'est pas bonne.

6. Le chat est dans _____ (your - inf) chambre.

7. Ce sont _____ (his) livres.

8. _____ (my) camion ne démarre plus.

9. _____ (your - form) valises sont ici.

10. Est-ce que tu as vu _____ (their) portefeuilles ?

Notes :

Count from 0 to 1000, and More
Compter de 0 à 1000, et Plus

0 to 100   AUDIO 11.1 🔊

0	**Zéro**	Zero		27	**Vingt-sept**	Twenty-seven
				28	**Vingt-huit**	Twenty-eight
1	**Un / Une**	One		29	**Vingt-neuf**	Twenty-nine
2	**Deux**	Two				
3	**Trois**	Three		30	**Trente**	Thirty
4	**Quatre**	Four		31	**Trente et un**	Thirty-one
5	**Cinq**	Five		32	**Trente-deux**	Thirty-two
6	**Six**	Six		33	**Trente-trois**	Thirty-three
7	**Sept**	Seven		34	**Trente-quatre**	Thirty-four
8	**Huit**	Eight		35	**Trente-cinq**	Thirty-five
9	**Neuf**	Nine		36	**Trente-six**	Thirty-six
10	**Dix**	Ten		37	**Trente-sept**	Thirty-seven
11	**Onze**	Eleven		38	**Trente-huit**	Thirty-eight
12	**Douze**	Twelve		39	**Trente-neuf**	Thirty-nine
13	**Treize**	Thirteen				
14	**Quatorze**	Fourteen		40	**Quarante**	Forty
15	**Quinze**	Fifteen		41	**Quarante et un**	Forty-one
16	**Seize**	Sixteen		42	**Quarante-deux**	Forty-two
17	**Dix-sept**	Seventeen		43	**Quarante-trois**	Forty-three
18	**Dix-huit**	Eighteen		44	**Quarante-quatre**	Forty-four
19	**Dix-neuf**	Nineteen		45	**Quarante-cinq**	Forty-five
				46	**Quarante-six**	Forty-six
20	**Vingt**	Twenty		47	**Quarante-sept**	Forty-seven
30	**Trente**	Thirty		48	**Quarante-huit**	Forty-eight
40	**Quarante**	Forty		49	**Quarante-neuf**	Forty-nine
50	**Cinquante**	Fifty				
60	**Soixante**	Sixty		50	**Cinquante**	Fifty
70	**Soixante-dix**	Seventy		51	**Cinquante et un**	Fifty-one
80	**Quatre-vingts**	Eighty		52	**Cinquante-deux**	Fifty-two
90	**Quatre-vingt-dix**	Ninety		53	**Cinquante-trois**	Fifty-three
100	**Cent**	One hundred		54	**Cinquante-quatre**	Fifty-four
				55	**Cinquante-cinq**	Fifty-five
20	**Vingt**	Twenty		56	**Cinquante-six**	Fifty-six
21	**Vingt et un**	Twenty-one		57	**Cinquante-sept**	Fifty-seven
22	**Vingt-deux**	Twenty-two		58	**Cinquante-huit**	Fifty-eight
23	**Vingt-trois**	Twenty-three		59	**Cinquante-neuf**	Fifty-nine
24	**Vingt-quatre**	Twenty-four				
25	**Vingt-cinq**	Twenty-five		60	**Soixante**	Sixty
26	**Vingt-six**	Twenty-six		61	**Soixante et un**	Sixty-one

62	**Soixante-deux**	Sixty-two	82	**Quatre-vingt-deux**	Eighty-two
63	**Soixante-trois**	Sixty-three	83	**Quatre-vingt-trois**	Eighty-three
64	**Soixante-quatre**	Sixty-four	84	**Quatre-vingt-quatre**	Eighty-four
65	**Soixante-cinq**	Sixty-five	85	**Quatre-vingt-cinq**	Eighty-five
66	**Soixante-six**	Sixty-six	86	**Quatre-vingt-six**	Eighty-six
67	**Soixante-sept**	Sixty-seven	87	**Quatre-vingt-sept**	Eighty-seven
68	**Soixante-huit**	Sixty-eight	88	**Quatre-vingt-huit**	Eighty-eight
69	**Soixante-neuf**	Sixty-nine	89	**Quatre-vingt-neuf**	Eighty-nine
70	**Soixante-dix**	Seventy	90	**Quatre-vingt-dix**	Ninety
71	**Soixante et onze**	Seventy-one	91	**Quatre-vingt-onze**	Ninety-one
72	**Soixante-douze**	Seventy-two	92	**Quatre-vingt-douze**	Ninety-two
73	**Soixante-treize**	Seventy-three	93	**Quatre-vingt-treize**	Ninety-three
74	**Soixante-quatorze**	Seventy-four	94	**Quatre-vingt-quatorze**	Ninety-four
75	**Soixante-quinze**	Seventy-five	95	**Quatre-vingt-quinze**	Ninety-five
76	**Soixante-seize**	Seventy-six	96	**Quatre-vingt-seize**	Ninety-six
77	**Soixante-dix-sept**	Seventy-seven	97	**Quatre-vingt-dix-sept**	Ninety-sept
78	**Soixante-dix-huit**	Seventy-eight	98	**Quatre-vingt-dix-huit**	Ninety-eight
79	**Soixante-dix-neuf**	Seventy-nine	99	**Quatre-vingt-dix-neuf**	Ninety-nine
80	**Quatre-vingts**	Eighty	100	**Cent**	One hundred
81	**Quatre-vingt-un**	Eighty-one			

EX. 1.31 *Écrivez les nombres en **lettres**.*   AUDIO 11.2 ◄))

1. 53 _____

2. 95 _____

3. 100 _____

4. 19 _____

5. 26 _____

6. 88 _____

7. 49 _____

8. 72 _____

9. 34 _____

10. 57 _____

*Remember to **download the audio** of the lists and to **watch the videos** – see Preface*

100 to 1000

In French, **cent** takes an **-s** when plural, but only when it stand alone. **Cent** doesn't take an **-s** when followed by another number.

AUDIO 11.3 ◄ঙ)

100	**Cent**	One hundred
200	**Deux cents**	Two hundred
300	**Trois cents**	Three hundred
400	**Quatre cents**	Four hundred
500	**Cinq cents**	Five hundred
600	**Six cents**	Six hundred
700	**Sept cents**	Seven hundred
800	**Huit cents**	Eight hundred
900	**Neuf cents**	Nine hundred
1000	**Mille**	One thousand

283	**Deux cent quatre-vingt-trois**	Two hundred and eighty-three
502	**Cinq cent deux**	Five hundred and two
627	**Six cent vingt-sept**	Six hundred and twenty-seven
891	**Huit cent quatre-vingt-onze**	Eight hundred and ninety-one

Mille never takes an **-s** when plural.

AUDIO 11.4 ◄)

2000	**Deux mille**	Two thousand
5000	**Cinq mille**	Five thousand
7000	**Sept mille**	Seven thousand

1005	**Mille cinq**	One thousand and five
1638	**Mille six cent trente-huit**	One thousand six hundred and thirty-eight
6582	**Six mille cinq cent quarte-vingt-deux**	Six thousand five hundred and eighty-two

Add **an -s** to **million** and **milliard** when plural.

Un million	A million
Deux millions	Two million

Un milliard	A billion
Deux milliards	Two billion

EX. 1.32 *Écrivez les nombres en chiffres.* AUDIO 11.5 ◀))

1. Mille huit cent quarante-neuf _____

2. Deux cent quatre-vingt-neuf _____

3. Sept cent soixante-dix-sept _____

4. Cent vingt et un _____

5. Mille cinq cent vingt-quatre _____

Ordinal Numbers

To form **ordinal numbers** in French. We simply add **-ième** to the number. Only **un** is fully irregular.
If the number ends with **-e,** such as **quatre**, remove the **e** before adding **-ième**.
In **neuf**, the **-f** becomes **-v.**
Cinq takes a **-u** before adding **-ième**.

AUDIO 11.6 ◀))

1er	**Premier / Première**	First	20e	**Vingtième**	Twentieth
2e	**Deuxième**	Second	30e	**Trentième**	Thirtieth
3e	**Troisième**	Third	40e	**Quarantième**	Fortieth
4e	**Quatrième**	Fourth	50e	**Cinquantième**	Fiftieth
5e	**Cinquième**	Fifth	60e	**Soixantième**	Sixtieth
6e	**Sixième**	Sixth	70e	**Soixante-dixième**	Seventieth
7e	**Septième**	Seventh	80e	**Quatre-vingtième**	Eightieth
8e	**Huitième**	Eighth	90e	**Quatre-vingt-dixième**	Ninetieth
9e	**Neuvième**	Ninth	100e	**Centième**	One hundredth
10e	**Dixième**	Tenth			

EX. 1.33 *Écrivez les nombres ordinaux en lettres.* AUDIO 11.7 ◀))

1. 57e _____

2. 12e _____

3. 63e _____

4. 75e _____

5. 100e _____

Notes :

Negation – Négation

The regular **negation** is made of two words in French : **ne** and **pas**.
Each word goes around the verb and after the pronoun / subject => **ne** + verb + **pas**

Here is a list of all the negations used in French nowadays.   **AUDIO 12.1** ◄))

Ne ... pas	Not
Ne ... plus	No longer / Not anymore / None left
Ne ... jamais	Never
Ne ... que	Only
Ne ... rien	Nothing
Ne ... pas encore	Not yet
Ne ... personne	Nobody / No one / Anyone
Ne ... ni ... ni	Neither ... nor

Ne will be shortened to **n'** when the verb starts with a vowel or a silent h.

ne / n' + verb + pas

Let's look at each negation in a few sentences: **AUDIO 12.2** ◄))

Ne ... pas   Not
Je **ne** mange **pas.** *I am not eating / I don't eat.*

Ne ... plus   No longer / Not anymore / None left
Tu **ne** fumes **plus.** *You no longer smoke.*

Ne ... jamais   Never
Il **ne** boit **jamais.** *He never drinks.*

Ne ... que   Only
Elle **n'**aime **que** le chocolat. *She only likes chocolate.*

Ne ... rien   Nothing
On **ne** donne **rien.** *We give nothing.*

Ne ... pas encore   Not yet
Elle **n'**est **pas encore** là. *She is not there yet.*

Ne ... personne   Nobody / No one / Anyone
Vous **n'**aimez **personne.** *You like nobody.*

Ne ... ni ... ni   Neither ... nor
Il **n'**a **ni** argent **ni** travail. *He has neither money nor a job.*

EX. 1.34 *Changez ces phrases en phrases **négatives**.* AUDIO 12.4 🔊

1. J'aime cette couleur.

   _____

2. Mon père fume encore tous les jours. (no longer)

   _____

3. Il est déjà arrivé. (not yet)

   _____

4. C'est le bon moment pour lui dire.

   _____

5. Tu travailles encore au même endroit ? (no longer)

   _____

6. Le bus est toujours en retard. (never)

   _____

7. Elle mange seulement bio. (only)

   _____

8. Tu habites près de chez moi.

   _____

9. Il dit quelque chose. (nothing)

   _____

10. C'est ma faute.

   _____

Negation Followed by De

When **pas** is followed by an indefinite article « **un – une – des** » or a partitive article « **du – de la – de l' – des** », any of these articles become **de**. **De** becomes **d'** before a word starting with a vowel or a silent h.

> **ne + verb + pas + de / d'**

AUDIO 12.4 🔊

Tu manges un ananas. *You are eating a pineapple.*
Tu **ne** manges **pas** d'ananas. *You are not eating a pineapple.*
Je veux du pain. *I want some bread.*

Je **ne** veux **pas** de pain. *I don't want bread.*
Il a des enfants. *He has children.*
Il **n'**a **pas** d'enfants. *He has no children.*

However, the definite articles « **le – la – l' – les** » don't change. When the negation includes **c'est**, the article doesn't change either, or after **être**.

Elle lit le livre. *She is reading the book.*
Il **ne** lit **pas** le livre. *She is not reading the book.*

C'est un chat. *It's a cat.*
Ce **n'**est **pas** un chat. *It's not a cat.*

Tu es une danseuse. *You are a dancer.*
Tu **n'**es **pas** une danseuse. *You are not a dancer.*

EX. 1.35 *Ajoutez le correct article dans la phrase :* **un – une – des – de – d'**   AUDIO 12.5 ◀))

1. Elle n'a pas _____ argent.

2. Ce n'est pas _____ bonne idée.

3. Elle ne veut plus _____ viande.

4. Nous faisons _____ basketball.

5. Tu ne portes jamais _____ écharpe.

6. Il ne joue plus _____ guitare.

7. Vous ne faites pas _____ études.

8. Elle ne prend pas _____ rendez-vous pour le moment.

9. Tu ne poses jamais _____ questions.

10. Ce n'est pas _____ bon jeu.

Negation in Speech

In everyday speech, **ne** tends to be left out and only **pas** is pronounced. But it's important to keep **ne** and **pas** when writing and in formal speech.

AUDIO 12.6 ◀))

ne + verb + **pas**	Not

J'ai un rendez-vous. *I have an appointment.*

Writing: Je **n'**ai **pas** de rendez-vous. *I don't have an appointment.*
Informal speech: J'ai **pas** de rendez-vous. *I don't have an appointment.*

ne + verb + **plus**   Not anymore / None left

Tu as de l'eau. *You have water.*

Writing: Tu **n'**as **plus** d'eau. *You don't have water anymore.*
Informal speech: T'as **plus** d'eau. *You don't have water anymore.*

ne + verb + **que**   Only

Il a une chance. *He has a chance.*

Writing: Il **n'**a **qu'**une chance. *He has only one chance.*
Informal speech: Il a **qu'**une chance. *He has only one chance.*

ne + verb + **jamais**   Never

Elle dort tard. *She sleeps late.*

Writing: Elle **ne** dort **jamais** tard. *She never sleeps late.*
Informal speech: Elle dort **jamais** tard. *She never sleeps late.*

ne + verb + **rien**   Nothing

On veut tout faire. *We want to do everything.*

Writing: On **ne** veut **rien** faire. *We want to do nothing.*
Informal speech: On veut **rien** faire. *We want to do nothing.*

ne + verb + **pas encore**   Not yet

Je suis arrivé. *I arrived.*

Writing: Je **ne** suis **pas encore** arrivé. *I didn't arrive yet.*
Informal speech: Je suis **pas encore** arrivé. *I didn't arrive yet.*

ne + verb + **personne**   No one / Nobody / Anyone

Ils parlent à tout le monde. *They talk to everyone.*

Writing: Ils **ne** parlent à **personne.** *They talk to no one.*
Informal speech: Ils parlent à **personne.** *They talk to no one.*

EX. 1.36 *Changez ces phrases en **phrases négatives** avec la négation donnée sur la première ligne. Sur la deuxième ligne, ajoutez la **négation parlée.*** AUDIO 12.7 ◄))

1. Il mange toujours du pain à midi.

   Ne ... jamais : _____

   Speech : _____

2. Ses blagues sont drôles !

   Ne ... pas : _____

   Speech : _____

3. Les acheteurs ont le choix entre plusieurs maisons.

   Ne ... plus : _____

   Speech : _____

4. Est-ce que tu peux te taire ?

   Ne ... pas : _____

   Speech : _____

5. Vous avez entendu ce bruit.

   Ne ... pas : _____

   Speech : _____

6. Il reste du fromage du repas d'hier.

   Ne ... plus : _____

   Speech : _____

7. Je suis impressionnée par ce spectacle.

   Ne ... pas du tout : _____

   Speech : _____

8. Elle veut tout apprendre !

   Ne ... rien : _____

   Speech : _____

9. Nous préparons les cadeaux pour Noël.

   Ne ... pas encore : _____

   Speech : _____

10. Elle étudie tous les jours.

    Ne ... pas : _____

    Speech : _____

Negation with an Infinitive Verb

When a verb is infinitive, the negation stays together and is placed before the verb.

> **ne pas / ne plus / ne jamais / ne rien + infinitive verb**

AUDIO 12.8 ◀»

ne pas + infinitive verb   Not

> Il me demande de <u>venir</u> maintenant. *He is asking me to come now.*
> Infinitive verb = **venir**
> Il me demande de **ne pas** <u>venir</u> maintenant. *He is asking me not to come now.*

We also find this construction in orders and instructions:

> Merci de **ne pas** <u>fumer</u>. *Thanks for not smoking.*
> **Ne pas** <u>déranger</u>. *Don't disturb.*
> **Ne pas** <u>marcher</u> sur la pelouse. *Don't walk on the grass.*

EX. 1.37 *Traduisez les ordres et instructions suivants.*   AUDIO 12.9 ◀»

1. Thanks for not closing the door.

   _____

2. Don't open.

   _____

3. Don't touch.

   _____

4. Thanks for not smoking.

   _____

5. Thanks for not using your phone.

   _____

Perfect Tense – Le Passé Composé

> This is a review of "*The Complete French Conjugation Course*". The review includes only a part of what is taught in the conjugation course.

The perfect tense, called the **passé composé**, doesn't follow a specific translation in English, but it has similarities with: the **present perfect** (he has forgotten) – the **simple past** (he forgot) – the **emphatic past** (he did forget) = **Il a oublié**.

Uses of the Passé Composé

We use the passé composé to: AUDIO 12.1.1 ◀))

- Describe something that took place in the past at a very specific moment:

    L'avion a atterri à 11 heures. *The plane landed at 11 p.m.*

- Describe an event that usually only happens once:

    Mon fils est né il y a quelques jours. *My son was born a few days ago.*

- Talk about something that happened repeatedly:

    J'ai appelé 3 fois mais personne n'a répondu. *I called 3 times but nobody answered.*

- Indicate something that happened suddenly:

    Soudainement, il a eu une crise cardiaque. *Suddenly, he had a heart attack.*

Conjugation of Verbs

The **passé composé** is a compound tense made of the verb **avoir** or the verb **être** conjugated in the present tense + the **past participle** of the verb.
Most of the verbs conjugated in the passé composé are built with the auxiliary avoir conjugated in the present tense.

AUDIO 12.1.2 ◀))

Avoir To have

J'**ai**
Tu **as**
Il-Elle-On **a**
Nous **avons**
Vous **avez**
Ils-Elles **ont**

A specific list of verbs, as well as **reflexive verbs**, are built with the auxiliary **être** conjugated in the present tense.

Être To be

Je **suis**
Tu **es**
Il-Elle-On **est**
Nous **sommes**
Vous **êtes**
Ils-Elles **sont**

Before seeing the different verbs conjugated in passé composé, we need to see the different **past participles**. The past participles change depending on the group of verbs and if the verb is irregular or not.

AUDIO 12.1.3 ◀))

Verbs ending in -er, regular and irregular: er = é

Regarder To look, To watch	regardé
Annoncer To announce	annoncé
Appeler To call	appelé
Peser To weigh	pesé

Verbs ending in -ir from the 2nd group: ir = i

Finir To finish	fini
Grandir To grow up	grandi

Verbs ending in -re from the 3rd group: re = u

Attendre To wait	attendu
Pendre To hang	pendu

Irregular verbs with irregular past participles:

Accueillir	**accueilli**	Éteindre	**éteint**
Avoir	**eu**	Être	**été**
Battre	**battu**	Faire	**fait**
Boire	**bu**	Falloir	**fallu**
Conduire	**conduit**	Fuir	**fui**
Connaître	**connu**	Joindre	**joint**
Courir	**couru**	Lire	**lu**
Craindre	**craint**	Mentir	**menti**
Croire	**cru**	Mettre	**mis**
Devoir	**dû**	Mourir	**mort**
Dire	**dit**	Naître	**né**
Dormir	**dormi**	Offrir	**offert**
Écrire	**écrit**	Ouvrir	**ouvert**

Pleuvoir	**plu**	Suivre	**suivi**
Pouvoir	**pu**	Tenir	**tenu**
Prendre	**pris**	Vaincre	**vaincu**
Recevoir	**reçu**	Valoir	**valu**
Rire	**ri**	Venir	**venu**
Savoir	**su**	Vivre	**vécu**
Servir	**servi**	Vouloir	**voulu**

EX. 1.38 *Donnez le participe passé des verbes suivants.*   AUDIO 12.1.4 ◄))

1. Connaître _____
2. Regarder _____
3. Être _____
4. Choisir _____
5. Dormir _____
6. Avoir _____
7. Prendre _____
8. Mettre _____
9. Aller _____
10. Pouvoir _____

11. Entendre _____
12. Lancer _____
13. Voir _____
14. Faire _____
15. Dire _____
16. Grandir _____
17. Tenir _____
18. Savoir _____
19. Parler _____
20. Apprendre _____

Passé Composé with Avoir

Subject + avoir + past participle

The past participle of verbs conjugated with **avoir** doesn't agree in gender and number with the subject.

AUDIO 12.1.5 ◄))

1st group	**2nd group**	**3rd group**
Regarder To watch / To look	**Finir** To finish	**Attendre** To wait
J'ai regardé	J'ai fini	J'ai attendu
Tu **as regardé**	Tu **as fini**	Tu **as attendu**
Il-Elle-On **a regardé**	Il-Elle-On **a fini**	Il-Elle-On **a attendu**
Nous **avons regardé**	Nous **avons fini**	Nous **avons attendu**
Vous **avez regardé**	Vous **avez fini**	Vous **avez attendu**
Ils-Elles **ont regardé**	Ils-Elles **ont fini**	Ils-Elles **ont attendu**

EX. 1.39 *Conjuguez les verbes suivants au passé composé.*   AUDIO 12.1.6 🔊

1. **Jouer**

   J'_____

   Tu _____

   On _____

   Nous _____

   Vous _____

   Elles _____

2. **Faire**

   J'_____

   Tu _____

   Il _____

   Nous _____

   Vous _____

   Ils _____

3. **Conduire**

   J'_____

   Tu _____

   Elle _____

   Nous _____

   Vous _____

   Elles _____

Passé Composé with Être

The **passé composé** of verbs conjugated with **être** combines the conjugation of the verb **être** in the **present tense** followed by the **past participle** of this verb.

> The **past participle** of verbs conjugated with **être** agrees in gender and number with the subject.

Not many verbs are conjugated with **être**. To remember them, remember the rule of **DR & MRS VANDERTRAMPP**, each letter corresponding to a verb conjugated with **être**.

AUDIO 12.1.7 🔊

Infinitive	Translation	Past participle
Devenir	To become	**devenu**
Revenir	To come back	**revenu**
&		
Monter	To go up	**monté**
Rester	To stay	**resté**
Sortir	To go out	**sorti**
Venir	To come	**venu**
Aller	To go	**allé**
Naître	To be born	**né**
Descendre	To go down	**descendu**
Entrer	To enter	**entré**
Rentrer	To go home	**rentré**
Tomber	To fall	**tombé**
Retourner	To return	**retourné**
Arriver	To arrive	**arrivé**
Mourir	To die	**mort**
Partir	To leave	**parti**
Passer	To pass by	**passé**

Venir To come

Je **suis venu(e)**

Tu **es venu(e)**

Il **est venu**

Elle **est venue**

On **est venu(e)s**

Nous **sommes venu(e)s**

Vous **êtes venu(e)s**

Ils **sont venus**

Elles **sont venues**

EX. 1.40 *Conjuguez les verbes entre parenthèses au **passé composé**.* AUDIO 12.1.8 ◀))

1. Elles _____ **(devenir)** célèbres l'année dernière.

2. Le valet _____ **(descendre)** avec les clients.

3. Les jumeaux _____ **(naître)** lundi.

4. Les clients _____ **(arriver)** il y a quelques heures.

5. Le patron _____ **(passer)** au bureau ce matin.

6. Nous _____ **(tomber)** dans le lac.

7. Le courrier _____ **(revenir)** car l'adresse était fausse.

8. Elles _____ **(partir)** aux alentours de 19 heures.

9. Jeff _____ **(retourner)** au bureau car il avait oublié ses clés.

10. Mes parents _____ **(monter)** se coucher.

Passé Composé of Reflexive Verbs

Reflexive verbs are always conjugated with the auxiliary **être**.

Reflexive pronoun + être + past participle

AUDIO 12.1.9 ◀))

Se souvenir To remember

Je **me suis souvenu(e)**
Tu **t'es souvenu(e)**
Il **s'est souvenu**
Elle **s'est souvenue**
On **s'est souvenu(e)s**
Nous **nous sommes souvenu(e)s**
Vous **vous êtes souvenu(e)s**
Ils **se sont souvenus**
Elles **se sont souvenues**

EX. 1.41 *Conjuguez les verbes entre parenthèses au passé composé.* AUDIO 12.1.10 ◄»)

1. Elle _____ **(se brosser)** les dents ce matin.

2. Je _____ **(se changer)** après l'entrainement.

3. Nous _____ **(s'imaginer)** quelque chose de différent.

4. Il _____ **(se rappeler)** de cette histoire hier.

5. On n'a rien fait ce week-end, on _____ **(se reposer)**.

6. Les enfants _____ **(se cacher)** sous le lit.

7. Ils _____ **(s'amuser)** avec la voiture électrique dans le jardin.

8. Tu _____ **(s'excuser)** auprès de ton ami ?

9. L'enfant _____ **(s'adapter)** en quelques semaines après l'adoption.

10. Vous _____ **(se coucher)** à quelle heure ?

Passé Composé and Negation

As we saw before, negation always goes around the verb. But what about when the verb is conjugated in a compound tense? **The negation is placed around the auxiliary** and is followed by the past participle.

> **Pronoun + ne / n' + avoir / être + pas + past participle**

AUDIO 12.1.11 ◄»)

Ne ... pas   Not
Je **n'ai pas** <u>vu</u> le chien. *I didn't see the dog.*

Ne ... jamais   Never
Il **n'a jamais** <u>bu</u> d'alcohol. *He never drank alcohol.*

Ne ... rien   Nothing
On **n'a rien** <u>changé</u>. *We changed nothing.*

*Exception:
Ne ... personne goes around the verb and the past participle.

Ne ... personne   Nobody, no one
Vous **n'**<u>avez rencontré</u> **personne.** *You met no one.*

When a reflexive verb is conjugated in the passé composé and in a negative sentence, we have this order:

Passé composé of reflexive verbs with negation:

ne / n' + reflexive pronoun + être + pas + past participle

Ne ... pas   Not
Je **ne** me suis **pas** changé(e). *I didn't get changed.*

Ne ... jamais   Never
Il **ne** s'est **jamais** intéressé à l'art. *He was never interested in art.*

Ne ... rien   Nothing
Elle **ne** s'est **rien** demandée. *She asked herself nothing.*

EX. 1.42 *Conjuguez le verbe entre parenthèses au passé composé et ajoutez la négation sur la deuxième ligne.*   AUDIO 12.1.12 ◀))

1. Il _____ **(se rappeler)** de Marc.

_____

2. Les ouvriers _____ **(se faire)** des sandwichs pour midi.

_____

3. Tu _____ **(se sécher)** les cheveux ?

_____

4. Elle _____ **(se lever)** de mauvaise humeur.

_____

5. On _____ **(se dépêcher)** et on est arrivés à temps.

_____

6. Sa femme _____ **(se précipiter)** quand elle l'a vu.

_____

7. Mon oncle _____ **(s'occuper)** du jardin cet été.

_____

8. Tout le monde _____ **(se taire)** quand il est entré.

    (Personne) _____

9. Je _____ **(se tromper)** dans la date.

_____

10. Tu _____ **(se souvenir)** de moi ?

_____

There is / There are – Il y a

The expression **il y a** is always singular and never changes.

It is made of the pronoun **IL + Y + AVOIR** conjugated. **Avoir** can be conjugated in other tenses such as the **imparfait:** il y avait, or the **futur:** il y aura.

In English, it changes depending on the number. It's either singular = there is, or plural = there are.

SINGULIER   PLURIEL

Il y a   ~~Il y ont~~

AUDIO 13.1 ◀))

Feminine:

Il y a <u>une voiture</u> devant la maison. *There is a car in front of the house.*
Il y a <u>deux voitures</u> devant la maison. *There are two cars in front of the house.*
Il y a <u>des voitures</u> devant la maison. *There are cars in front of the house.*

Masculine:

Il y a <u>un chien</u> dans le jardin. *There is a dog in the yard.*
Il y a <u>trois chiens</u> dans le jardin. *There are three dogs in the yard.*
Il y a <u>des chiens</u> dans le jardin. *There are dogs in the yard.*

Il y a in a negative sentence:

Articles will change to **de** in a negative sentence:

Il + n' + y + a + pas + de / d'

Il n'y a pas **de** voiture devant la maison. *There is no car in front of the house.*
Il n'y a pas **de** chien dans le jardin. *There is no dog in the yard.*

Il y a = ago

When talking about time, we also use **il y a**, the same way as ago in English.

Je suis arrivé(e) **il y a** une heure. *I arrived an hour ago.*
Ils se sont parlés **il y a** quelques temps. *They talked some time ago.*

EX. 1.43 *Traduisez les phrases suivantes avec **il y a**.*   AUDIO 13.2 ◀))

1. There is a bottle in my car.

   _____

2. *He arrived 2 hours ago.*

   _____

3. *There isn't enough space.*

   _____

4. *There is a bed and a desk.*

   _____

5. *She was born a few hours ago.*

   _____

*Remember to **download the audio** of the lists and to **watch the videos** – see Preface*

Chapter 1 – Review
Chapitre 1 – Révision

EX. 1.44 *Remplacez le groupe de mots par un pronom sujet et conjuguez le verbe au temps donné.*

AUDIO 13.1.1 🔊

1. **Nicole** (payer – passé composé) les salaires la semaine dernière.

   _____

2. **Les pompiers** (se précipiter – présent) pour l'aider.

   _____

3. **La voiture** (ralentir – présent) avant le feu rouge.

   _____

4. **Le chien et le chat** (jouer – passé composé) tout l'après-midi.

   _____

5. **Les voisines** (louer – présent) depuis quelques années.

   _____

6. **Ma sœur et son mari** (quitter – passé composé) le restaurant à 21 heures.

   _____

7. **Ce plat** (sentir – présent) bizarre.

   _____

8. **La petite fille** (trembler – présent) de froid.

   _____

9. **L'infirmier** (se couper – passé composé) le doigt en travaillant.

   _____

10. **La policière** (laisser – passé composé) partir le suspect.

    _____

EX. 1.45 *Changez le sujet du **singulier** au **pluriel** et accordez le verbe.* AUDIO 13.1.2 🔊

1. Il a quitté sa femme après 3 ans de mariage. (leurs femmes)

   _____

2. Le patient guérit très vite avec ce nouveau traitement.

   _____

3. La fleur ne pousse pas comme elle devrait. (elles devraient)

   _____

4. Tu t'es réveillée de mauvaise humeur ?

   _____

5. Le piéton traverse la rue quand le feu est vert.

   _____

6. Le juge déduit que cette histoire est fausse.

   _____

7. La victime a pardonné son agresseur. (leur agresseur)

   _____

8. L'oie protège ses œufs. (leurs œufs)

   _____

9. L'immigrant espère trouver un travail assez vite.

   _____

10. L'élève a oublié de faire ses devoirs. (leurs devoirs)

    _____

EX. 1.46 *Ajoutez le pays d'origine des personnes. N'oubliez pas l'article.* AUDIO 13.1.3 🔊

1. Il est mexicain, il vient _____.
2. Elle est australienne, elle vient _____.
3. Il est chinois, il vient _____.
4. Elle est espagnole, elle vient _____.
5. Il est suisse, il vient _____.

*Remember to **download the audio** of the lists and to **watch the videos** – see Preface*

6.   Elle est indienne, elle vient _____

7.   Il est luxembourgeois, il vient _____

8.   Elle est thaïlandaise, elle vient _____

9.   Il est anglais, il vient _____

10.   Elle est coréenne, elle vient _____

EX. 1.47 *Changez les phrases affirmatives en négatives et les phrases négatives en affirmatives.*

AUDIO 13.1.4 ◀))

1.   Tu as de la chance.

   _____

2.   Elle n'est jamais en retard.

   _____

3.   C'est bien de manger du sucre.

   _____

4.   Il n'y a pas assez de farine dans ce gâteau.

   _____

5.   Les Jeux Olympiques sont annulés.

   _____

6.   Le bébé mange des fruits tous les jours.

   _____

7.   La barrière n'est pas assez haute pour protéger le jardin.

   _____

8.   Le centre commercial est construit depuis janvier.

   _____

9.   J'ai hâte d'être samedi !

   _____

10.   Cette clé ouvre cette porte.

   _____

EX. 1.48 *Choisissez un des adjectifs ci-dessous et ajoutez-le à la bonne phrase – plusieurs possibilités.* AUDIO 13.1.5 🔊

mon – cette – ses – son – sa – leurs – cet – cette - ces – son

1. Ils ont réussi _____ examens.

2. C'est le chien de ma voisine. C'est _____ chien.

3. Elle a laissé _____ affaires dans le casier.

4. _____ idée est géniale !

5. J'ai oublié _____ parapluie.

6. Tu as vu _____ ours dans le jardin ?

7. C'est _____ voiture je crois.

8. _____ soldats reviennent de l'entrainement.

9. Ce n'est pas ton problème, c'est _____ problème.

10. J'ai reçu _____ invitation par courrier.

EX. 1.49 *Traduisez les phrases suivantes.* AUDIO 13.1.6 🔊

1. It's possible.

   _____

2. We drink wine.

   _____

3. The cat is eating a fish.

   _____

4. Luxembourg is a country.

   _____

5. We accepted the offer.

   _____

6. It's 2 a.m.

   _____

7. Breakfast is delicious.

   _____

8. I don't remember this movie.

    _____

9. I am hungry, I am thirsty.

    _____

10. There is a deer in the yard.

    _____

EX. 1.50 *Faites des phrases avec **il y a** pour décrire ce qu'**il y a**.*

Attention de transformez « votre » :
*Exemple : Dans **votre** jardin*
*Dans **mon** jardin, il y a des fleurs.*

1. Dans votre frigo

    _____

2. Dans votre chambre

    _____

3. Dans votre portefeuille

    _____

4. Dans votre téléphone

    _____

5. Dans votre bureau

    _____

6. Dans votre cahier

    _____

7. Dans votre bouteille

    _____

8. Dans votre voiture

    _____

9. Dans votre grenier

    _____

10. Dans votre armoire

    _____

CHAPTER 2

Prepositions
Les Prépositions

The Preposition À – La Préposition À

The preposition **à** is one of the most used prepositions in French but has few characteristics that confuse a lot of French learners.

First, **à** has a few translations in English: to, at, in but also for, from, or per.
Second, **à** can be by itself or have different forms if followed by an indefinite article.

AUDIO 14.1 ◀))

à + le = au + singular masculine noun
à + les = aux + plural masculine or feminine noun

à + la = à la + singular feminine noun
à + l' = à l' + singular masculine or feminine noun starting with a vowel or a silent h

Only **à + le** and **à + les** change forms.

À = to, at, or in but also for, from, per

AUDIO 14.2 ◀))

Location:

J'habite **au** Canada. *I live in Canada.*
Je vais **à** Paris. *I am going to Paris.*
Nous sommes **à la** piscine. *We are at the swimming pool.*

Distance, time, age, and rate:

J'arrive **à** 5 heures. *I'll arrive at 5 o'clock.*
Il s'est marié **à** 35 ans. *He got married at 35 years old.*
Le marché est **à** 5 minutes. *The market is 5 minutes away.*
La ville est **à** 10 kilomètres d'ici. *The city is 10 kilometers from here.*
L'employé est payé **à l'**heure. *The employee is paid per hour.*
À midi. *At noon.*
À minuit. *At midnight.*

Manner and characteristic:

Une femme **aux** cheveux blonds. *A woman with blond hair.*
Ce pull est fait **à l'**ancienne. *This sweater is vintage / made in a traditional way.*
Laver ce manteau **à la** machine à laver. *Wash this coat in the washing machine.*

Possession:

Cette voiture est **à** Jean. *This car belongs to Jean.*
C'est **à** toi ? *Is this yours?*

Food and how it is made:

Un sandwich **au** thon – A tuna sandwich
Un thé **à** la vanille – A vanilla tea
Une tarte **aux** fraises – A strawberry pie

Specific ways of transportation:

Je suis venu(e) **à** pied. *I came on foot.*
Il est venu **à** cheval. *He came by horse.*
Elles sont venues **à** vélo. *They came by bike.*

To express pain:

J'ai mal **au** pied. *I have foot pain.*
Tu as mal **à l'**estomac. *You have stomach pain.*
Elle a mal **à la** tête. *She has a headache.*

Names of festivities:

À Noël – At Christmas
À Paques – At Easter

To show the purpose of something:

Un sac **à** main – A handbag
Un verre **à** vin – A wine glass
Un couteau **à** steak – A steak knife

Ways to say goodbye:

À demain – See you tomorrow
À vendredi – See you on Friday
À bientôt – See you soon
À plus tard – See you later
À la prochaine – Until next time
À la semaine prochaine – See you next week
À tout de suite – See you right away
À tout à l'heure – See you later

A few expressions with être :

Être à (qqn) – To belong to sb
Être à l'heure – To be on time
Être au courant – To be informed

Il est toujours **à l'**heure. *He is always on time.*
Ce stylo est **à** mon père. *This pencil belongs to my dad.*

A few expressions with c'est and à:

C'est bon **à** savoir. *It's good to know.*
C'est difficile **à** dire. *It's difficult to say.*
C'est impossible **à** dire. *It's impossible to say.*

EX. 2.1 *Ajoutez la préposition* ***à – au – à l' – à – aux.*** AUDIO **14.3** 🔊

1. Le rendez-vous est _____ 16 heures.

2. _____ tout de suite !

3. Nous habitons _____ Portugal.

4. Je suis _____ librairie.

5. Cet enfant _____ cheveux roux.

6. Tu _____ mal à la tête ?

7. Est-ce que c'est _____ Nicole ?

8. C'est bon _____ savoir !

9. Veux-tu un thé _____ framboise ?

10. Est-ce qu'il est _____ courant ?

Verbs Followed by the Preposition à

AUDIO **14.4** 🔊

Acheter qqch **à** qqn	To buy sth from or for sb
Arracher qqch **à** qqn	To tear away from sb
Aller à qqn	To suit sb
Assister qqn **à** qqch	To assist sb to do sth
S'attendre à qqch	To expect sth
Croire à qqch	To believe sth
Conseiller qqch **à** qqn	To advise sb
Convenir à qqn	To be suitable for sb
Demander qqch **à** qqn	To ask sth to sb
Défendre à qqn	To forbid sb
Désobéir à qqn	To disobey sb
Dire qqch **à** qqn	To tell sb
Donner qqch **à** qqn	To give to sb
Écrire à qqn	To write to sb
Emprunter qqch **à** qqn	To borrow sth from sb
Envoyer qqch **à** qqn	To send to sb
Être à qqn	To belong to sb
Faire attention **à** qqn	To pay attention to / be careful with sb
Faire confiance **à** qqn	To trust sb
Faire mal **à** qqn	To hurt sb
Se fier à qqn / qqch	To trust sb /sth
Goûter à qqch	To taste sth
S'habituer à qqn	To get used to sb
Interdire qqch **à** qqn	To forbid sb
S'intéresser à qqn	To be interested by sb
Jouer à qqch	To play sth
Manquer à qqn	To miss sb
Nuire à qqn	To harm sb
Obéir à qqn	To obey sb

S'opposer à qqn	To oppose sb
Ordonner à qqn	To order sb
Pardonner à qqn	To forgive sb
Parler à qqn	To talk to sb
Penser à qqn / qqch	To think about sb / sth
Permettre à qqn	To allow sb
Plaire à qqn	To please sb
Profiter à qqn	To benefit sb
Promettre à qqn	To promise sb
Raconter qqch **à** qqn	To tell sth to sb
Rappeler qqch **à** qqn	To remind sth to sb
Réfléchir à qqch	To consider / reflect upon sth
Rendre visite **à** qqn	To visit sb
Répondre à qqn	To answer sb
Reprocher qqch **à** qqn	To reproach sb for sth
Résister à qqn	To resist sb
Ressembler à qqn	To look like sb
Servir à qqn	To be useful for sb
Songer à qqn / qqch	To dream of / To think of sb / sth
Sourire à qqn	To smile to sb
Succéder à qqn	To take over from sb
Survivre à qqn	To outlive sb
Téléphoner à qqn	To call sb
Voler qqch **à** qqn	To steal sth from sb

Il **a fait** mal **à** sa sœur. *He hurt his sister.*
Le touriste **demande** son chemin **à** un officier de police. *The tourist is asking a police officer for the way.*
Le secrétaire **répond aux** emails. *The secretary answers emails.*
On **a envoyé** une carte de Noël **à** nos amis. *We sent a Christmas card to our friends.*
Cette jupe **va** bien **à la** journaliste. *This skirt suits the journalist.*

EX. 2.2 *Choisissez un verbe dans la liste ci-dessus, conjuguez-le au **passé composé** et ajoutez la préposition.*   AUDIO 14.5 ◀))

1. Elle _____ un collier sa mère.

2. Cet outil _____ la construction.

3. Le commerçant _____ policier.

4. Tu _____ ton frère de fermer la porter ?

5. Les enfants _____ une lettre _____ Père Noël.

6. L'agresseur _____ pardon victime.

7. Est-ce que tu _____ dessert ?

8. J' _____ chien de dormir sur le lit.

9. Il _____ une histoire _____ enfants.

10. Elle _____ téléphone.

Verbs Followed by à and an Infinitive Verb

As seen in the conjugation course, verbs following the preposition **à** are always infinitive.

AUDIO 14.6 🔊

Aider à faire qqch	To help to do sth
S'amuser à faire qqch	To have fun doing sth
Apprendre à faire qqch	To learn how to do sth
Arriver à faire qqch	To manage / succeed in doing sth
Aspirer à faire qqch	To aspire to do sth
S'attendre à faire qqch	To expect doing sth
S'autoriser à faire qqch	To allow oneself to do sth
Avoir à faire qqch	To have to / be obliged to do sth
Chercher à faire qqch	To attempt to do sth
Commencer à faire qqch	To begin to do sth
Consentir à faire qqch	To agree to do sth
Continuer à faire qqch	To continue to do sth
Se décider à faire qqch	To make up one's mind to do sth
Encourager qqn **à** faire qqch	To encourage sb to do sth
S'engager à faire qqch	To commit to do sth
S'épuiser à faire qqch	To exhaust oneself doing sth
Forcer qqn **à** faire qqch	To force sb to do sth
S'habituer à faire qqch	To get used to doing sth
Hésiter à faire qqch	To hesitate to do sth
Inviter qqn **à** faire qqch	To invite sb to do sth
Se mettre à faire qqch	To start doing sth
Obliger qqn **à** faire qqch	To force sb to do sth
Parvenir à faire qqch	To succeed in doing sth
Passer du temps **à** faire qqch	To spend time doing sth
Perdre du temps **à** faire qqch	To waste time doing sth
Persister à faire qqch	To persist in doing sth
Pousser qqn **à** faire qqch	To push sb to do sth
Se préparer à faire qqch	To prepare oneself to do sth
Recommencer à faire qqch	To start doing sth again
Réfléchir à faire qqch	To think of doing sth
Renoncer à faire qqch	To give up doing sth
Résister à faire qqch	To resist doing sth
Réussir à faire qqch	To succeed in doing sth
Servir à faire qqch	To be used to do sth
Songer à faire qqch	To think of doing sth
Tenir à faire qqch	To insist on doing sth
En **venir à** faire qqch	To come to do sth

J'hésite **à** <u>quitter</u> mon travail. *I hesitate to quit my job.*
Cet outil sert **à** <u>couper</u> du bois. *This tool is used to cut wood.*
Cela commence **à** <u>m'embêter</u>. *It's starting to bother me.*
J'apprends **à** <u>méditer</u>. *I am learning to meditate*
Les équipes aident **à** <u>contrôler</u> le feu. *The teams help to control the fire.*

EX. 2.3 *Choisissez un verbe dans la liste ci-dessus, conjuguez-le au temps donné et ajoutez la préposition.*   AUDIO 14.7 ◀)

1. Il _____ appeler pour un rendez-vous. (passé composé)

2. Nous _____ changer un pneu. (passé composé)

3. Les parents _____ les enfants _____ finir leurs assiettes. (présent)

4. Il _____ acheter le cadeau tout seul. (passé composé)

5. On _____ changer de voiture. (présent)

6. Ma famille _____ les voisins _____ dîner. (passé composé)

7. J' _____ mon petit frère _____ nager. (passé composé)

8. Tu _____ partir plus tôt ? (présent)

9. Il _____ ses parents _____ déménager. (passé composé)

10. Elle _____ devenir scientifique. (présent)

Être + Adjective + à

Être + adjective / past participle + à + infinitive is used to describe the state of someone or something, not feelings.

In French, the adjective agrees in gender and number with the subject. The feminine version is added after the masculine form of the adjective.

Here is the list of commonly used expressions: AUDIO 14.8 ◀)

Être prêt (prête) **à**	To be ready to
Être autorisé (autorisée) **à**	To be authorized to
Être habitué (habituée) **à**	To be used to
Être occupé (occupée) **à**	To be busy with
Être déterminé (déterminée) **à**	To be determined to

Je suis prêt **à** <u>partir</u>. *I am ready to leave.*
On est habitués **à** <u>dormir</u> tard. *We are used to sleep late.*
Elle est occupée **à** <u>travailler</u>. *She is busy with work.*

EX. 2.4 *Reliez les deux parties pour former des phrases.*   AUDIO **14.9** ◀))

1. Nous sommes occupés à   voyager avec Air Canada.
2. Tu es prête à   réussir.
3. Elle est déterminée à   te marier ?
4. Vous êtes habitués à   retirer de l'argent.
5. Il est autorisé à   lire un livre.

Le seul à

In this case and as well as ordinal numbers in the next point, we don't have a verb before the preposition **à**. **Le seul** is a pronoun and will change depending on if the subject is masculine, feminine, singular, or plural. The change in gender and number doesn't affect the following verb since it's an infinitive.

It also happens with **nombreux**, which will change to **nombreuses** when feminine. **Nombreux** and **nombreuses** are always plural.

Here are the 6 possibilities with different gender and number: AUDIO **14.10** ◀))

Le seul à (m)	The only one who
La seule à (f)	The only one who
Les seuls à (m)	The only ones who
Les seules à (f)	The only ones who
Nombreux à (m)	Many are
Nombreuses à (f)	Many are

Il était **le seul à** venir me voir. *He was the only one who came to see me.*
Ils sont **nombreux à** chercher la réponse. *Many are looking for the answer.*

EX. 2.5 *Choisissez la bonne réponse dans la liste ci-dessous :*   AUDIO **14.11** ◀))

la seule à – nombreux à – nombreuses à – le seul à – les seuls à

1. Elle ne veut pas être _____ aller à la plage.
2. Ce ne sont pas _____ créer ces produits.
3. Les femmes sont _____ faire attention à leur apparence.
4. Il est _____ connaître le secret.
5. Les oiseaux _____ passer l'hiver ici.

Ordinal Number + à

Like the last point, we don't have a verb before the preposition **à**. **The article before the ordinal number** will change depending on if the subject is masculine, feminine, singular, or plural, as well as the ordinal number. The change in gender and number doesn't affect the following verb since it's infinitive.

Here are a few possibilities with different gender and number: AUDIO **14.12** 🔊

Le premier à (m)	The first one to
La première à (f)	The first one to
Les premiers à (m)	The first ones to
Les premières à (f)	The first ones to
Le deuxième à (m)	The second one to
La deuxième à (f)	The second one to
Les deuxièmes à (m)	The second ones to
Les deuxièmes à (f)	The second ones to
Le dernier à (m)	The last one to
La dernière à (f)	The last one to
Les derniers à (m)	The last ones to
Les dernières à (f)	The last ones to

Ils sont **les derniers à** <u>se coucher</u>. *They are the last ones to go to bed.*
Je suis **la deuxième à** <u>arriver</u>. *I am the second one to arrive.*

EX. 2.6 *Choisissez la bonne réponse dans la liste ci-dessus.*   AUDIO **14.13** 🔊

1. Le _____ arriver a perdu !

2. C'est _____ me dire ça.

3. Il est _____ aller aux Jeux Olympiques.

4. Je suis _____ aller à l'université.

5. Ils sont toujours _____ se lever.

The Preposition De – La Préposition De

The preposition **de** is very similar to **à**. It's also one of the most used prepositions in French and changes depending on if it's followed by an indefinite article as well.

In English, **de** translates to: from, of, about.

AUDIO 15.1 🔊

de + le = du + singular masculine noun
de + les = des + plural masculine or feminine noun
de + la = de la + singular feminine noun
de + l' = de l' + singular masculine or feminine noun starting with a vowel or a silent h

Only **de + le** and **de + les** change forms.

De = from, of, or about.

AUDIO 15.2 🔊

Starting point and origin:

Je viens **de la** Belgique. *I am coming from Belgium.*
Il arrive **du** Luxembourg. *He is arriving from Luxembourg.*
Elle part **de** New York. *She is leaving from New York.*

To indicate what something contains:

Un verre **de** vin. *A glass of wine.*
Une bouteille **d'**eau. *A water bottle.*
Une tasse **de** café. *A cup of coffee.*
Une boîte **de** mouchoirs. *A tissue box.*
Un pot **de** fleurs. *A flower planter.*

To describe the use of something:

Un sac **de** couchage. *A sleeping bag.*
Une plaine **de** jeux. *A playground.*
Des chaussures **de** sport. *Sport shoes.*

Possession:

French doesn't use 's to talk about possession. Instead, **de** is used between the 2 words:

La voiture **de** Marie. *Marie's car.*
Le livre **de** Paul. *Paul's book.*
Le mari **de** Jeanne. *Jeanne's husband.*

From ... to with à:

De Paris **à** Bruxelles. *From Paris to Brussels.*
Nous partons **du** mardi **au** vendredi. *We are leaving from Tuesday to Friday.*
J'ai lu le livre **du** début **à** la fin. *I read the book from the beginning to the end.*

Superlatives:

La plus belle femme **du** monde. *The most beautiful woman in the world.*
Le meilleur hôtel **de la** ville. *The best hotel in the city.*
La plus chanceuses **des** mamans. *The luckiest of the moms.*

Quantities:

Beaucoup **de** – A lot of
Peu **de** – A little bit of
Moins **de** – Less of
La majorité **de** – The majority of
Trop **de** – Too much of / Too many of
Une douzaine **de** – A dozen of
Un litre **de** – A liter of
Un mètre **de** – A meter of

Expressions with être and de:

Être d'accord – To agree
Être de bonne humeur – To be in a good mood
Être de mauvaise humeur – To be in a bad mood
Être de retour – To be back

Je suis **de** bonne humeur aujourd'hui. *I am in a good mood today.*
Ils sont déjà **de** retour. *They are already back.*

EX. 2.7 *Ajoutez la préposition **de – d' – du – de la – de l' – des.*** `AUDIO 15.3 ◄))`

1. Je suis _____ accord avec toi !

2. Ce train va _____ New York à Montréal.

3. Moins _____ moitié des étudiants réussissent.

4. Je suis la plus chanceuse _____ monde !

5. Pour une fois, il est _____ bonne humeur.

6. C'est la maison _____ ma tante.

7. Cet avion arrive _____ Madrid.

8. J'ai regardé ce film _____ début à la fin.

9. Ce sac _____ couchage est confortable.

10. Est-ce que tu veux aller à la plaine _____ jeux ?

Verbs Followed by the Preposition De

Descendre de qqch	To get off / down from sth
S'agir de qqn / qqch	To be about sb / sth
S'apercevoir de qqch	To notice sth
S'approcher de qqn / qqch	To approach sb / sth
Arriver de + endroit	To arrive from + place
Avoir besoin **de** qqn / qqch	To need sb / sth
Avoir envie **de** qqch	To want sth
Avoir l'air **de** qqn	To look like sb
Avoir peur **de** qqn / qqch	To be afraid of sb / sth
Changer de + qqch	To change + sth
Dépendre de qqn / qqch	To depend on sb / sth
Douter de qqn / qqch	To doubt sb / sth
S'emparer de qqn / qqch	To garb sb / sth
S'étonner de qqn / qqch	To be amazed by sb / sth
Être responsable **de** qqn /qqch	To be responsible for sb
Hériter de qqn / qqch	To inherit from sb / To inherit sth
Jouer de + instrument	To play + instrument
Manquer de qqn / qqch	To lack of sb / sth
Se méfier de qqn	To mistrust sb
Se moquer de qqn	To make fun of sb
S'occuper de qqn / qqch	To take care of sb / sth
Parler de qqn / qqch	To talk about sb / sth
Partir de + endroit	To leave + place
Se passer de qqn / qqch	To do without sb / sth
Penser de qqn / qqch	To think of sb / sth
Se plaindre de qqn / qqch	To complain about sb / sth
Profiter de qqn / qqch	To take advantage of sb / sth
Raffoler de qqch	To be crazy of sth
Rêver de qqn / qqch	To dream of sb / sth
Rire de qqn / qqch	To laugh at sb / sth
Se servir de qqn / qqch	To use sb / sth
Se souvenir de qqn / qqch	To remember sb / sth
Se tromper de + objet	To take the wrong / To buy the wrong + object
Tenir qqch **de** qqn	To take sth after sb
Vivre de qqch	To live on sth

Je me souviens **de** cette histoire. *I remember this story.*
Le directeur parle **du** projet avec enthousiasme. *The director talks about the project with enthusiasm.*
Nous avons besoin **de** temps. *We need time.*
Mon père descend **de** l'échelle. *My dad comes down the ladder.*
Il a profité **d'**elle pendant longtemps. *He took advantage of her for a long time.*

EX. 2.8 *Choisissez un verbe dans la liste ci-dessus, conjuguez-le au temps donné et ajoutez la préposition.* AUDIO 15.5 🔊

1. Il _____ violon depuis des années. (présent)

2. Nous _____ une année sans problèmes. (présent)

3. Je _____ numéro. (passé composé)

4. Il _____ carrière il y a quelques années. (passé composé)

5. Vous _____ toutes ces affaires ? (présent)

6. Il _____ sa volonté. (présent)

7. Elle _____ enfants tous les jours. (présent)

8. On _____ viande depuis quelques années déjà. (présent)

9. Tu _____ une glace ? (présent)

10. Je _____ brownies ! (présent)

Verbs Followed by De and an Infinitive Verb

AUDIO 15.6 🔊

Just like the preposition **à**, **de** is required before adding the infinitive verb.

Accepter de faire qqch	To accept to do sth
Accuser qqn **de** faire qqch	To accuse sb of doing sth
Achever de faire qqch	To finish doing sth
Arrêter de faire qqch	To stop doing sth
Attendre de faire qqch	To wait to do sth
Avoir besoin **de** faire qqch	To need to do sth
Avoir envie **de** faire qqch	To feel like doing sth
Avoir l'air **de** faire qqch	To seem to be doing sth
Avoir l'intention **de** faire qqch	To intend to do sth
Avoir peur **de** faire qqch	To be afraid of doing sth
Avoir raison **de** faire qqch	To be right to do sth
Avoir tort **de** faire qqch	To be wrong to do sth
Cesser de faire qqch	To cease doing sth
Choisir de faire qqch	To choose to do sth
Commander à qqn **de** faire qqch	To order sb to do sth
Conseiller de faire qqch	To advise to do sth
Se contenter de faire qqch	To be happy to do sth
Continuer de faire qqch	To keep doing sth
Convaincre qqn **de** faire qqch	To convince sb to do sth
Convenir de faire qqch	To agree to do sth
Craindre de faire qqch	To fear doing sth
Décider de faire qqch	To decide to do sth
Défendre à qqn **de** faire qqch	To forbid sb to do sth

Se dépêcher de faire qqch	To hurry to do sth
Demander à qqn **de** faire qqch	To ask sb to do sth
Dire à qqn **de** faire qqch	To tell sb to do sth
S'efforcer de faire qqch	To try hard to do sth
Empêcher qqn **de** faire qqch	To keep/ prevent sb from doing sth
S'empresser de faire qqch	To hurry to do
Envisager de faire qqch	To contemplate doing sth
Essayer de faire qqch	To try to do sth
Être en train de faire qqch	To be in the process of doing sth
Être sur le point de faire qqch	To be about to do sth
Éviter de faire qqch	To avoid doing sth
S'excuser de faire qqch	To apologize for doing sth
Faire semblant **de** faire qqch	To pretend doing sth
Feindre de faire qqch	To feign to / To pretend doing sth
Finir de faire qqch	To finish doing sth
Se hâter de faire qqch	To hurry to do sth
Interdire à qqn **de** faire qqch	To forbid sb to do sth
Manquer de faire qqch	To neglect doing sth
Menacer qqn **de** faire qqch	To threaten sb to do sth
Mériter de faire qqch	To deserve to do sth
Offrir de faire qqch	To offer to do sth
Oublier de faire qqch	To forget to do sth
Parler de faire qqch	To talk about doing sth
(Se) permettre de faire qqch	To allow sb to do sth
Persuader qqn **de** faire qqch	To convince sb to do sth
Se plaindre de faire qqch	To complain about doing sth
Prier de faire qqch	To beg to do sth
Projeter de faire qqch	To plan on doing sth
Promettre de faire qqch	To promise to do sth
Proposer de faire qqch	To suggest doing sth
Refuser de faire qqch	To refuse to do sth
Regretter de faire qqch	To regret doing sth
Remercier de faire qqch	To thank for doing sth
Reprocher à qqn **de** faire qqch	To reproach sb for doing sth
Rêver de faire qqch	To dream of doing sth
Risquer de faire qqch	To risk doing sth
Soupçonner qqn **de** faire qqch	To suspect sb of doing sth
Se souvenir de faire qqch	To remember doing sth
Supplier de faire qqch	To beg to do sth
Tâcher de faire qqch	To try to do sth
Venir de faire qqch	To have just done sth

J'ai offert **d'**<u>aider</u> ma grand-mère ce week-end. *I offered to help my grandmother this weekend.*
Elle rêve **de** <u>travailler</u> au centre-ville. *She dreams of working in the city center.*
L'élève refuse **de** <u>faire</u> ses devoirs. *The student refuses to do his homework.*
On envisage **de** <u>passer</u> le DELF bientôt. *We contemplate on taking the DELF soon.*
Les enfants ont besoin **de** <u>faire</u> la sieste. *Children need to nap.*

EX. 2.9 *Choisissez un verbe dans la liste ci-dessus, conjuguez-le au temps donné et ajoutez la préposition.* AUDIO 15.7 ◀))

1. Je _____ vider le lave-vaisselle. (passé composé)
2. Elle _____ s'exposer au soleil sans crème solaire. (présent)
3. Les employés _____ rester tard au travail. (présent)
4. Elle _____ le docteur _____ sauver la vie de son fils. (passé composé)
5. Il _____ faire un infarctus. (présent)
6. Il _____ demander une augmentation. (passé composé)
7. La banque _____ débloquer les fonds. (passé composé)
8. J' _____ déménager. (passé composé)
9. On _____ manger avant de partir. (présent)
10. Je _____ recevoir une augmentation ! (présent)

Être + en train + De + Infinitive

Since there is no equivalent of the English continuous present, if you want to emphasize an ongoing action, you can use **Être + en train + de + infinitive**. It translates to To be + in the process + of but the easiest translation is To be _____ing.

Train is also the word for "train" but this expression has nothing to do with trains and rails.

AUDIO 15.8 ◀))

Je suis **en train d'**écrire un livre. *I am writing a book.*
Nous sommes **en train d'**y réfléchir. *We are thinking about it.*
Le chat est **en train de** se laver. *The cat is cleaning himself.*

Être + sur le point + De + Infinitive

Être + sur le point + de + infinitive translates to To be about to.

AUDIO 15.9 ◀))

Je **suis sur le point de** partir. *I am about to leave.*
La branche **est sur le point de** tomber. *The branch is about to fall.*

EX. 2.10 *Achevez les phrases suivantes.*

1. Je suis sur le point de

   _____

   _____

   _____

2. Je suis en train de

   _____

   _____

   _____

Être + Adjective + De + Infinitive / Noun

Être + adjective + de + infinitive / noun is a common way to express feelings. It translates almost word by word to To be + adjective + to. (Except for To be sure <u>of</u>, To be tired <u>of</u>, To be proud <u>of</u>)

In French, the adjective agrees in gender and number with the subject, the feminine version is added after the masculine form of the adjective.

Here is the list of commonly used expressions: AUDIO 15.10 ◀))

Être anxieux (anxieuse) de	To be anxious to
Être content (contente) de	To be happy to
Être désolé (désolée) de	To be sorry to
Être enchanté (enchantée) de	To be delighted to
Être fatigué (fatiguée) de	To be tired of
Être fier (fière) de	To be proud of
Être heureux (heureuse) de	To be happy to
Être impatient (impatiente) de	To be impatient to
Être libre de	To be free to
Être obligé (obligée) de	To be obligated to
Être ravi (ravie) de	To be delighted to
Être reconnaissant (reconnaissante) de	To be thankful to
Être satisfait (satisfaite) de	To be satisfied to
Être sûr (sûre) de	To be sure to
Être surpris (surprise) de	To be surprised to
Être triste de	To be sad to

Nous **sommes tristes de** partir. *We are sad to leave.*
Elle **est anxieuse de** prendre l'avion. *She is anxious to fly.*
La caissière **est fatiguée de** travailler. *The cashier is tired to work.*
Les enfants **sont impatients d'**être en vacances. *The children are impatient to be on vacation.*
Je **suis désolé de** vous réveiller. I am sorry to wake you up.

EX. 2.11 *Conjuguez le verbe **être** au **présent** et ajouté la préposition **de – du**.* AUDIO 15.11 ◄))

1. Il _____ ravi _____ résultat.
2. Tu _____ sûr _____ ton choix ?
3. Je _____ heureux _____ choix que j'ai fait.
4. Nous _____ impatients _____ te voir !
5. Elle _____ enchantée _____ te rencontrer.

Il est + Adjective + De + Infinitive

Il est + adjective + de + infinitive is a formal way to speak French. The informal way is explained in the next point.

Here **être** is an impersonal verb. Therefore the adjective stays masculine / singular.

Here is the list of commonly used expressions: AUDIO 15.12 ◄))

Il est bon de	It's good to
Il est dangereux de	It's dangerous to
Il est défendu de	It's forbidden to
Il est interdit de	It's forbidden to
Il est difficile de	It's difficult to
Il est dur de	It's hard to
Il est facile de	It's easy to
Il est important de	It's important to
Il est nécessaire de	It's necessary to
Il est impossible de	It's impossible to
Il est possible de	It's possible to
Il est utile de	It's useful to
Il est inutile de	It's useless to

Il est possible de <u>retourner</u> ces articles. *It's possible to return these items.*
Il est interdit de <u>fumer</u> à l'intérieur. *It's forbidden to smoke inside.*
Il est inutile de se <u>mettre</u> en colère. *It's useless to be angry.*

C'est + Adjective + De + Infinitive

C'est + adjective + de + infinitive is the informal way to talk, as opposed to **il est**.

Here **être** is an impersonal verb. Therefore the adjective stays masculine / singular.

Here is the list of commonly used expressions:　　**AUDIO 15.13** ◀))

C'est interdit de	It's forbidden to
C'est difficile de	It's difficult to
C'est bien de	It's good to
C'est dommage de	It's a pity to

EX. 2.12 *Choisissez un adjectif dans la liste ci-dessus et complétez la phrase.*　　**AUDIO 15.14** ◀))

1. C'est _____ de déposer des ordures ici.
2. C'est _____ de se détendre après le travail.
3. Il est _____ d'apprendre la méditation.
4. C'est _____ de se téléporter.
5. Il est _____ de traverser la rue sans regarder.
6. C'est _____ de vendre de la drogue.
7. Il est _____ d'aider la planète.
8. C'est _____ de jeter ces légumes.
9. C'est _____ de se lever tôt.
10. Il est _____ de prendre l'air.

Notes :

The Preposition En – La Préposition En

The preposition **en** refers to **location, time, material**, and more. **EN** translates to in, on and to. **En** is easier to use than **à** and **de** because it doesn't change when followed by articles.

AUDIO 16.1 🔊

Location and destination (especially feminine countries and region):

Ils vont **en** France. *They are going to France.*
J'habite **en** Colombie Britannique. *I live in British Columbia.*
Elle est née **en** Allemagne. *She was born in Germany.*

Years, months, and seasons:

En 1987 – In 1987
En mars – In March
En été – In summer
En hiver – In winter
En automne – In autumn
Except: Au printemps – In spring

The time that something will take:

Le dîner sera prêt **en** 5 minutes. *Dinner will be ready in 5 minutes.*
On mange toujours **en** 10 minutes. *We always eat in 10 minutes.*

Transportations:

Elle vient **en** voiture. *She is coming by car.*
Elles vont en vacances **en** avion. *They are going on vacation by plane.*
Je vais au travail **en** train. *I am going to work by train.*

As a way to say "in" a language:

Le formulaire est **en** anglais. *The form is in English.*
Je regarde la télé **en** espagnol. *I am watching TV in Spanish.*
Il lit un livre **en** français. *He is reading a book in French.*

Material:

Un collier **en** argent – A silver necklace
Une veste **en** cuir – A leather jacket
Une étagère **en** bois – A wood shelf

EX. 2.13 *Traduisez les phrases ci-dessous.*   AUDIO 16.2 ◄»

1. My birthday is in November.

   _____

2. He moved to Colombia.

   _____

3. I can be ready in 5 minutes.

   _____

4. She wants this leather jacket.

   _____

5. It happened in 1990.

   _____

Common Expressions with Être and En

AUDIO 16.3 ◄»

Être en avance – To be early
Être en vacances – To be on vacation
Être en retard – To be late
Être en colère – To be angry
Être en vie – To be alive
Être en train de (+ inf) – To be in the process of (doing)
Être en forme – To be in shape
Être en bonne santé – To be healthy
Être en panne – To be out of order

Les clients sont arrivés **en** retard. *The clients arrived early.*
Le bébé est né **en** bonne santé. *The baby was born healthy.*
On a hâte d'être **en** vacances. *We can't wait to be on vacation.*

EX. 2.14 *Choisissez une expression dans la liste ci-dessus et conjuguez le verbe au présent.*

AUDIO 16.4 ◄»

1. Elle a de la chance d' _____ .

2. On _____ à partir de ce samedi.

3. Tu _____ aujourd'hui !

4. Il _____ depuis qu'il prend soin de lui.

5. Cette voiture _____ .

The Verb To Go – Le Verbe Aller

AUDIO 17.1 🔊

Aller is of course used as a verb of motion, To go somewhere. It's always followed by a preposition:

Aller + à la   Use **à la** when followed by a feminine noun (**à l'** when the noun starts with a vowel or a silent h)

Aller à la pharmacie – To go to the pharmacy
Aller à la gare – To go to the train station

Aller + au   Use **au** when followed by a masculine noun

Aller au cinéma – To go to the theater
Aller au musée – To go to the museum

Aller + aux   Use **aux** when followed by a plural noun

Aller aux courses – To go grocery shopping
Aller aux toilettes – To go to the washroom

Aller + en   Use **en** when followed by a feminine country

Aller en Suisse – To go to Switzerland
Aller en Italie – To go to Italy

Aller + au   Use **au** when followed by a masculine country

Aller au Mexique – To go to Mexico
Aller au Japon – To go to Japan

Aller + aux   Use **aux** when followed by a plural country

Aller aux Philippines – To go to the Philippines
Aller aux Seychelles – To go to Seychelles

Aller + à   Use **à** when followed by a city

Aller à Amsterdam – To go to Amsterdam
Aller à Berlin – To go to Berlin

Aller + chez   Use **chez** when followed by a person, a business, a store

Aller chez le dentiste – To go to the dentist
Aller chez la voisine – To go to the neighbor('s house)

EX. 2.15 *Ajoutez le verbe **aller** et **la préposition** adéquate.* AUDIO 17.2 ◀

1. Je _____ marché demain matin.

2. Il _____ cinéma avec ses amis.

3. Tu _____ bibliothèque ce matin ?

4. Nous _____ le docteur.

5. Ils _____ États-Unis pour le documentaire.

6. On _____ Londres pour le week-end.

7. Est-ce que tu _____ épicerie ?

8. Mes amis et moi _____ Japon en mai.

9. Je _____ le dentiste ce soir.

10. Tu _____ Australie en décembre ?

Prepositions of Place
Les Prépositions de Lieu

Simple Prepositions

I like to separate prepositions of place into two different categories. The first one includes prepositions with only **one word.** They will usually be followed by an article:

AUDIO 18.1 🔊

Contre   against

La télévision est **contre** le mur. *The television is against the wall.*

Dans   in

Le couteau est **dans** le tiroir. *The knife is in the drawer.*

Derrière   behind

Le garage est **derrière** la maison. *The garage is behind the house.*

Devant   in front of

La voiture est **devant** la sortie. *The car is in front of the exit.*

Entre   between

La lampe est **entre** le mur et le canapé. *The lamp is between the wall and the couch.*

Sous   under

Le monstre est **sous** le lit. *The monster is under the bed.*

Sur   on

La pomme est **sur** la table. *The apple is on the table.*

EX. 2.16 *Choisissez la préposition adéquate dans la liste ci-dessus.*   **AUDIO 18.2** 🔊

1. Le chat dort _____ le lit.

2. Le train est arrêté _____ deux villes.

3. Je t'attends _____ le magasin.

4. Est-ce que tu as regardé _____ le meuble ?

5. Il est appuyé _____ la porte.

6. J'ai mis des serviettes propres _____ la salle de bain.

7. Le garage est _____ la maison.

---

*Remember to **download the audio** of the lists and to **watch the videos** – see Preface*

Prepositions Followed by De

The second type of prepositions of place are the ones made of **more than one word**, especially the ones including **de.**

In this case, **de** will also change if followed by **le** or **les**, just like **de:**

AUDIO 18.3 ◄))

de + le = du + singular masculine noun
de + les = des + plural masculine or feminine noun

de + la = de la + singular feminine noun
de + l' = de l' + singular masculine or feminine noun starting with a vowel or a silent h

AUDIO 18.4 ◄))

À côté de   next to
  Le verre d'eau est **à côté du** livre. *The glass of water is next to the book.*

À droite de   to the right of
  Le magasin est **à droite de la** banque. *The store is to the right of the bank.*

À gauche de   to the left of
  Je suis **à gauche du** la sortie. *I am to the left of the exit.*

Au bord de   by, on the edge of
  Nous sommes **au bord de la** plage. *We are by the beach.*

Au-dessous de   below
  L'athlète est **au-dessous de** ses performances. *The athlete is below his performances.*

Au-dessus de   above
  Le nounours est **au-dessus de l'**armoire. *The teddy bear is above the dresser.*

Au milieu de   in the middle of
  L'enfant est **au milieu du** parc. *The child is in the middle of the park.*

En face de   facing, in front of
  Je suis **en face du** restaurant. *I am in front of the restaurant.*

Loin de   far from
  C'est **loin d'**ici. *It's far from here.*

Près de   near
  Nous sommes **près de l'**aéroport. *We are near the airport.*

EX. 2.17 *Choisissez la préposition adéquate dans la liste ci-dessus.* AUDIO 18.5 ◀》

1. La maison est _____ magasin.
2. Je range toujours les biscuits _____ armoire.
3. Nous étions _____ monument.
4. Le lac est _____ pays.
5. Je suis _____ toi.
6. L'appartement a été vendu _____ prix demandé.
7. Elle habite _____ ce restaurant.
8. Est-ce que l'appartement _____ plage ?
9. Ils sont _____ rupture.
10. L'avion s'est posé _____ mes grands-parents.

Notes :

*Remember to **download the audio** of the lists and to **watch the videos** – see Preface*

Prepositions of Time
Les Prépositions de Temps

Simple Prepositions

Prepositions of time don't necessarily refer to a specific timing in the sentence, more of an action happening at a certain time.

AUDIO 19.1 🔊

Rappel: **à – en - dans**

À   at

   To indicate the exact time when something will happen or happened:
   Le rendez-vous est **à** midi. *The meeting is at noon.*

En   in

   To indicate the amount of time that it takes to do something:
   Il a fini son examen **en** une heure. *He finished his exam in an hour.*

Dans   in

   To indicate the amount of time before the beginning of something:
   Nous partons **dans** 10 minutes. *We are leaving in 10 minutes.*

Après   after

   On regarde la télévision **après** le dîner. *We watch TV after dinner.*

Avant   before

   On prend un café **avant** le travail. *We have a coffee before work.*

Depuis   since, for

   To talk about an ongoing action – used with the present tense:
   J'enseigne en ligne **depuis** 2019. *I have been teaching online since 2019.*

EX. 2.18 *Choisissez la préposition adéquate dans la liste ci-dessus.* AUDIO 19.2 ◀))

1. Je travaille ici _____ plusieurs mois.

2. Il n'est jamais _____ heure.

3. _____ que tu ne partes, est-ce que tu peux m'aider ?

4. Nous nous reposons _____ la chambre.

5. Vous étiez _____ moi.

6. La ville était détruite _____ la tempête.

7. Je suis _____ marché, tu veux me rejoindre ?

8. On se verra _____ le travail.

9. Ce document est _____ moi.

10. Mon voyage _____ Allemagne était incroyable.

Jusqu'à – au – ...

AUDIO 19.3 ◀))

Jusqu'à – au – aux – où – en   until, before, to, up to

- To talk about a duration = **Jusqu'à – au – aux**

  Nous serons en vacances **jusqu'au** 19 mars. *We will be on vacation until the 19th of March.*
  Plus que deux mois **jusqu'à** Noël. *Only 2 months until Christmas.*

- To talk about a distance = **Jusqu'à – au – aux**

  On voyage **jusqu'à** Londres. *We are traveling to London.*
  Il court **jusqu'au** parc. *He is running to the park.*

- To talk about a distance, mostly in questions = **Jusqu'où**

  Jusqu'où est-ce qu'il doit aller ? *How far should he go?*

- To talk about a time frame from a moment to another, including months or years = **Jusqu'en**

  Il a **jusqu'en** juin pour étudier. *He has until June to study.*

- To talk about a destination, including a feminine country = Jusqu'en

  Cette personne a marché **jusqu'en** Chine. *This person walked to China.*

EX. 2.19 *Choisissez parmi les différentes formes de **jusqu'**.*   AUDIO 19.4 ◄»

1. Il est allé _____ ?

2. _____ Amérique.

3. On a _____ dimanche pour faire une offre.

4. Il restera là-bas _____ Noël.

5. Cette réservation est valide _____ premier janvier.

Durant – Pendant – Pour

AUDIO 19.5 ◄»

Durant, pendant and **pour**   during / for

Durant and **pendant** indicate the entire duration of an action, a specific timeframe. They can be used with other tenses:

> J'ai dormi **pendant** 8 heures. *I slept for 8 hours.*
> Il a nagé **durant** une heure. *He swam for an hour.*

To talk about general situations or vague future actions:

> Je commanderai ce livre **pendant** la semaine. *I will order this book during the week.*
> Je ne travaille jamais **durant** les fêtes. *I never work during the Holidays.*

Pour   for

> The preposition **pour** usually translates to for.

To express duration in the future. It can be replaced by **pendant** as well:

> Je serai partie **pour** 3 jours. *I will be gone for 3 days.*
> Il viendra **pour** une semaine. *He will come for a week.*

EX. 2.20 *Choisissez entre **durant – pendant – pour** (plusieurs possibilités).*   AUDIO 19.6 ◄»

1. Ce chien sera en traitement _____ quelques semaines.

2. Il est venu _____ que tu étais parti.

3. J'ai paniqué _____ l'examen.

4. On a étudié _____ des semaines pour cet examen !

5. Elle jouait avec son téléphone _____ le speech.

EX. 2.21 *Choisissez parmi les prépositions ci-dessous.* AUDIO 19.7 🔊

au bord de – durant – dans – avant – sur – devant – après – en – à cause de jusqu'à

1. Nous prévoyons d'aller _____ Espagne cet été.

2. Le livre est _____ la table, tu ne l'as pas trouvé.

3. Le train est parti _____ l'heure prévue.

4. Nous sommes en manque d'eau _____ canicule.

5. Je suis restée _____ toi au travail.

6. Il y a un moustique _____ la tente.

7. Nous avons beaucoup de choses à faire _____ le week-end.

8. Est-ce que tu peux attendre _____ semaine prochaine ?

9. Nous restons toujours _____ plage.

10. J'ai laissé le sachet _____ la porte.

Other Prepositions – Les Autres Prépositions

Besides the prepositions **à**, **de**, **en**, prepositions of place, and time, there are many more useful prepositions.

Par

The preposition **par** usually translates to through, by, per, for or even around. We use the preposition **par**:

AUDIO 20.1 ◀))

To talk about a reason:

> Je fais ça **par** habitude. *I do that by habit.*
> Il a fait ça **par** amour. *He did that for love.*
> Il a trouvé la solution **par** hasard. *He found the solution by chance.*

To talk about measures:

> C'est mieux d'acheter **par** kilo. *It's better to buy per kilo.*
> Le tissu coûte 3 euros **par** mètre. *The fabric costs 3 euros per meter.*

To talk about directions:

> Tu marches **par** le chemin derrière la maison ? *Do you walk by the path behind the house?*
> Il regarde **par** la fenêtre. *He is looking out the window.*
> Nous habitons **par** ici. *We are living around here.*

Verbs with par:

A list of verbs use the preposition **par**, some of the most common French verbs are: **AUDIO 20.2** ◀))

Arriver par	To come in by
Commencer par	To begin by _____-ing
Entrer par	To enter by
Faire par	To do out of (pity, love)
Finir par + infinitive	To end up _____-ing / to finally do something
Habiter par ici	To live around here
Jurer par	To swear by
Obtenir qqch **par**	To obtain sth by
Prendre qqun **par** (la main)	To take sb by (the hand)
Sortir par	To leave by
Venir par	To come by

Les voisins ont fini **par** vendre la maison. *The neighbor ended up selling the house.*
Les moustiques rentrent **par** la porte. *Mosquitoes are coming in through the door.*

EX. 2.22 *Traduisez les phrases suivantes.*   AUDIO 20.3 ◀))

1. She answered by chance.

    _____

2. Do you (est-ce que tu) live around here?

    _____

3. We came by the old road.

    _____

4. They (m) obtained the money by force.

    _____

5. He entered through the door.

    _____

Pour

The preposition **pour** usually translates to for but can also translate to per, in favor of, or on behalf of. We use the preposition **pour**:

AUDIO 20.4 ◀))

To talk about a destination, people, place, or abstract goal:

Le cadeau est **pour** mon frère. *The gift is for my brother.*
C'est le train **pour** Paris. *It's the train for Paris.*
Les aides sont **pour** les réfugiés. *The help is for the refugees.*
Il se bat **pour** les droits de l'homme. *He fights for human rights.*

To talk about percentage:

50 **pour** cent – 50 percent

Verbs with pour:

A list of verbs use the preposition **pour**, some of the most common French verbs are: AUDIO 20.5 ◀))

Acheter pour	To buy for
Compter pour	To be worth
Craindre pour	To fear for
Être pour	To be in favor of
Parler pour	To speak on behalf of
Partir pour	To leave for
Payer pour (qqun)	To pay for (sb)
Se pencher pour	To bend over to

Remercier pour	To thank for
Travailler pour	To work for
Voter pour	To vote for

If **pour** is followed by a verb, the verb will always be in its infinitive form.

Ça compte **pour** du beurre. *It counts for nothing.*
Parler **pour** ne rien dire. *Talking to say nothing.*
On a voté **pour** le président. *We voted for the president.*

EX. 2.23 *Choisissez parmi les verbes ci-dessus et conjuguez-les au temps donné.*   AUDIO 20.6 ◀))

1. _____ les cadeaux _____ les enfants. (passé composé)

2. Nous _____ l'avortement. (présent)

3. Est-ce que tu _____ Julie _____ son aide ? (passé composé)

4. Elle _____ Barcelone. (passé composé)

5. Toute la province _____ la gauche. (passé composé)

Other Prepositions

AUDIO 20.7 ◀))

À propos de / au sujet de   about

Il faut faire quelque chose **à propos de la** toiture. *We must do something about the roof.*
Le gouvernement sait beaucoup de choses **au sujet des** entreprises. *The government knows a lot of things about companies.*

Avec   with

Il est **avec** les enfants. *He is with the children.*
Je mange toujours **avec** mon mari. *I always eat with my husband.*

D'après   according to

Il va pleuvoir **d'après** la météo. *It's going to rain according to the weather forecast.*
D'après moi, il n'est pas honnête. *According to me, he is not honest.*

Environ   approximatively, about

Les ventes représentent **environ** 50% des revenus. *Sales represent approximatively 50% of the income.*
Je dors **environ** 6 heures par nuit. *I sleep about 6 hours per night.*

Malgré   despite

La voiture fonctionne **malgré** les problèmes. *The car works despite the issues.*
Malgré le retard, on est arrivés à l'heure. *Despite the delay, we arrived on time.*

Parmi among

Elle est la seule fille **parmi** les garçons. *She is the only girl among boys.*
Le virus se propage **parmi** les personnes âgées. *The virus is spreading among old people.*

Sans without

Nous passons un week-end **sans** les enfants. *We spend a weekend without the children.*
J'essaie de manger **sans** gluten. *I try to eat without gluten.*

Sauf except

Ils ont trouvé tous les trésors **sauf** un. *They found all the treasures except one.*
Il aime tous les légumes, **sauf** les courgettes. *He likes all vegetables, except zucchinis.*

Selon according to

Selon le documentaire, les voitures électriques sont l'avenir. *According to the documentary, electric cars are the future.*
Laver le chapeau **selon** les instructions. *Wash the hat according to instructions.*

Vers / Envers towards, around (time)

L'avion se dirige **vers** la ville. *The plane is directed towards the city.*
Cette photo a été prise **vers** 2005. *This picture was taken around 2005.*

EX. 2.24 *Choisissez parmi les **prépositions** ci-dessus.* AUDIO 20.8 ◄))

1. Il a réalisé le film _____ les directions.

2. J'ai tout acheté _____ les bananes.

3. On prendra une pizza _____ du jambon.

4. _____ leurs efforts, ils n'ont pas réussi.

5. _____ la météo, il va faire beau toute la semaine.

6. Elle gagne _____ 3000 dollars.

7. C'est possible de vivre _____ manger de viande.

8. Cette attaque était dirigée _____ les diplomates.

9. Je rêve d'une semaine _____ travailler.

10. J'ai grandi _____ des garçons.

EX. 2.25 *Choisissez parmi les prépositions ci-dessous.* **AUDIO 20.9** 🔊

par – malgré – pour - avec – selon – sans – pour – à propos de – aux environ de – par

1. Le mariage était magnifique _____ la pluie.

2. _____ l'article, le politicien a démissionné.

3. Elle est arrivée _____ minuit.

4. J'écris toujours _____ ma main droite.

5. Est-ce que tu as entendu quelque chose _____ cette histoire ?

6. Le contrat est signé _____ tous les participants.

7. Ce n'est pas _____ toi.

8. Qu'est-ce qu'on mange _____ le déjeuner ?

9. La plupart des élèves réussissent _____ difficulté.

10. La souris est passé _____ le trou pour rentrer.

Notes :

When Not to Use an Article
Quand Ne Pas Utiliser un Article

As said before, French requires articles in front of nouns most of the time. In some very specific cases, we don't add an article :

AUDIO 21.1 🔊

To indicate a profession (except after c'est):

Il est docteur. *He is a doctor.*
Elle est avocate. *She is a lawyer.*
Il est devenu infirmier. *He became a nurse.*
Elle est devenue mère au foyer. *She became a stay-at-home mom.*

After **de**, if the noun is plural and after references of quantity:

Il a beaucoup de problèmes. *He has a lot of problems.*
Elle a reçu plusieurs invitations. *She got several invitations.*

After some prepositions when talking in a general way:

Avec	**Elle cherche un appartement avec balcon.**	*She is looking for an apartment with a balcony.*
Sans	**Tu ne te sentiras pas mieux sans étirements.**	*You won't feel better without stretching.*
Sous	**L'Europe est sous eau.**	*Europe is under water.*
En	**Nous sommes en classe.**	*We are in class.*
Par	**Il fait ça par habitude.**	*He does that by habit.*

After **parler** when talking about languages:

Je parle français depuis plusieurs années. *I have been speaking French for a few years.*
Il aimerait parler espagnol. *He would like to speak Spanish.*

EX. 2.26 *Ajoutez un article si nécessaire.*   **AUDIO 21.2** 🔊

1. J'apprends _____ chinois depuis janvier.

2. Il parle _____ luxembourgeois et _____ allemand.

3. _____ commandes sont arrivées.

4. C'est _____ docteur incroyable !

5. Elle s'est mariée par _____ obligation.

6. Elle a gagné _____ gros lot !

7. Tu manges beaucoup trop de _____ sel.

8. Elle a acheté plusieurs _____ chapeaux.

Notes :

Same Verb - Different Prepositions
Même Verbe – Prépositions Différentes

Aller

Aller to go
Nous **allons** en France ce week-end. *We are going to France this weekend.*

Aller vers + time to go at around + time
Je **vais** au lit **vers** 21 heures. *I am going to bed at around 9 p.m.*

Aller vers + location to go toward + location
L'avion **va vers** Bruxelles. *The plan is going toward Brussels.*

Apprendre

Apprendre à to learn to
Les enfants **apprennent à** dessiner. *Children learn to draw*

Apprendre par to learn from
Elle a **appris** la nouvelle **par** sa sœur. *She heard the news from her sister.*

Arriver

Arriver à to manage/succeed in
Il n'**arrive** pas **à** étudier tout seul. *He can't study alone.*

Arriver de + location to arrive from + location
Ce colis **arrive de** Chine. *This package is arriving from China.*

Chercher

Chercher to look for
Les étudiants **cherchent** un travail pour l'été. *Students are looking for a job for the summer.*

Chercher à to attempt to / to try to
Elle **cherche à** nous persuader. *She is trying to persuade us.*

Chercher dans to look in
Cherche dans la boîte. *Look in the box.*

Commencer

Commencer à to begin to / to start to
Il **commence à** faire chaud. *It's starting to get hot.*

Commencer par to begin by / to start by
Commence par ranger ta chambre et après je déciderai. *Begin by tidying up your room and after I will decide.*

---

*Remember to **download the audio** of the lists and to **watch the videos** – see Preface*

Compter

Compter — to expect / to intend
Le maire **compte** être réélu. *The maire is expecting to be re-elected.*

Compter pour — to count / to be worth
Cela **compte pour** du beurre. *That counts for nothing.*

Compter sur — to count on
Il peut **compter sur** moi. *He can count on me.*

Croire

Croire — to think / to believe
Il **croit** tout ce que je dis. *He believes everything I say.*

Croire à — to believe something
Il ne **croit** pas **à** cette théorie. *He doesn't believe this theory.*

Croire en — to believe in
Il **croit en** Dieu. *He believes in God.*

Donner

Donner — to give
Donner sur — to overlook / to open onto
Elle lui a **donné** la chambre qui **donne sur** la piscine. *She gave him the room that overlooks the pool.*

Être

Être à — to belong to
C'**est à** lui. *It's his.*

Être pour — to be in favor of
Je **suis pour** le vaccin. *I am in favor of the vaccine.*

Être vers + time — to be around/near + time
C'**est vers** 15 heures. *It's around 3 p.m.*

Finir

Finir de — to finish
Finir par — to end up
Je **viens de** finir de travailler mais je vais **finir par** démissionner. *I just finished work, but I will end up quitting.*

Parler

Parler à — to talk to
Parler de — to talk about
Il parle **à** sa sœur **de** son projet. *He is talking to his sister about his project.*

Parler pour — to speak on behalf of
Il **parle pour** tout le monde. *He is speaking on behalf of everyone.*

Partir

Partir de	to leave
Partir dans + time	to leave in + time
Partir pour	to leave for / to be off to

Nous **partons de** l'hôtel **dans** 10 minutes **pour** la gare. *We are leaving the hotel in 10 minutes for the train station.*

Tenir

Tenir à to insist on / to be attached to

Je **tiens à** ce collier. *I am attached to this necklace.*

Tenir de to take after

Je **tiens** ça **de** mon père. *I took that after my dad.*

Venir

Venir de to have just

Tu **viens de** partir. *You have just left.*

Venir par to come by

Il **vient par** la vieille route. *He is coming by the old road.*

EX. 2.27 *Choisissez parmi les deux prépositions pour chaque verbe.* AUDIO 22.2 ◀))

1. (de – par) Il va finir _____ se faire arrêter.

2. (/ – sur) Le balcon donne _____ la mer.

3. (de – pour) C'est _____ moi.

4. (à – par) J'ai appris _____ peindre très tôt.

5. (à – de) Elle tient son caractère _____ son père.

Notes :

The Recent Past – Le Passé Récent

The recent past is called **passé récent** in French, simply because it just happened.

To build the **passé récent**, conjugate the verb **venir** in the present tense, add **de** and the infinitive verb of the action you want to describe. It's also common to have **juste** between **venir** and **de**.

Attention that **venir de + location** translates to coming from + location, and we add the infinitive after the verb **venir**.

> **Je viens de** + infinitive = I have just done / I just did
> **Je viens juste de** + infinitive = I have just done / I just did

The verb **venir** – present tense: AUDIO **22.1.1** ◀))

Je **viens**	Nous **venons**
Tu **viens**	Vous **venez**
Il-Elle-On **vient**	Ils-Elles **viennent**

De becomes **d'** when followed by an infinitive verb starting with a vowel or a silent h.

Elle **vient juste de** <u>partir</u>. *She just left.*
Je **viens d'**<u>acheter</u> cette voiture. *I just bought this car.*
Il **vient de** <u>commencer</u>. *He just started.*
On n'a pas faim, on **vient juste de** <u>manger</u>. *We aren't hungry, we just ate.*

EX. 2.28 *Remettez les phrases dans l'ordre et conjuguez le verbe au passé récent.*   AUDIO **22.1.2** ◀))

1. concert / chanter / une / au / elle / chanson

   _____

2. parc / se promener / on / au / juste

   _____

3. son / réaliser / il / erreur

   _____

4. travail / finir / nous / le

   _____

5. bébé / le / boire / biberon / son

   _____

6. train / passager / manquer / le / son

_____

7. les / découvrir / planète / chercheurs / une

_____

8. les / contrat / signer / le / parents

_____

9. valise / elle / préparer / la

_____

10. administration / le / soumettre / l' / dossier

_____

How to Ask a Question
Comment Poser Une Question

Just like in English, we have different ways to ask a question. We have questions with a yes-no answer and questions for specific information, such as time. On top of that, we also have formal and informal questions. Let's start with the yes/no questions.

Yes-no Questions

For **yes-no questions**, we have **3 different ways** to ask a question. The easiest and most common way in everyday French is simply to **raise your voice at the end of the sentence** to turn it into a question. This is what you will encounter the mos.

AUDIO 23.1 ◄))

Tu es prête ? Oui, je suis prête.
Are you ready? Yes, I am ready.

Elle peut venir avec nous ? Non, elle ne peut pas venir avec nous.
Can she come with us? No, she can't come with us.

C'est disponible ? Oui, c'est disponible.
Is it available? Yes, it's available.

Now that you know how to make a question by simply raising your voice at the end of the question, the next step is to add **est-ce que in front of the subject**. This is also a yes-no question.

AUDIO 23.2 ◄))

Tu es prête ?
Est-ce que tu es prête ? Oui, je suis prête.
Are you ready? Yes, I am ready.

Elle peut venir avec nous ?
Est-ce qu'elle peut venir avec nous ? Non, elle ne peut pas venir avec nous.
Can she come with us? No, she can't come with us.

C'est disponible ?
Est-ce que c'est disponible ? Oui, c'est disponible.
Is it available? Yes, it's available.

The third way to ask a yes-no question is by using the **inversion**. It's the most formal way to ask a question. The verb is placed before the pronoun, and a hyphen joins the two. The auxiliary goes first when the verb is a compound tense such as **passé composé**.

AUDIO 23.3 ◄))

Tu es prête ?
Es-tu prête ? Oui, je suis prête.
Are you ready? Yes, I am ready.

Elle peut venir avec nous ?

Peut-elle venir avec nous ? Non, elle ne peut pas venir avec nous.

Can she come with us? No, she can't come with us.

C'est disponible ? (Ce + est)

Est-ce disponible ? Oui, c'est disponible.

Is it available? Yes, it's available.

EX. 2.29 *Changez les phrases en **question**. Sur la première ligne, ajoutez **est-ce que**. Sur la deuxième ligne, ajoutez **l'inversion**.* AUDIO 23.4 ◀))

1. Elles ont vu le papier sur la table.

   Est-ce que _____

   Inversion : _____

2. Tu as gagné à la loterie.

   Est-ce que _____

   Inversion : _____

3. Vous êtes arrivés à temps.

   Est-ce que _____

   Inversion : _____

4. Ils ont déjà signé le contrat.

   Est-ce que _____

   Inversion : _____

5. Vous économisez assez d'argent.

   Est-ce que _____

   Inversion : _____

6. Tu as accordé la bourse aux familles.

   Est-ce que _____

   Inversion : _____

7. Vous avez gardé cette vieille valise ?

   Est-ce que _____

   Inversion : _____

8. Ils ont quitté la maison il y a une heure.

   Est-ce que _____

   Inversion : _____

*Remember to **download the audio** of the lists and to **watch the videos** – see Preface*

9. Vous avez visité ce château.

    Est-ce que _____

    Inversion : _____

10. Tu as répondu à la question correctement.

    Est-ce que _____

    Inversion : _____

EX. 2.30 *Écrivez la question avec **est-ce que** pour obtenir la réponse donnée.* AUDIO 23.5 ◀))

1. _____

    Oui, j'ai vu ce film.

2. _____

    Non, il n'a pas répondu au téléphone.

3. _____

    Oui, la police a prévenu ses parents.

4. _____

    Oui, ils ont remercié les invités.

5. _____

    Oui, nous avons marché toute la journée.

Note that when the verb ends with a vowel and the pronoun starts with a vowel, we add **-t-** between the verb and the pronoun. **-t-** doesn't have any meaning; we add it only for phonetic reasons.

AUDIO 23.6 ◀))

Il aime le jus d'orange ?
Aime-t-il le jus d'orange ? Oui, il aime le jus d'orange.
Does he like orange juice? Yes, he likes orange juice.

Elle est en retard ?
Est-elle en retard ? Oui, elle est en retard.
Is she late? Yes, she is late.

EX. 2.31 *Transformez ces phrases en question avec inversion.* **AUDIO 23.7** ◀))

1. Il est arrivé dans la soirée.
   _____

2. Elle a établi un plan pour réussir ses études.
   _____

3. Il a laissé le chien dehors.
   _____

4. Elle a donné son salaire à une association.
   _____

5. Il a essayé de se faire pardonner.
   _____

Interrogative Adverbs

Here is the list of the **interrogative adverbs**:

AUDIO 24.1 ◀))

Quand	When
Comment	How
Pourquoi	Why
Où	Where
Combien (de)	How many – How much

To use an interrogative adverb, you have two possibilities for more formal questions. The first one and the easiest is to use **est-ce que** after the interrogative adverb, the second one is to use the **inversion**.
To ask an informal question with an interrogative adverb, simply add the adverb after, but sometimes at the beginning of the question.

AUDIO 24.2 ◀))

Quand   When

When are you leaving?

Quand est-ce que tu pars ?
Quand pars-tu ?
Informal: Tu pars **quand** ?

Comment   How

How are you?

Comment allez-vous ?
Comment est-ce que vous allez ?
Informal: Comment tu vas ?

Pourquoi   Why

Why are they doing that?

Pourquoi est-ce qu'ils font ça ?
Pourquoi font-ils ça ?
Informal: Pourquoi ils font ça ?

Où   Where

Where do you live?

Où est-ce que tu vis ?
Où vis-tu ?
Informal: Tu vis **où** ?

Combien   How many / How much

How much did you get?

Combien est-ce que tu as reçu ?
Combien as-tu reçu ?
Informal: Tu as reçu **combien** ?

Combien de   How many / How much

Use **de** or **d'** after combien when followed by a noun or an adjective:

How many friends do you have?

Combien d'amis est-ce que tu as ?
Combien d'amis as-tu ?
Informal: Tu as **combien d'**amis ?

Here, because we have « **combien de** », the pronoun is in the middle of the informal question since you can't finish de question by « **de** ».

EX. 2.32 *Traduisez ces questions avec **est-ce que** et en **question informelle**.*   AUDIO 24.3 ◄ఱ

1. When are you going to the store? (tu)

     _____

     _____

2. How does he study?

     _____

     _____

3. Why are you late? (tu)

     _____

     _____

---

4. How many houses does he own?

_____

_____

5. Where is she going?

_____

_____

6. Where are you working? (tu)

_____

_____

7. How many dogs does she have?

_____

_____

8. Where do your parents live?

_____

_____

9. How many months do you work during the year? (tu)

_____

_____

10. When is your brother coming back?

_____

_____

Interrogative Pronouns

The use of **interrogative pronouns** is very specific to each pronoun.

Here is the list of the interrogative pronouns:

Qui	Who – Whom
Qui est-ce qui	Who
Qui est-ce que	Whom
Que / Qu'	What
Qu'est-ce qui	What
Qu'est-ce que	What
De – à – avec … quoi	What

How to use qui?

Qui means both who and whom and also have different forms in French. It all depends if **Qui** is the **subject** or the **object**.

Qui as the subject:

To ask the question who?, you can either use **qui**, or **qui est-ce qui**. Inversion isn't allowed in this case.

Qui	Who
Qui est-ce qui	Who

Who saw this movie?

Qui a vu ce film ?
Qui est-ce qui a vu ce film ?

⇨ Here **qui** and **qui est-ce qui** are both <u>subjects of the question</u>.

Qui as the object:

To ask the question whom ?, you can either use **qui**, or **qui est-ce que**. Inversion is allowed with **qui** when it represents the object.

Qui	Who
Qui est-ce que	Whom

Whom did you see?

Qui as-tu vu ?
Qui est-ce que tu as vu ?

⇨ Here **qui** and **qui est-ce que** are both objects of the question.

EX. 2.33 *Choisissez entre* **qui est-ce qui** *and* **qui est-ce que.** AUDIO 25.2 🔊

1. _____ est là ?
2. _____ tu vas voir ?
3. _____ le chien a mordu ?
4. _____ a adopté un enfant ?
5. _____ vous aimez voir le week-end ?
6. _____ a téléphoné ce matin ?
7. _____ a mangé mon plat ?
8. _____ tu as appelé ?
9. _____ est arrivée la première ?
10. _____ vous avez vu ?

Qui with prepositions:

To know when to use a preposition such as **à**, **de**, **avec**, etc., go back to the list of verbs followed by a preposition.

AUDIO 25.3 🔊

À qui	To whom
À qui est-ce que	To whom

Whom are you speaking to?

À qui parles-tu ?
À qui est-ce que tu parles ?

⇨ A few verbs with à: **penser à, être à, demander à,** etc.

De qui	About whom
De qui est-ce que	About whom

Whom are you talking about?

De qui parles-tu ?
De qui est-ce que tu parles ?

⇨ A few verbs with de: **avoir peur de, s'agir de, se méfier de,** etc.

Avec qui	With whom
Avec qui est-ce que	With whom

With whom are you talking?

Avec qui parles-tu ?
Avec qui est-ce que tu parles ?

EX. 2.34 *Choisissez entre **à qui est-ce que** - **de qui est-ce que** - **avec qui est-ce que**.* AUDIO 25.4 ◀))

1. _____ tu as donné l'enveloppe ?

2. _____ vous êtes au cinéma ?

3. _____ il s'agit ?

4. _____ vous avez téléphoné ?

5. _____ il est parti ?

6. _____ vous avez fait mal ?

7. _____ tu as rêvé ?

8. _____ cet argent a servi ?

9. _____ tu as mangé ?

10. _____ elle a profité ?

How to use que?

AUDIO 25.5 ◀))

Que means what and can also be the **subject** or the **object**.

Que as subject:

When **que** acts as a **subject**, the only way to ask the question is to use **qu'est-ce qui**.
No inversion is allowed with **qu'est-ce qui**.

Qu'est-ce qui   What

What's wrong?

Qu'est-ce qui ne va pas ?

Que as object:

When **que** acts like an **object**, we can use **que** with **inversion** or just **qu'est-ce que**.

Que   What

What do you want?

Que veux-tu ?
Qu'est-ce que tu veux ?

EX. 2.35 *Choisissez entre* **qu'est-ce qui** *ou* **qu'est-ce que** *et complétez la question.*   AUDIO 25.6 ◄))

1. _____ tu as reçu pour Noël ?
2. _____ pèse 10 kilos ?
3. _____ il aime faire le week-end ?
4. _____ arrivera si elle ne vient pas ?
5. _____ tu attends ?
6. _____ t'arrive ?
7. _____ lui a plu ?
8. _____ vous faites ce soir ?
9. _____ est arrivé à la voiture ?
10. _____ tu écoutes ?

Another way to ask a question when **que is the object is to change que for quoi** and place it at the end of the sentence. This is, of course, an informal question:

AUDIO 25.7 ◄))

Que = quoi

What do you want?

Tu veux **quoi** ?

Que with prepositions:

After a preposition, **que** becomes **quoi**. To know when to use a preposition such as **à**, **de**, **avec**, etc., go back to the list of verbs followed by a preposition.

À quoi   What

What are you thinking about?

À quoi penses-tu ?
À quoi est-ce que tu penses ?
Tu penses **à quoi** ?

⇨ A few verbs with à: **jouer à, croire à, servir à**, etc.

De quoi   What

What are you talking about?

De quoi parles-tu ?
De quoi est-ce que tu parles ?
Tu parles **de quoi** ?

⇨ A few verbs with de: **manquer de, s'occuper de, profiter de**, etc.

Avec quoi   What

With what are you cooking?

Avec quoi cuisines-tu ?
Avec quoi est-ce que tu cuisines ?
Tu cuisines **avec quoi** ?

EX. 2.36 *Choisissez entre **à quoi** - **de quoi** - **avec quoi** et formez une question.*   AUDIO 25.8 ◄))

1. _____ est-ce que ce monument ressemble ?

2. _____ est-ce que vous avez hérité ?

3. _____ est-ce que tu veux jouer ?

4. _____ est-ce que tu parles ?

5. _____ est-ce que tu cuisines ?

6. _____ est-ce que tu as peur ?

7. _____ est-ce que vous pensez ?

8. _____ est-ce qu'il se sert pour travailler ?

9. _____ est-ce qu'elle nourrit les chevaux ?

10. _____ est-ce que tu penses ?

The Interrogative Adjective – Quel

Quel is an **interrogative adjective** that translates to which and what. French interrogative adjectives agree in gender and number with the noun they describe.

AUDIO 26.1 ◄))

Masculine singular = Quel   What / Which
Feminine singular = Quelle   What / Which

Masculine plural = Quels   What / Which
Feminine plural = Quelles   What / Which

How to use quel?

As an adjective, **quel** is (almost) always **followed by a noun** but can also be **followed by a verb**.

Quel followed by a noun:

When **quel** is followed by a **noun**, **inversion** and the use of **est-ce que** are allowed.

Quel — What / Which

What dish did you order?

Quel <u>plat</u> as-tu commandé ?
Quel <u>plat</u> **est-ce que** tu as commandé ?

But **quel** can also be in the **middle of the sentence** in an informal question. Even then, it's followed by the noun:

Tu as commandé **quel** plat ?

Quel followed by a verb:

Quel — What / Which

What is your favorite movie?

Quel est ton film préféré ?

Quel is used in a very similar way as in English. When what is followed by a noun in English, it will be the same in French. The same applies to verbs.

Quel with prepositions:

De quel — From what / Which

Which city are you from?

De quelle ville viens-tu ?
De quelle ville est-ce que tu viens ?
Tu viens **de quelle** ville ?

Quel alone with a noun:

Quel can be used alone with only a noun to ask for more information about something previously mentioned.

What do you think of my idea? What idea?

Qu'est-ce que tu penses de mon idée ?
Quelle idée ?

EX. 2.37 *Ajoutez **quel** – **quelle** – **quels** – **quelles** – **de quel** – **de quelle** pour compléter les questions.*

AUDIO 26.2 ◀))

1. _____ est votre nom ?

2. _____ idée est la meilleure ?

3. _____ film est-ce que tu parles ?

4. _____ est votre chanteur préféré ?

5. J'ai reçu un appel de l'avocat. _____ avocat ?

6. _____ heure est-il ?

7. _____ sont les meilleures fraises ?

8. _____ personne es-tu responsable ?

9. _____ temps fait-il aujourd'hui ?

10. _____ livres est-ce que vous avez lu ?

The interrogative Pronoun – Lequel

I have been asked so many questions about **lequel**, but it's pretty simple when we look at its main purpose.
Lequel is simply used to not repeat something that we are already talking about.
It translates to which one. Let's see an example:

AUDIO 26.3 🔊

Zach: **J'ai envie d'acheter ce pull.** *I want to buy this sweater.*
Me (not really looking): **Lequel ?** *Which one?*

⇨ **Lequel** is simply the contraction of **le pull + quel** = **Le + quel** = **Lequel**

As you can guess, **lequel** will change with gender and number, but also with prepositions:

	Masc. Sing	Fem. Sing.	Masc. Pl.	Fem. Pl
	Lequel	**Laquelle**	**Lesquels**	**Lesquelles**
à + lequel	**Auquel**	**À laquelle**	**Auxquels**	**Auxquelles**
de + lequel	**Duquel**	**De laquelle**	**Desquels**	**Auxquelles**

I usually advise to know how to use **lequel - laquelle - lesquels and lesquelles**. But **auquel - duquel** and variations aren't used that much in spoken French. You can find them mostly in written French, so be sure to recognize them but don't worry too much about them.

Laquelle (de ces peintures) est-ce que tu préfères ? *Which one (of these paintings) do you prefer?*
Lequel est-ce que tu veux ? *Which one do you want?*
Lesquelles (de ces fleurs) veux-tu ? *Which ones (of these flowers) do you want?*

EX. 2.38 *Ajoutez lequel – laquelle – lesquels – lesquelles.* AUDIO 26.4 ◀))

1. (un pull) _____ est-ce que tu as commandé ?

2. (une personne) _____ de vous est responsable ?

3. (les maisons) _____ est-ce que tu as visité ?

4. (les médicaments) _____ sont à toi ?

5. (un parapluie) _____ est-ce que vous avez acheté ?

6. (une université) _____ est-ce que tu as choisi ?

7. (les chaussures) _____ sont les plus confortables ?

8. (un auteur) _____ est-ce que tu préfères ?

9. (les poires) _____ sont les meilleures ?

10. (une idée) _____ est-ce que le patron a aimé le plus ?

Tag Questions

Tag questions are words or groups of words added at the end of an affirmative sentence to turn it into a question.

AUDIO 26.5 ◀))

N'est-ce pas ?

The French language doesn't use "aren't you?, isn't she?, etc." Instead, we have other ways to end a question if we want to make sure that the other person heard us.

Il est bien arrivé, **n'est-ce pas ?** *He arrived safely, didn't he?*
C'est ta sœur, **n'est-ce pas ?** *This is your sister, isn't she?*

N'est-ce pas is quite formal and barely used in spoken French. Instead, we have many other ways to ask a final question. In spoken French, we will use more "**hein**" or "**non**":

Il est bien arrivé, **hein ?** *He arrived safely, didn't he?*
C'est ta sœur, **non ?** *She's your sister, isn't she?*

Other little words that we add at the end of a question:

OK / D'accord

On part bientôt, **ok ?** *We are leaving soon, ok?*
Tu vas te coucher dans 5 minutes, **d'accord ?** *You are going to bed in 5 minutes, ok?*

Non

Son anniversaire est en décembre, **non ?** *His birthday is in December, isn't it?*
Il a réussi, **non ?** *He made it, didn't he?*

Si - with a negative question

Ils ne sont pas mariés, **si ?** *They aren't married, are they?*

How to Answer a Negative Question?

To answer a negative question, we use **si** to make sure that the negative question is reversed into a positive statement.

AUDIO 26.6 🔊

Ils ne sont pas mariés ? *Aren't they married?*
Si, ils sont mariés depuis quelques années. *Yes, they have been married for a few years.*

Tu n'as pas raté ton avion ? *Didn't you miss your flight?*
Si, j'ai dû attendre le prochain vol. *Yes, I had to wait for the next flight.*

EX. 2.39 *Répondez à ces questions avec **si, je ...***   **AUDIO 26.7** 🔊

1. Tu ne parles pas espagnol ?

   _____

2. Tu n'es pas mariée ?

   _____

3. Tu ne travailles plus ? (encore)

   _____

4. Tu n'habites plus en ville ? (toujours)

   _____

5. Tu n'as pas fait les courses ce matin ?

   _____

Chapter 2 – Review
Chapitre 2 – Révision

EX. 2.40 *Formez une question avec les éléments de la première ligne et répondez avec **oui** ou **non** sur la deuxième ligne.* AUDIO 26.1.1 ◀️))

1. Tu as essayé cette robe.

    Est-ce que _____

    Non, _____

2. Nous avons réservé nos vacances d'été.

    Inversion (vous) : _____

    Oui, _____

3. Elle aime cueillir les fruits de son jardin.

    Est-ce que _____

    Oui, _____

4. Il a forcé l'homme à rentrer dans la voiture.

    Inversion : _____

    Non, _____

5. Tu vas bien ?

    Est-ce que _____

    Oui, _____

6. Mon grand-père a fondé l'entreprise en 1990.

    Est-ce que (ton) _____

    Non, _____

7. L'employé a descendu la poubelle.

    Inversion (il) :_____

    Oui, _____

8. Je dors tard tous les samedis.

   Est-ce que (tu) _____

   Non, _____

9. Tu as menti aux enquêteurs.

   Inversion : _____

   Oui, _____

10. Cette route mène à la vieille ville.

    Est-ce que _____

    Non, _____

CHAPTER 3

Adjectives
Les Adjectifs

Adjectives – Les Adjectifs

But first, what is an adjective?

An **adjective** is a word that modifies or describes a noun. In other words, it helps to give information about the noun.

Adjectives in English only change when used for comparison:

⇨ A **lucky** woman = She is the **luckiest**

In French, adjectives agree in gender and number with the noun they modify, which will change the spelling and the pronunciation.

> French adjectives agree in gender and number with the noun they modify.

Gender and Number

Do you remember the lesson about French nouns with all the different endings? The process is the same here. Let's start with adjectives ending in E, the easiest.

Adjectives ending in E: AUDIO 27.1 ◀))

When an adjective ends in **E**, the masculine and feminine are the same, for the plural, add only an S:

	Masc. Sing	Fem. Sing.	Masc. Pl.	Fem. Pl
Free	**Libre**	**Libre**	**Libres**	**Libres**
Famous	**Célèbre**	**Célèbre**	**Célèbres**	**Célèbres**
Clean	**Propre**	**Propre**	**Propres**	**Propres**

⇨ The pronunciation stays the same for all forms.

Adjectives ending in É – I – U: AUDIO 27.2 ◀))

When an adjective ends in **É – I** or **U**, the feminine will take an E, for the plural, add only an S.

	Masc. Sing	Fem. Sing.	Masc. Pl.	Fem. Pl
Old	**Âgé**	**Âgée**	**Âgés**	**Âgées**
True	**Vrai**	**Vraie**	**Vrais**	**Vraies**
Missing	**Disparu**	**Disparue**	**Disparus**	**Disparues**

⇨ The pronunciation stays the same for all forms.

Adjectives ending in T – D – N – S: AUDIO 27.3 ◀»

When an adjective ends in **T – D – N** or **S**, the feminine will take an E. For the plural, add only an S.

	Masc. Sing	Fem. Sing.	Masc. Pl.	Fem. Pl
Funny	**Amusant**	**Amusante**	**Amusants**	**Amusantes**
Blond	**Blond**	**Blonde**	**Blonds**	**Blondes**
Next	**Prochain**	**Prochaine**	**Prochains**	**Prochaines**
English	**Anglais**	**Anglaise**	**Anglais**	**Anglaises**

⇨ In this case, the pronunciation of the feminine form of the adjective changes. The last consonant is pronounced (**T – D – N – S**), but not **E**. The plural of adjectives ending in S doesn't change since French doesn't allow double S.

Adjectives ending in EUX: AUDIO 27.4 ◀»

When an adjective ends in **EUX**, the masculine singular and plural are the same, but the feminine forms turn into **EUSE(S)**.

	Masc. Sing	Fem. Sing.	Masc. Pl.	Fem. Pl
Happy	**Heureux**	**Heureuse**	**Heureux**	**Heureuses**

⇨ The masculine plural of adjectives ending in EUX doesn't change since French doesn't allow X to be followed by an S.

EX. 3.1 *Remplissez les cases vides avec les adjectifs.* AUDIO 27.5 ◀»

Masc. Sing	Fem. Sing.	Masc. Pl.	Fem. Pl
Lâche			
	Désolée		
		Grands	
			Bleues
		Bruns	
	Dorée		
Gris			
	Suivante		
		Ravis	
			Vivantes

Adjectives ending in F: AUDIO 27.6 🔊

When an adjective ends in **F** (**if** and **euf**), the feminine forms change to **VE** (**ive** and **euve**)

	Masc. Sing	Fem. Sing.	Masc. Pl.	Fem. Pl
Active	**Actif**	**Active**	**Actifs**	**Actives**
Athletic	**Sportif**	**Sportive**	**Sportifs**	**Sportives**
New	**Neuf**	**Neuve**	**Neufs**	**Neuves**
Widowed	**Veuf**	**Veuve**	**Veufs**	**Veuves**

Adjectives ending in ER: AUDIO 27.7 🔊

When an adjective ends in **ER**, the feminine forms change to **ÈRE**.

	Masc. Sing	Fem. Sing.	Masc. Pl.	Fem. Pl
Proud	**Fier**	**Fière**	**Fiers**	**Fières**
Expensive	**Cher**	**Chère**	**Chers**	**Chères**
First	**Premier**	**Première**	**Premiers**	**Premières**

⇨ For **fier** and **cher**, the pronunciation is the same for all forms, not **premier – première**.

Adjectives ending in AL: AUDIO 27.8 🔊

Adjectives ending in **AL** take an **E** for the feminine form but change to **AUX** when masculine plural.

	Masc. Sing	Fem. Sing.	Masc. Pl.	Fem. Pl
Special	**Spécial**	**Spéciale**	**Spéciaux**	**Spéciales**
Social	**Social**	**Sociale**	**Sociaux**	**Sociales**
National	**National**	**Nationale**	**Nationaux**	**Nationales**

Double final consonant: AUDIO 27.9 🔊

Some adjectives will **double the last consonant** before adding an **E** or an **S** for the plural.

	Masc. Sing	Fem. Sing.	Masc. Pl.	Fem. Pl
Former	**Ancien**	**Ancienne**	**Anciens**	**Anciennes**
Low	**Bas**	**Basse**	**Bas**	**Basses**
Big	**Gros**	**Grosse**	**Gros**	**Grosses**
Kind	**Gentil**	**Gentille**	**Gentils**	**Gentilles**

⇨ Remember that if the adjective ends with an **S**, the plural form doesn't take a second S.

EX. 3.2 *Ajoutez l'adjectif féminin.* AUDIO 27.10 🔊

1. Gentil _____
2. Naïf _____
3. Gros _____
4. Entier _____
5. Pareil _____

6. Premier _____
7. Banal _____
8. Cher _____
9. Gros _____
10. Ancien _____

Irregular Adjectives

Some adjectives don't follow the masculine / feminine / plural rule explained in this lesson. Their feminine form is irregular.

AUDIO 27.11 🔊

	Masc. Sing	Fem. Sing.	Masc. Pl.	Fem. Pl
Beautiful	**Beau**	**Belle**	**Beaux**	**Belles**
White	**Blanc**	**Blanche**	**Blancs**	**Blanches**
Complete	**Complet**	**Complète**	**Complets**	**Complètes**
Soft	**Doux**	**Douce**	**Dou<u>x</u>**	**Douces**
Wrong	**Faux**	**Fausse**	**Fau<u>x</u>**	**Fausses**
Favorite	**Favori**	**Favorite**	**Favoris**	**Favorites**
Crazy	**Fou**	**Folle**	**Fous**	**Folles**
Fresh	**Frais**	**Fraîche**	**Frais**	**Fraîches**
Frank	**Franc**	**Franche**	**Francs**	**Franches**
Worried	**Inquiet**	**Inquiète**	**Inquiets**	**Inquiètes**
Long	**Long**	**Longue**	**Longs**	**Longues**
New	**Nouveau**	**Nouvelle**	**Nouveaux**	**Nouvelles**
Public	**Public**	**Publique**	**Publics**	**Publiques**
Redhead	**Roux**	**Rousse**	**Rou<u>x</u>**	**Rousses**
Dry	**Sec**	**Sèche**	**Secs**	**Sèches**
Secret	**Secret**	**Secrète**	**Secrets**	**Secrètes**
Old	**Vieux**	**Vieille**	**Vieu<u>x</u>**	**Vieilles**

Two adjectives don't change:

	Masc. Sing	Fem. Sing.	Masc. Pl.	Fem. Pl
Brown	**Marron**	**Marron**	**Marron**	**Marron**
Orange	**Orange**	**Orange**	**Orange**	**Orange**

EX. 3.3 *Ajoutez un des adjectifs irréguliers de la liste ci-dessus.* AUDIO 27.12 ◀》

1. Quelle _____ maison !

2. Mes petits-enfants sont _____.

3. Ce _____ château doit être rénové.

4. Sa couleur préférée est le _____.

5. Les matins sont _____ au Canada.

6. Les températures sont _____ aujourd'hui.

7. Ce fleuve est _____ de 10 kilomètres.

8. Elle a reçu des _____ informations.

9. C'est _____ !

10. Je pense que cette réponse est _____.

Adjectives with a Fifth Choice

Three adjectives have a specific ending if the <u>following masculine noun starts with a vowel or a silent h</u>:

AUDIO 27.13 ◀》

	Masc. Sing	Fem. Sing.	Masc. Sing. Vowel or silent h	Masc. Pl.	Fem. Pl
New	**Nouveau**	**Nouvelle**	**Nouvel**	**Nouveaux**	**Nouvelles**
Old	**Vieux**	**Vieille**	**Vieil**	**Vie<u>ux</u>**	**Vieilles**
Beautiful	**Beau**	**Belle**	**Bel**	**Beaux**	**Belles**

Un nouveau canapé – A new couch
Un nouvel ordinateur – A new computer

Un vieux téléphone – An old phone
Un vieil arbre – An old tree

Un beau manteau – A beautiful coat
Un bel oiseau – A beautiful bird

EX. 3.4 *Ajoutez un des adjectifs nouveau – vieux – beau.* AUDIO 27.14 ◀》

1. C'est un _____ ami.

2. Elle a des _____ yeux.

3. Le _____ employé est malade.

4. Quel _____ endroit !

5. Ces papiers sont _____ et fragiles.

Tout

Tout translates to all / whole in English. It, of course, agrees in gender and number with the noun it describes. Note that tout as a pronoun means everything and doesn't agree in gender and number.

AUDIO 27.15 ◀))

	Masc. Sing	Fem. Sing.	Masc. Pl.	Fem. Pl
All / Whole	**Tout**	**Toute**	**Tous**	**Toutes**

Je me repose toute la journée. *I am relaxing all day.*
Il a mangé tout le gâteau. *He ate the whole cake.*

Tous ses amis sont venus à son anniversaire. *All his friends came to his birthday.*
Toutes les danseuses sont souples. *All dancers are flexible.*

Common Adjectives

AUDIO 27.16 ◀))

Âgé – Âgée	Old	**Différent – Différente**	Different
Amical – Amicale	Friendly	**Difficile – Difficile**	Difficult
Ancien – Ancienne	Old / Former / Antique	**Doré – Dorée**	Gold
Argenté – Argentée	Silver	**Doux – Douce**	Soft / Sweet
Autre – Autre	Other	**Droit – Droite**	Straight
		Drôle – Drôle	Funny / Strange
Bas – Basse	Low	**Dur – Dure**	Hard
Beau – Belle	Beautiful / Handsome		
Bizarre – Bizarre	Strange / Odd	**Effrayant – Effrayante**	Scary
Blanc – Blanche	White	**Ennuyeux – Ennuyeuse**	Annoying
Bleu – Bleue	Blue	**Entier – Entière**	Whole / Entire
Bon – Bonne	Good	**Épuisé – Épuisée**	Exhausted
Bronzé – Bronzée	Tan	**Étrange – Étrange**	Strange / Odd
Brun – Brune	Brown		
Bruyant – Bruyante	Noisy	**Fâché – Fâchée**	Angry
		Facile – Facile	Easy
Certain – Certaine	Certain / Clear	**Faible – Faible**	Weak
Chaud – Chaude	Hot, warm	**Fatigué – Fatiguée**	Tired
Cher – Chère	Expensive / Dear	**Faux – Fausse**	Wrong
Clair – Claire	Clear / Light / Pale	**Foncé – Foncée**	Dark
Confus – Confuse	Confused	**Fort – Forte**	Strong
Content – Contente	Happy	**Frais – Fraîche**	Cool / Fresh
Courageux – Courageuse	Brave	**Français – Française**	French
Courant – Courante	Common	**Froid – Froide**	Cold
Dangereux – Dangereuse	Dangerous	**Généreux – Généreuse**	Generous
Dernier – Dernière	Last	**Gentil – Gentille**	Kind / Nice / Sweet
Désolé – Désolée	Sorry	**Grand – Grande**	Tall
Désorienté – Désorientée	Confused	**Grave – Grave**	Grave / Serious
Détendu – Détendue	Relaxed		

Gris – Grise	Grey	**Ouvert – Ouverte**	Open
Gros – Grosse	Big / Large	**Pareil – Pareille**	The same / Alike
		Paresseux – Paresseuse	Lazy
Haut – Haute	High / Tall	**Patient – Patiente**	Patient
Heureux – Heureuse	Happy	**Pauvre – Pauvre**	Poor
Honnête – Honnête	Honest	**Petit – Petite**	Small
Humain – Humaine	Human	**Plein – Pleine**	Full
Humide – Humide	Humid	**Poli – Polie**	Polite
		Possible – Possible	Possible
Impatient – Impatiente	Impatient	**Précédent – Précédente**	Previous
Impoli – Impolie	Rude	**Premier – Première**	First
Important – Importante	Important	**Pressé – Pressée**	In a hurry
Impossible – Impossible	Impossible	**Prêt – Prête**	Ready
Inquiet – Inquiète	Worried	**Prochain – Prochaine**	Next
Intelligent – Intelligente	Smart	**Propre – Propre**	Clean / Neat
Intéressant – Intéressante	Interesting		
Inutile – Inutile	Useless	**Rapide – Rapide**	Fast
		Rare – Rare	Rare
Jaune – Jaune	Yellow	**Ravi – Ravie**	Delighted
Jeune – Jeune	Young	**Romantique – Romantique**	Romantic
Joli – Jolie	Pretty	**Rose – Rose**	Pink
Joyeux – Joyeuse	Happy	**Rouge – Rouge**	Red
Juste – Juste	Just / Fair		
		Sage – Sage	Wise / Calm
Lâche – Lâche	Coward	**Sale – Sale**	Dirty
Laid – Laide	Ugly	**Sec – Sèche**	Dry
Léger – Légère	Light	**Sérieux – Sérieuse**	Serious
Lent – Lente	Slow	**Seul – Seule**	Alone
Libre – Libre	Free	**Silencieux – Silencieuse**	Silent
Long – Longue	Long	**Simple – Simple**	Simple
Lourd – Lourde	Heavy	**Solitaire – Solitaire**	Lonely
		Sportif – Sportive	Athletic
Maigre – Maigre	Skinny	**Stupide – Stupide**	Stupid
Malade – Malade	Ill / Sick	**Suivant – Suivante**	Next
Malhonnête – Malhonnête	Dishonest	**Super – Super**	Great
Mauvais – Mauvaise	Bad / Poor	**Sympa – Sympa**	Nice
Méchant – Méchante	Mean		
Meilleur – Meilleure	Better	**Timide – Timide**	Shy
Même – Même	Same	**Tout – Toute**	All
Mignon – Mignonne	Cute	**Tranquille – Tranquille**	Calm
Mince – Mince	Thin	**Travailleur – Travailleuse**	Hard-working
Moderne – Moderne	Modern	**Triste – Triste**	Sad
Mort – Morte	Dead		
Mou – Molle	Soft	**Utile – Utile**	Useful
Mouillé – Mouillée	Wet		
		Vert – Verte	Green
Naïf – Naïve	Naive	**Vide – Vide**	Empty
Navré – Navrée	Sorry	**Vieux – Vieille**	Old
Nerveux – Nerveuse	Nervous	**Violet – Violette**	Purple
Noir – Noire	Black	**Vivant – Vivante**	Alive / Lively
Nuageux – Nuageuse	Cloudy	**Vrai – Vraie**	True / Genuine
Orageux – Orageuse	Stormy		
Orange – Orange	Orange		

Adjectives and Brands

It's common to talk about different products by calling them by their brand names. In this case, the adjective will agree in gender and number with the noun that the brand replaces.

AUDIO 27.17 ◀ッ

J'ai une nouvelle voiture = J'ai une nouvelle Mercedes.
I have a new car = I have a new Mercedes.

J'ai un nouvel iPhone = J'ai un nouveau téléphone.
I have a new iPhone = I have a new phone.

Here **nouveau** turns into **nouvel** since iPhone starts with a vowel.

EX. 3.5 *Choisissez un des adjectifs dans la liste ci-dessous et accordez-le si nécessaire.*

AUDIO 27.18 ◀ッ

orageux – vieux – sec – léger – mignon – mou – inquiet – joli – rose – beau – patient – meilleur – noir – dur – prochaine – heureux – laid – nouveau – étrange – seul

1. Cette chienne est tellement _____ !

2. Tu es (m) _____ comme une plume.

3. Les couvertures sont déjà _____.

4. Mon père est un homme _____.

5. Nous (f) sommes très _____ pour toi.

6. Ma _____ voiture n'est pas encore arrivée.

7. Tu as vu ce _____ homme ?

8. Pourquoi est-ce que tu gardes cette _____ chemise ?

9. C'est le _____ athlète dans sa catégorie.

10. Les fleurs _____ sont les plus belles.

11. C'est mon opinion mais ces chaussures sont _____.

12. Il fait _____ aujourd'hui.

13. Ma grand-mère est _____ quand je ne donne pas de nouvelles.

14. Cette pâtisserie est trop _____ à manger.

15. C'est une histoire _____.

16. Je (f) préfère étudier _____ dans ma chambre.

17. Le _____ train est à 10 heures.

18. On a acheté de la peinture _____ pour la buanderie.

19. Je préfère les matelas _____.

20. Elle a acheté une _____ robe pour le mariage.

Where to Place the Adjective?
Où Placer l'Adjectif ?

Most adjectives are placed after the noun in French, which can be confusing for English speakers since the adjective is placed before the noun in English.

AUDIO 28.1 ◄))

Un chien blanc – A white dog
Un plat délicieux – A delicious dish

However, just like most French rules, there are exceptions. Some adjectives are placed before the noun, and while there aren't that many that are placed before the noun, they are also the most common ones. Because of that, you will come across them a lot. However, in reality, most of them are placed after the verb.

Before the Noun

The adjectives placed before the noun usually express **Beauty**, **Age**, **Number**, **Goodness**, and **Size**. Remember it with the acronym **BANGS**.

AUDIO 28.2 ◄))

BEAUTY

	Masc. Sing	Fem. Sing.	Masc. Pl.	Fem. Pl
Beautiful	**Beau**	**Belle**	**Beaux**	**Belles**
Pretty	**Joli**	**Jolie**	**Jolis**	**Jolies**

Un <u>beau</u> chat – A beautiful cat
Un <u>joli</u> paysage – A beautiful landscape

AGE

	Masc. Sing	Fem. Sing.	Masc. Pl.	Fem. Pl
Young	**Jeune**	**Jeune**	**Jeunes**	**Jeunes**
Old	**Vieux**	**Vieille**	**Vieux**	**Vieilles**
New	**Nouveau**	**Nouvelle**	**Nouveaux**	**Nouvelles**

Les <u>jeunes</u> enfants – Young children
Un <u>vieux</u> château – An old castle
Un <u>nouveau</u> produit – A new product

NUMBER

	Masc. Sing	Fem. Sing.	Masc. Pl.	Fem. Pl
First	**Premier**	**Première**	**Premiers**	**Premières**
Second	**Deuxième**	**Deuxièmes**	**Deuxième**	**Deuxièmes**
Last	**Dernier**	**Dernière**	**Derniers**	**Dernières**

Le <u>premier</u> jour des vacances – The first day of vacation
Le <u>deuxième</u> chanteur – The second singer
Le <u>dernier</u> jour – The last day

GOODNESS

	Masc. Sing	Fem. Sing.	Masc. Pl.	Fem. Pl
Good	**Bon**	**Bonne**	**Bons**	**Bonnes**
Bad	**Mauvais**	**Mauvaise**	**Mauvais**	**Mauvaises**
Best / Better	**Meilleur**	**Meilleure**	**Meilleurs**	**Meilleures**
Kind / Nice	**Gentil**	**Gentille**	**Gentils**	**Gentilles**

Une <u>bonne</u> tarte – A good pie
Un <u>mauvais</u> choix – A bad choice
Une <u>meilleure</u> note – A better grade
Un <u>gentil</u> monsieur – A nice gentleman

SIZE

	Masc. Sing	Fem. Sing.	Masc. Pl.	Fem. Pl
Small	**Petit**	**Petite**	**Petits**	**Petites**
Tall	**Grand**	**Grande**	**Grands**	**Grandes**
Big	**Gros**	**Grosse**	**Gros**	**Grosses**
Long	**Long**	**Longue**	**Longs**	**Longues**

Un <u>petit</u> livre – A little book
Un <u>grand</u> building – A tall building
Une <u>grosse</u> facture – A big bill
Des <u>longs</u> cheveux – Long hair

Note on **long:**
Des cheveux longs and **des longs cheveux** are both right. The difference is very subtle. Make sure to limit the use of **long** after the noun to **cheveux**, if you want to.

EX. 3.6 *Ajoutez l'adjectif donné à la phrase. L'adjectif peut être placé avant ou après le nom. Accordez l'adjectif avec le nom.* **AUDIO 28.3** ◀))

1. (nouveau) C'est un _____ manteau _____.

2. (amusant) Il a raconté une _____ blague _____.

3. (meilleur) Je cherche le _____ restaurant _____ de la ville.

4. (impossible) C'est un _____ problème _____ à résoudre.

5. (dernier) Le _____ survivant _____ de l'accident est décédé récemment.

6. (ouvert) La _____ porte _____ laisse entrer de l'air frais.

7. (long) Elle a les _____ cheveux _____ pour son âge.

8. (lourd) Fais attention c'est un _____ colis _____.

9. (courageux) Les pompiers sont des _____ personnes _____.

10. (bon) C'est une _____ idée _____.

More than One Adjective

If the adjectives are supposed to be placed before or after the noun, place them this way. If they are both after the noun, add **et** between the two. If they are before, you can simply have them one after the other.

AUDIO 28.4 ◀))

Un gros meuble blanc – A big white piece of furniture
Le grand méchant loup – The big bad wolf
Un petit livre magnifique – A beautiful little book

Il fait chaud et humide. *It's hot and humid.*
Ce plat est salé et épicé. *This dish is salty and spicy.*

If two or more adjectives accompany a noun, they are placed <u>after</u> the noun if they are connected by a conjunction such as mais, donc, or, car, et, ou, ni ... ni, etc. This means that even if the noun is supposed to be placed before, it can be placed after using conjunction.

EX. 3.7 *Ajoutez les deux adjectifs dans la phrase, changez les adjectifs au féminin si besoin.*
AUDIO 28.5 ◀))

1. C'est un colis - (important – prioritaire)

_____

2. C'est une femme - (gentil et patient)

_____

3. C'est une journée - (froid et nuageux)

_____

4. C'est un gâteau - (bon – gros)

_____

5. C'est une histoire - (long et stupide)

_____

Adjective with Two Different Meanings

Some adjectives have a different meaning depending on if it's placed before or after the noun.

<u>Before</u> the noun usually implies a **figurative meaning.**
<u>After</u> the noun implies a **literal meaning.**

AUDIO 28.6 ◀))

Ancien:

> **Mon <u>ancienne</u> voiture** – My old (former) car
> **Une voiture <u>ancienne</u>** – An antique car

Dernier:

> **Le <u>dernier</u> mardi** – The last Tuesday
> **Mardi <u>dernier</u>** – Last Tuesday

Drôle

> **Une <u>drôle</u> de personnne** – A strange person
> **Une personne <u>drôle</u>** – A funny person

Grand

> **Une <u>grand</u> homme** – A great man
> **Un homme <u>grand</u>** – A tall man

Pauvre

> **Un <u>pauvre</u> enfant** – A poor child (pity)
> **Un enfant <u>pauvre</u>** – A poor child (money)

Propre

> **Ma <u>propre</u> maison** – My own house
> **Une assiette <u>propre</u>** – A clean plate

Seul

> **La <u>seule</u> solution** – The only solution
> **Une personne <u>seule</u>** – A single person

Vrai

> **Un <u>vrai</u> tableau** – An authentic painting
> **Une histoire <u>vraie</u>** – A true story

The Imperfect Tense – L'Imparfait

This is a review of "*The Complete French Conjugation Course*". The review includes only a part of what is taught in the conjugation course.

The **imparfait** is used to talk about the past, mostly actions and situations without a specific timeframe, that happened an unspecified amount of time or were in progress when something else happened.

The imperfect tense, called **imparfait**, replaces 3 tenses in English: the **past progressive** (he was drawing), the **simple past** (he drew) as well as he used to draw / he would draw = **Il dessinait**.

Uses of the Imparfait:

AUDIO 28.1.1 ◆))

We use the imparfait:

- To describe **habits** and **repeated actions** in the past:
  Elle était policière. *She was a police officer.*

- To talk about **repeated actions** in the past that you could translate to used to or would. Once again, without a specific timeframe:
  On regardait la télévision tous les soirs. *We used to watch TV every night.*

- To describe a person, a property, the weather or even a physical state or an emotion:
  Il n'était pas grand. *He wasn't tall.*

- To talk about actions happening at the same time:
  Je rangeais la cuisine pendant qu'il nettoyait la salle de bain. *I was tidying up the kitchen while he was cleaning the bathroom.*

- After si:
  Et si tu marchais plus souvent ? *What if you walked more?*

How to Conjugate Verbs in the Imparfait

Verbs of the 1st group – regular verbs ending in -er:

To form the **imparfait**, we are going to look at the **verb conjugated in the present tense with nous**, remove the **-ons** and add the endings for the imparfait: **-ais, -ais, -ait, -ions, iez** and **-aient**. **Être** is the only verb not following the stem rule.

Dessiner To draw

Je **dessinais**
Tu **dessinais**
Il-Elle-On **dessinait**
Nous **dessinions**
Vous **dessiniez**
Ils-Elles **dessinaient**

Verbs of the 2nd group – Regular verbs ending in -ir:

The stem of the verb **réussir** is **réussiss-** (Nous réussissons – Present tense)
To conjugate the verb, add the endings to the stem: **-ais -ais -ait -ions -iez -aient**

Réussir To succeed

Je **réussissais**
Tu **réussissais**
Il-Elle-On **réussissait**
Nous **réussissions**
Vous **réussissiez**
Ils-Elles **réussissaient**

Verbs of the 3rd group – regular verbs ending in -re:

The stem of the verb **vendre** is **vend-** (Nous vendons – Present tense)
To conjugate the verb, add the endings to the stem: **-ais -ais -ait -ions -iez -aient**

Vendre To sell

Je **vendais**
Tu **vendais**
Il-Elle-On **vendait**
Nous **vendions**
Vous **vendiez**
Ils-Elles **vendaient**

EX. 3.8 *Conjuguez les verbes suivants à l'imparfait.*   AUDIO 28.1.5 ◀))

1. **Écouter**

   J'_____

   Tu _____

   On _____

   Nous _____

Vous _____

Elles _____

2. **Choisir**

Je_____

Tu _____

Il _____

Nous _____

Vous _____

Ils _____

3. **Vendre**

Je_____

Tu _____

Il _____

Nous _____

Vous _____

Ils _____

Other irregular verbs: AUDIO 28.1.6 ◄))

Verb	Présent	Imparfait
Être To be	Nous **sommes**	**J'étais***irregular
Avoir To have	Nous **av**ons	**J'avais**
Aller To go	Nous **all**ons	**J'allais**
Faire To do / To make	Nous **fais**ons	**Je faisais**
Prendre To take	Nous **pren**ons	**Je prenais**
Mettre To put	Nous **mett**ons	**Je mettais**
Venir To come	Nous **ven**ons	**Je venais**
Tenir To hold	Nous **ten**ons	**Je tenais**
Savoir To know	Nous **sav**ons	**Je savais**
Connaître To know	Nous **connaiss**ons	**Je connaissais**
Devoir To have to	Nous **dev**ons	**Je devais**
Vouloir To want	Nous **voul**ons	**Je voulais**
Pouvoir To be able to	Nous **pouv**ons	**Je pouvais**
Dire To tell	Nous **dis**ons	**Je disais**

EX. 3.9 *Traduisez les phrases suivantes à l'imparfait.* AUDIO 28.1.7 ◀))

1. He knew the right answer.

   _____

2. This man was tall and skinny.

   _____

3. He was holding the book in his hands.

   _____

4. She always bought beautiful clothes.

   _____

5. This man believed strange stories.

   _____

6. We lived in Canada between 1995 and 2005.

   _____

7. I didn't understand difficult problems.

   _____

8. The gardener watered the dry plants.

   _____

9. You were drinking hot chocolate.

   _____

10. The baby seemed to be tired.

    _____

EX. 3.10 *Réécrivez la phrase en conjuguant le verbe à **l'imparfait** et ajoutez le ou les adjectifs (accordez si nécessaire).* **AUDIO 28.1.8** 🔊

1. Elle (peindre) des tableaux (magnifique).

   _____

2. Ta grand-mère (être) une très fille (joli – jeune).

   _____

3. La fenêtre (donner) sur un jardin (petit).

   _____

4. Il (mettre) la vaisselle dans le lave-vaisselle (sale).

   _____

5. Tu ne (porter) jamais de lunettes (ronde).

   _____

6. On (aimer) les films (romantique).

   _____

7. Le panneau (signaler) des travaux (gros).

   _____

8. Elle (faire) toujours des gâteaux (délicieux).

   _____

9. Il (finir) son petit déjeuner quand le bus est arrivé (rouge)

   _____

10. Le clown (rendre) les enfants (joyeux).

    _____

Notes :

*Remember to **download the audio** of the lists and to **watch the videos** – see Preface*

Comparatives & Superlatives
Comparatifs & Superlatifs

What are the comparative and the superlative?

| **The comparative allows us to compare two things, two persons, etc.** |

| **The superlative is used to talk about the extreme.** |

The Comparative

AUDIO 29.1 🔊

We use the comparative ... to compare! Easy! The difference between English and French is that the comparative goes around the adjective. Let's see the 3 possible comparatives:

As ... as	**Aussi ... que**	**Aussi** + <u>adjective</u> + **que**
More ... than	**Plus ... que**	**Plus** + <u>adjective</u> + **que**
Less ... than	**Moins ... que**	**Moins** + <u>adjective</u> + **que**
As much as / As many as	**Autant que**	**Autant** + **que**

Don't forget that the adjective always agrees in gender and number. The comparative is no exception. **Autant** doesn't take an adjective.

Elle est **aussi** <u>grande</u> **que** sa sœur. *She is as tall as her sister.*
Il est **aussi** <u>intelligent</u> **que** moi. *He is as smart as me.*

Elle est **plus** <u>grande</u> **que** sa sœur. *She is taller than her sister.*
Il est **plus** <u>intelligent</u> **que** moi. *He is smarter than me.*

Elle est **moins** <u>grande</u> **que** sa sœur. *She is shorter than her sister.*
Il est **moins** <u>intelligent</u> **que** moi. *He is less intelligent than me.*

Je travaille **autant que** mon collègue. *I work as much as my colleague.*

If you already know what you are comparing to, you don't always need to add **que + complement**.

Elle est **aussi** <u>grande</u>. *She is as tall.*
Il est **aussi** <u>intelligent</u>. *He is as smart.*

Elle est **plus** <u>grande</u>. *She is taller.*
Il est **plus** <u>intelligent</u>. *He is smarter.*

Elle est **moins** <u>grande</u>. *She is shorter.*
Il est **moins** <u>intelligent</u>. *He is less intelligent.*

Je travaille **autant.** *I work as much.*

EX. 3.11 *Remplissez les cases avec le comparatif donné – changez l'adjectif si nécessaire.*

AUDIO 29.2 ◄))

1. L'avion est _____ le train. (+, rapide).

2. Le bus est _____ le train. (+, confortable).

3. Les singes sont _____ les cochons. (+, intelligent)

4. Ce matelas est _____ celui-là. (=, mou).

5. Elle est _____ sa compétitrice. (-, doué)

6. Les vraies fleurs sont _____ les fausses. (+, jolie)

7. Je gagne _____ que mon collègue. (=)

8. Cette maison est _____ la maison où j'habitais avant. (-, grand)

9. Je suis (f) _____ l'année dernière. (+, heureux)

10. Elle est _____ toi. (=, grand)

The comparative followed by a noun:

AUDIO 29.3 ◄))

The comparative followed by a noun or a number changes from **que** to **de**, or **d'** when the noun or the number starts with a vowel or a silent h. Aussi doesn't exist in this case, only autant.

As much ... as	**Autant de ... que**	**Autant de** + <u>noun</u> + **que**
More ... than	**Plus de ... que**	**Plus de** + <u>noun</u> + **que**
Less ... than	**Moins de ... que**	**Moins de** + <u>noun</u> + **que**

On a **autant d'**<u>argent</u> **que** mon frère. *We have as much money as my brother.*
Je veux avoir **autant de** <u>chance</u> **que lui.** *I want to have as much luck as him.*

On a **plus d'**<u>argent</u> **que** mon frère. *We have more money than my brother.*
Je veux avoir **plus de** <u>chance</u> **que** lui. *I want to have more luck than him.*

On a **moins d'**<u>argent</u> **que** mon frère. *We have less money than my brother.*
Je veux avoir **moins de** <u>problèmes</u> **que** lui. *I want to have less problems than him.*

EX. 3.12 *Traduisez les phrases suivantes avec les comparatifs ci-dessus.*   AUDIO 29.4 ◄))

1. He has more hair than his brother.

   _____

2. I need less sleep than my husband.

   _____

*Remember to **download the audio** of the lists and to **watch the videos** – see Preface*

3. She wears more makeup than before.

_____

4. We have as many opportunities as others.

_____

5. She has more resources than her sister.

_____

The Superlative

We use the superlative to talk about the extreme. Just like in English, we are going to use an article in front of **plus** (most) or **moins** (less). The adjective agrees with the noun but doesn't change because of the superlative.

AUDIO 29.5 🔊

| The most | le / la / les plus ... | le / la / les plus + <u>adjective</u> |
| The least | le / la / les moins ... | le / la / les moins + <u>adjective</u> |

Elle est **la plus** <u>âgée</u>. *She is the oldest.*
Il est **le plus** <u>petit</u>. *He is the smallest.*

Elle est **la moins** <u>difficile</u>. *She is the least difficult.*
Il est **le moins** <u>rapide</u>. *He is the slowest.*

If you want to add some context, you can add **de** after the adjective. **De** can change to **du / de la / des / de l'**.

| The most | le / la / les plus ... de | le / la / les plus + adjective + **de** |
| The least | le / la / les moins ... de | le / la / les moins + adjective + **de** |

Elle est **la plus** âgée **de la** famille. *She is the oldest of the family.*
Il est **le plus** petit **de** ses frères. *He is the smallest of his brothers.*

Elle est **la moins** difficile **du** groupe. *She is the least difficult of the group.*
Il est **le moins** rapide **de l'**équipe. *He is the slowest of the team (the less fast).*

EX. 3.13 *Remplissez les cases avec le superlatif donné.*   **AUDIO 29.6** 🔊

1. Cette voiture est _____ magasin. (+, abordable)

2. Elle est _____ princesses. (+, joli)

3. Ma grand-mère est _____ famille. (+, sociable)

4. C'est le voyage _____ monde. (+, long)

5. Elle est _____ groupe. (-, chanceux)

Irregular Comparatives & Superlatives

A few comparatives and superlatives are irregular. Try to remember them by heart:

AUDIO 29.7 ◀))

	Comparative	Superlative
Bon Good	**Meilleur**	**Le meilleur**
Mauvais Bad	**Pire**	**Le pire**
Petit Little	**Moindre (weaker)**	**Le moindre**

Bon:

Il est **meilleur que** l'autre coureur. *He is better than the other runner.*
C'est **le meilleur** athlète. *He is the best athlete.*
Il est **le meilleur**. *He is the best.*

Mauvais:

Le résultat est **pire que** tout. *The result is worse than everything.*
C'est **le pire** résultat. *This is the worst result.*

Moindre:

Ses notes sont **moindres**. *Her grades are weaker.*
C'est **la moindre** des choses. *It's the least we can do.*

EX. 3.14 *Remplissez les cases avec la liste d'irréguliers ci-dessus.* AUDIO 29.8 ◀))

1. Ce sont les _____ croissants de la ville.

2. Sa participation était _____.

3. Marc a les _____ notes de la classe. Quelle honte.

4. Il est le _____ chef de l'hôtel.

5. C'est _____ que ce que je ne pensais.

*Remember to **download the audio** of the lists and to **watch the videos** – see Preface*

Indefinite Adjectives – Les Adjectifs Indéfinis

What is an indefinite adjective?

> **An indefinite adjective helps to describe a noun in a non-specific way**

Indefinite adjectives are always placed before the noun. They are mostly (but not always) used instead of an article, and they, of course, agree in gender and number with the noun they describe.

AUDIO 30.1 ◀))

	Masc. Sing	Fem. Sing.	Masc. Pl.	Fem. Pl
Other / Another	**Autre**	**Autre**	**Autres**	**Autres**
Certain	**Certain**	**Certaine**	**Certains**	**Certaines**
Each	**Chaque**	**Chaque**		
Various			**Divers**	**Diverses**
Several			**Plusieurs**	**Plusieurs**
Some / A few	**Quelque**	**Quelque**	**Quelques**	**Quelques**
Such / Like	**Tel**	**Telle**	**Tels**	**Telles**
All / Every	**Tout**	**Toute**	**Tous**	**Toutes**

AUDIO 30.2 ◀))

Autre:

Est-ce que tu as un **autre** chargeur ? *Do you have another charger?*
Il veut une **autre** console de jeux. *He wants another game console.*
Les **autres** fleurs sont plus jolies. *The other flowers are prettier.*

Certain:

J'avais peur à **certains** moments. *I was scared at certain moments.*
Certaines personnes sont difficiles à vivre. *Certain people are difficult to live with.*

Chaque:

Chaque jeu a ses propres règles. *Each game has its own rules.*
On y va **chaque** année. *We go there every year.*

Divers:

Tu peux choisir entre **divers** matériaux. *You can choose between various materials.*
L'employé est en charge de **diverses** tâches. *The employee is in charge of diverse tasks.*

Plusieurs:

L'association a reçu **plusieurs** donations. *The association got several donations.*
Elle a **plusieurs** rendez-vous ce matin. *She has several appointments this morning.*

Quelques:

J'ai perdu **quelques** kilos. *I have lost a few kilos.*
Le stagiaire a **quelques** bonnes idées. *The trainee has a few good ideas.*

Tel:

On ne fabrique plus de **telles** machines. *We don't make such machines anymore.*
J'ai besoin d'une amie **telle** que toi. *I need a friend like you.*

Tout:

Il dort **tout** le temps. *He sleeps all the time.*
Tous les indices ont été collectés. *All the evidence has been collected.*
Sa montre sonne **toutes** les heures. *His watch rings every hour.*

EX. 3.15 *Choisissez un **adjectif indéfini** dans la liste ci-dessus et mettez-le au féminin ou au pluriel si nécessaire.*   AUDIO 30.3 ◀))

1. _____ les élèves participeront au spectacle.

2. J'ai _____ idées si tu veux les entendre.

3. Il a réussi _____ test depuis le début de l'année.

4. Nous avons _____ projets pour le mois de décembre.

5. Il reste _____ macarons si tu veux.

6. On risque d'avoir une _____ tornade ce week-end.

7. Elle était _____ de l'avoir pris.

8. Il y a _____ personne à la porte.

The Future Tense – Le Futur Simple

> This is a review of "*The Complete French Conjugation Course*". The review includes only a part of what is taught in the conjugation course.

The future tense, called **futur simple** in French, is the equivalent of will in English.

Uses of the Futur Simple

AUDIO 30.1.1 ◀))

- To talk about something that is going to happen in the future:
  On achètera une maison bientôt. *We will buy a house soon.*

- To make suppositions about the future:
  Je pense qu'on sera heureux ici. *I think we will be happy here.*

How to Conjugate Verbs in the Futur Simple

Verbs of the 1st group and 2nd group – regular verbs ending in -er and -ir:

To form the **futur simple**, we keep the infinitive verb and add the endings: **-ai, -as, -a, -ons, ez** and **-ont.**

AUDIO 30.1.2 ◀))

Chanter To sing

Je **chanterai**
Tu **chanteras**
Il-Elle-On **chantera**
Nous **chanterons**
Vous **chanterez**
Ils-Elles **chanteront**

Grandir To grow up

Je **grandirai**
Tu **grandiras**
Il-Elle-On **grandira**
Nous **grandirons**
Vous **grandirez**
Ils-Elles **grandiront**

---

*Remember to **download the audio** of the lists and to **watch the videos** – see Preface*

Verbs of the 3rd group – regular verbs ending in -re:

For verbs ending in **-re**, we only remove the **-e** and add the endings to the stem: **-ai, -as, -a, -ons, ez** and **-ont**.

Entendre To hear

J'**entendrai**
Tu **entendras**
Il-Elle-On **entendra**
Nous **entendrons**
Vous **entendrez**
Ils-Elles **entendront**

Including irregular verbs endings in **-re**: AUDIO **30.1.3** ◀))

Prendre	Je prendr**ai**	Nous prendr**ons**	Ils prendr**ont**
Craindre	Je craindr**ai**	Nous craindr**ons**	Ils craindr**ont**
Éteindre	J'éteindr**ai**	Nous éteindr**ons**	Ils éteindr**ont**
Joindre	Je joindr**ai**	Nous joindr**ons**	Ils joindr**ont**
Battre	Je battr**ai**	Nous battr**ons**	Ils battr**ont**
Mettre	Je mettr**ai**	Nous mettr**ons**	Ils mettr**ont**
Boire	Je boir**ai**	Nous boir**ons**	Ils boir**ont**

Other irregular verbs: AUDIO **30.1.4** ◀))

Aller	J'**ir**ai	Nous **ir**ons	Ils **ir**ont
Avoir	J'**aur**ai	Nous **aur**ons	Ils **aur**ont
Courir	Je **courr**ai	Nous **courr**ons	Ils **courr**ont
Devoir	Je **devr**ai	Nous **devr**ons	Ils **devr**ont
Envoyer	J'**enverr**ai	Nous **enverr**ons	Ils **enverr**ont
Être	Je **ser**ai	Nous **ser**ons	Ils **ser**ont
Faire	Je **fer**ai	Nous **fer**ons	Ils **fer**ont
Mourir	Je **mourr**ai	Nous **mourr**ons	Ils **mourr**ont
Pouvoir	Je **pourr**ai	Nous **pourr**ons	Ils **pourr**ont
Recevoir	Je **recevr**ai	Nous **recevr**ons	Ils **recevr**ont
Savoir	Je **saur**ai	Nous **saur**ons	Ils **saur**ont
Tenir	Je **tiendr**ai	Nous **tiendr**ons	Ils **tiendr**ont
Valoir	Je **vaudr**ai	Nous **vaudr**ons	Ils **vaudr**ont
Venir	Je **viendr**ai	Nous **viendr**ons	Ils **viendr**ont
Vouloir	Je **voudr**ai	Nous **voudr**ons	Ils **voudr**ont

EX. 3.16 *Conjuguez les verbes suivants au futur simple.* AUDIO **30.1.5** ◀)

1. **Parler**

   Je _____

   Tu _____

   On _____

   Nous _____

   Vous _____

   Elles _____

2. **Choisir**

   Je _____

   Tu _____

   Il _____

   Nous _____

   Vous _____

   Ils _____

3. **Perdre**

   Je _____

   Tu _____

   Il _____

   Nous _____

   Vous _____

   Ils _____

EX. 3.17 *Traduisez les phrases suivantes au futur simple.* AUDIO **30.1.6** 🔊

1. I will be there at 3 p.m. (15 heures)

   _____

2. We will see if we can leave tomorrow.

   _____

3. We (on) will eat lasagna this weekend.

   _____

4. It will rain tonight.

   _____

5. At this time next Monday, we will be in Mexico.

   _____

6. My friend will walk the dog when we are away.

   _____

7. They will get married next year.

   _____

8. I will do the cleaning (ménage) later.

   _____

9. I hope it will snow this winter.

   _____

10. It will be late when we arrive.

    _____

The Near Future – Le Futur Proche

> This is a review of "*The Complete French Conjugation Course*". The review includes only a part of what is taught in the conjugation course.

The near future is called **futur proche** in French, simply because it's going to happen in the **near future**.

To build the **futur proche**, all you need to do is conjugate the verb **aller** in the present tense and add the infinitive verb of the action you want to describe.

> **Je vais** + infinitive = I am going to + infinitive

AUDIO 30.2.1 ◀»

The verb **aller** - present tense:

Je **vais**	Nous **allons**
Tu **vas**	Vous **allez**
Il-Elle-On **va**	Ils-Elles **vont**

On **va être** en retard. *We are going to be late.*
Tu **vas acheter** du pain ? *Are you going to buy some bread?*

When the infinitive verb (second verb) is reflexive, the reflexive pronoun agrees with the subject.

Je **vais <u>me</u> coucher**. *I am going to sleep.*
Tu **vas <u>te</u> coucher**. *You are going to sleep.*
Il **va <u>se</u> coucher**. *He is going to sleep.*
Nous **allons <u>nous</u> coucher**. *We are going to sleep.*

EX. 3.18 *Remettez les phrases dans l'ordre, conjuguez le verbe au futur proche et changez l'adjectif si nécessaire.* AUDIO 30.2.2 ◀»

1. livre / passionnant / il / lire / un

   _____

2. cette / je / réfléchir / à / proposition

   _____

3. de la / tu / branche / tomber

   _____

4. au / manger / soir/ on / restaurant / ce

_____

5. famille / se coucher / toute / la

_____

6. en retard / être / trafic / nous / à cause du

_____

7. s'il / il / mal / se faire / continue

_____

8. si / dans / quelques / tu / partir / ne ... pas / arrives / ils / minutes

_____

9. bientôt / avion / arriver / l'

_____

10. tu / aller / université / est-ce que / à l' / ?

_____

Chapter 3 – Review
Chapitre 3 – Révision

EX. 3.19 *Choisissez un des adjectifs, accordez-le dans la liste et ajoutez-le à la phrase.*

AUDIO 30.3 ◄))

**incroyable – clair – blanc – paresseux – léger – drôle – sérieux –
prêt – faux – heureux – électrique**

1. (f) Est-ce que tu es _____ ?

2. Les voitures _____ deviennent sales plus vite.

3. L'eau du lac est _____.

4. Ce n'est pas _____.

5. La réponse que tu as donnée est _____.

6. Cette crème au chocolat est _____.

7. Ils sont _____ d'être arrivés.

8. Les voitures _____ sont une
   invention _____.

9. Je suis _____, je n'ai envie de ne rien faire.

10. Tu penses qu'elle était _____ ?

EX. 3.20 *Décrivez ce que vous allez faire ce week-end en utilisant le futur proche. N'oubliez pas d'ajouter quelques adjectifs et des prépositions.*

Ce week-end, je vais _____

_____

_____

_____

_____

_____

_____

CHAPTER 4

Direct & Indirect Pronouns
Les Pronoms Directs et Indirects

Direct Object & Direct Object Pronoun
L'Objet Direct et Le Pronom Objet Direct

Direct object

A **direct object** is a noun or a group of words including a noun, referring to people or things, usually placed directly after the verb and is found by asking the direct question **Quoi** What - **Qui** Who.

> **Subject + verb + direct object**

AUDIO 31.1 🔊

Direct object with the question Quoi ?

Je lis un livre. *I am reading a book.*
Je lis quoi ? *What am I reading?*
Un livre – A book
Un livre is the direct object

Elle écrit une lettre. *She is writing a letter.*
Elle écrit quoi ? *What is she writing?*
Une lettre – A letter
Une lettre is the direct object

Direct object with the question Qui ?

Il appelle Ashley. *He is calling Ashley.*
Il appelle qui ? *Whom is he calling?*
Ashley
Ashley is the direct object

J'aime Jack. *I am in love with Jack.*
J'aime qui ? *Whom am I in love with?*
Jack
Jack is the direct object

EX. 4.1 *Entourez (circle) l'objet direct dans les phrases ci-dessous.*   **AUDIO 31.2** 🔊

1. J'aime la vanille.

2. On voit la mer.

3. J'appelais Paul et Marc tous les jours.

4. Nous achetons un pain.

5. Tu remplis le dossier.

6. Est-ce que tu entends la chanson ?

7. Je dessine une tortue.

8. Il donne ses vieux habits.

9. Elle prépare le petit déjeuner.

10. Tu connais tes résultats ?

Direct Object Pronouns

A direct object can be replaced by a **Direct Object Pronoun (DOP)**. The **DOP** is always placed before the verb in French.

> **Subject + <u>direct object pronoun</u> + verb**

Why knowing the **Direct Object Pronouns** is important:

If we look at the 2 sentences that we used before in English, but this time we change the direct object by a pronoun:

I am reading <u>a book</u>	I am reading **it**
He is calling <u>Ashley</u>	He is calling **her**

The DOP replaces the direct object when the object is known in the conversation. It avoids repetition, especially when answering a question including a direct object.
As you see, the pronoun in English goes after the verb, while it goes before the verb in French.

Here is the list of **Direct Object Pronouns**. Study them by heart: AUDIO 31.3 ◄»

Singular		Plural	
me - m'	me	**nous**	us
te - t'	you	**vous**	you
le - l'	him - it	**les**	them
la - l'	her - it		

AUDIO 31.4 ◄»)

Je lis un livre. *I am reading a book.*
Je <u>le</u> lis. *I am reading it.*

Elle écrit une lettre. *She is writing a letter.*
Elle <u>l'</u>écrit. *She is writing it.*

Il appelle Ashley. *He is calling Ashley.*
Il <u>l'</u>appelle. *He is calling her.*

J'aime Jack. *I am in love with Jack.*
Je <u>l'</u>aime. *I am in love with him.*

Nous attendons le bus. *We are waiting for the bus.*
Nous <u>l'</u>attendons. *We are waiting for it.*

Of course, the direct object can include more information such as an adjective:

Elle lave sa nouvelle voiture. *She is washing her new car.*
Elle <u>la</u> lave. *She is washing it.*

EX. 4.2 *Utilisez les phrases de l'exercice 4.1 et changez l'objet direct en pronom.* AUDIO 31.5 ◀))

1. _____
2. _____
3. _____
4. _____
5. _____
6. _____
7. _____
8. _____
9. _____
10. _____

Some verbs such as **Attendre**, take a direct object in French but a preposition in English such as for, at, to. Remember them as **REDCAP.**

AUDIO 31.6 ◀))

Regarder qqch / qqn	To look <u>at</u> sth / sb
Écouter qqch / qqn	To listen <u>to</u> sth / sb
Demander qqch / qqn	To ask <u>for</u> sth / sb
Chercher qqch / qqn	To search <u>for</u> sth / sb
Attendre qqch / qqn	To wait <u>for</u> sth / sb
Payer qqch	To pay <u>for</u> sth

Direct Object Pronouns and Negation

In the case of a negative sentence, the direct object pronoun is placed immediately before the verb.

> **Subject + ne + Direct Object Pronoun + verb + pas**

AUDIO 31.7 ◀))

Est-ce que tu regardes la télévision ? Non, je ne la regarde pas.
Are you watching TV? No, I am not watching it.

Je ne trouve pas mon téléphone, est-ce que tu l'as vu ? Non je ne l'ai pas vu.
I can't find my phone, have you seen it? No, I haven't seen it.

EX. 4.3 *Changez l'objet direct en **pronom** sur la première ligne et ajoutez la **négation** sur la deuxième ligne.* AUDIO 31.8 ◀))

1. Est-ce que tu connais son frère ?

   _____

   _____

2. Le chien mange ses croquettes.

   _____

   _____

3. Vous dégustez les pâtisseries.

   _____

   _____

4. L'étudiant finit ses devoirs.

   _____

   _____

5. Je lis un livre tranquillement.

   _____

   _____

6. Toute la famille regarde la télévision.

   _____

   (personne) _____

7. Les passagers attendent le bus.

   _____

   _____

8. Il pose une question au professeur.

   _____

   _____

9. Tu termines ton assiette.

   _____

   _____

10. Je vois mon fils cet après-midi.

    _____

    _____

*Remember to **download the audio** of the lists and to **watch the videos** – see Preface*

Direct Object Pronouns with the Passé Composé

If you remember the lesson about the passé composé, the past participle of verbs conjugated with **avoir** doesn't agree in gender and number with the subject. However, it agrees in gender and number with the **direct object if the direct object or the direct object pronoun is before the verb**.

> **Direct object + avoir + past participle + e, s, es**

The direct object can be: AUDIO 31.9 ◀))

⇨ A direct object pronoun = **le, la, les, l', nous, ...**

J'ai commandé **un thé.**	I ordered a tea.
Je l'ai commandé.	I ordered it.

In this first example, **un thé** is singular masculine. Therefore, nothing changes, even if the DOP is before the verb.

J'ai commandé **deux thés.**	I ordered two teas.
Je les ai commandé**s**.	I ordered them.

Deux thés is masculine plural, so the past participle takes **-s** in the second sentence.

J'ai commandé **une glace.**	I ordered an ice cream.
Je l'ai commandé**e**.	I ordered it.

Une glace is feminine singular, so the past participle takes **-e** in the second sentence.

J'ai commandé **deux glaces.**	I ordered two ice creams.
Je les ai commandé**es**.	I ordered them.

Deux glaces is feminine plural, so the past participle takes **-es** in the second sentence.

⇨ A relative pronoun = **Que / Qu'**

The relative pronoun replaces the direct object.

J'ai commandé **un thé.**	I ordered a tea.
Le thé **que** j'ai commandé.	The tea that I ordered.

J'ai commandé **deux thés.**	I ordered two teas.
Les deux thés **que** j'ai commandé**s**.	The two teas that I ordered.

J'ai commandé **une glace.**	I ordered an ice cream.
La glace **que** j'ai commandé**e**.	The ice cream that I ordered.
J'ai commandé **deux glaces.**	I ordered two ice creams.
Les deux glaces **que** j'ai commandé**es**.	The two ice creams that I ordered.

If it's easier for you, remember only the direct object which you can still find easily in the sentence instead of remembering the relative pronoun.

Note:
The past participle of verbs conjugated with **avoir** never agrees with other pronouns, only the direct object pronouns.

EX. 4.4 *Changez la phrase comme dans l'exemple ci-dessous.* AUDIO **31.10** 🔊

Exemple : J'ai commandé un thé.
Le thé que j'ai commandé.

1. J'ai acheté une rose.

   _____

2. J'ai vu les filles au magasin.

   _____

3. Luc a gagné sa course.

   _____

4. Michel a commandé les t-shirts.

   _____

5. Ils ont gagné le match.

   _____

6. Elle a reçu la balle sur la tête.

   _____

7. Nous avons mangé une tarte en famille.

   _____

8. Les papiers que l'avocat a signés.

   _____

9. J'ai invité Marie à manger. (C'est Marie ...)

   _____

10. Il a acheté la voiture.

    _____

EX. 4.5 *Répondez aux questions en changer l'objet direct en **pronom**. Accordez le participe passé en fonction.*   AUDIO 31.11 ◀))

Exemple : Tu as commandé **le thé** ?
         Oui, je **l'**ai commandé.

1. Tu as acheté les pommes ?

   Oui, _____

2. Vous avez compris la leçon ?

   Oui, _____

3. Tu as fini tes devoirs ?

   Oui, _____

4. Vous avez suivi la course ?

   Oui, _____

5. Tu as accepté les conditions ?

   Oui, _____

6. Vous avez appelé Julie ?

   Oui, _____

7. Tu as perdu ton jouet préféré ?

   Oui, _____

8. Vous avez mangé votre part de gâteau ?

   Oui, _____

9. Tu as invité les voisins ?

   Oui, _____

10. Vous avez aimé les fleurs ?

    Oui, _____

Indirect Object and Indirect Object Pronoun – L'Objet Indirect et Le Pronom Objet Indirect

Indirect object

An **indirect object** is usually preceded by the preposition **à**. We found it by asking the question **à qui**.

Subject + verb + indirect object

The **indirect object** can be placed after the verb or after the direct object. It's found by asking the <u>indirect</u> question **à qui** to who, for who. Most of the time, the indirect object starts with **à**.

À qui

AUDIO 32.1 ◀))

Je donne un conseil à Jean => Je donne un conseil à qui ?
I give advice to Jean.
À qui = à Jean

Elle achète un cadeau à ses parents => Elle achète un cadeau à qui ?
She is buying a gift for her parents.
À qui = à ses parents

While catching **à** in a sentence is easy, this preposition sometimes takes other forms:

à la	+	feminine noun starting with a consonant
à l'	+	feminine noun starting with a vowel or a silent h
au	+	masculine noun starting with a consonant
à l'	+	masculine noun starting with a vowel or a silent h
aux	+	masculine or feminine noun but plural

Elle achète un cadeau aux enfants. => Elle achète un cadeau à qui ?
She is buying a gift for the children.
À qui = aux enfants

EX. 4.6 *Entourez (circle) l'objet indirect dans les phrases ci-dessous.* AUDIO 32.2 ◀))

1. J'ai acheté un bouquet de fleurs à mes parents.

2. Le juge ordonne à l'avocat de se taire.

3. On fait confiance à nos amis.

4. Elle sourit aux passants dans la rue.

5. Elle a promis aux élèves de trouver une solution.

6. Il interdit à ses enfants de manger du sucre.

7. Tu as téléphoné à tes parents.

8. J'ai répondu au client par email.

9. Elle donne des conseils aux personnes âgées.

10. Je conseille à mes voisins de prendre soin de leur pelouse.

Indirect Object Pronouns

An indirect object can be replaced by an **Indirect Object Pronoun (IOP)**. Like the direct object pronoun (DOP), the **IOP** is always placed before the verb.

> **Subject + indirect object pronoun + verb**

Let's look at a sentence in English, but this time we change the indirect object to a pronoun: 32.3

L'infirmier donne les médicaments <u>au patient</u>. *The nurse is giving the medicine <u>to the patient</u>.*
To the patient is the indirect object but can be turned into a pronoun which is **him = lui.**

L'infirmier <u>lui</u> donne les médicaments. *The nurse is giving him the medicine.*

The Indirect Object Pronouns replace the indirect object when the object is known in the conversation.

Here is the list of **indirect object pronouns**. Study them by heart:

Singular		Plural	
Me - m'	me	**Nous**	us
Te - t'	you	**Vous**	you
Lui	him - her - it	**Leur**	them

Elle **me** parle	She is talking to **me**
Elle **te** parle	She is talking to **you**
Elle **lui** parle	She is talking to **him - her**
Elle **nous** parle	She is talking to **us**
Elle **vous** parle	She is talking to **you**
Elle **leur** parle	She is talking to **them**

EX. 4.7 *Utilisez les phrases de l'exercice **4.6** et changez l'objet indirect en **pronom**.*   AUDIO 32.4 ◄))

1. _____

2. _____

3. _____

4. _____

5. _____

6. _____

7. _____

8. _____

9. _____

10. _____

Indirect Object Pronouns and Negation

In the case of a negative sentence, the indirect object pronoun is placed immediately before the verb, just like the direct object pronouns.

| **Subject + ne + indirect object pronoun + verb + pas** |

AUDIO 32.5 ◀))

Est-ce que tu offres souvent des fleurs **à ta femme** ? Non, je ne **lui** offre jamais de fleurs.
Do you often give flowers to your wife? No, I never give her flowers.

EX. 4.8 *Traduisez le **pronom** en français sur la première ligne et ajoutez la négation **ne ... pas** sur la deuxième ligne.* AUDIO 32.6 ◀))

1. Elle a appelé hier. (me)

   _____

   _____

2. Cela plaît beaucoup. (him)

   _____

   _____

3. Cette robe va très bien. (her)

   _____

   _____

4. Il a apporté un cadeau. (us)

   _____

   _____

5. L'hôtesse a servi un café. (you – pl)

_____

_____

6. Il succède bientôt. (him)

_____

_____

7. Il rappelle ça tous les jours. (me)

_____

_____

8. Tu as volé cette bouteille de vin ? (them)

_____

_____

9. Elle a envoyé un paquet pour Noël. (you – sing)

_____

_____

10. C'est fou comme tu ressembles. (him)

_____

_____

Like RECAP, some verbs take an indirect object in French but no preposition in English. 32.7

Conseiller à qqn	To advise sb
Dire à qqn	To tell sb
Demander à qqn	To ask sb
Obéir à qqn	To obey sb
Rendre visite à qqn	To visit sb
Répondre à qqn	To answer sb
Ressembler à qqn	To resemble sb
Téléphoner à qqn	To call sb

Note:
The verbs **être à, penser à** and **faire attention à** will be followed by an **emphatic pronoun.**

Être à	To belong to
Penser à	To think of
Faire attention à	To pay attention to

Remember to **download the audio** of the lists and to **watch the videos** – see Preface

More examples:

J'ai offert un cadeau **aux invités.** *I offered a gift to the guests.*
Je **leur** ai offert un cadeau. *I offered them a gift.*

Ils **nous** ont donné leur canapé. *They gave us their couch.*
Elle **vous** a envoyé la facture la semaine dernière. *She sent you the bill last week.*

On est en train de **lui** parler. *We are talking to her.*
Les locataires **nous** ont rendu les clés. *The tenants gave us the keys back.*

EX. 4.9 *Répondez aux questions en changer l'objet indirect en* **pronom.** AUDIO 32.8 ◄))

1. Tu es en train de parler à l'employé ?

   Oui, _____

2. Vous avez envoyé la facture au fournisseur ?

   Oui, _____

3. Tu as offert des fleurs à ta femme ?

   Oui, _____

4. Il a écrit une lettre à ses parents ?

   Oui, _____

5. Est-ce que les voisines ont rendu les clés au propriétaire ?

   Oui, _____

The Pronouns Y & En – Les Pronoms Y & En

Y is a pronoun used to replace an object indicating **a place** or **a thing**. Like the other pronouns we saw, it has to be placed before the verb.

Y to Replace Places

AUDIO 33.1 🔊

For places, we will mostly use **Y** to replace the following prepositions:

À	To, at
En	To
Dans	In
Chez	At someone's place

> ### Subject + Y + verb

On est **au magasin**. *We are at the store.*
On **y** est.

Je vais **en France** ce week-end. *I am going to France this weekend.*
J'**y** vais ce week-end.

Est-ce qu'il est **dans sa chambre** ? *Is he in his bedroom?*
Oui, il **y** est.

Elle est **chez le docteur**. *She is at the doctor.*
Elle **y** est.

EX. 4.10 *Changez l'endroit par le pronom* **Y.** AUDIO 33.2 🔊

1. Je vais au marché ce samedi.
   _____

2. Tu vas à Londres dans quelques semaines.
   _____

3. Elle va au cabaret pour son anniversaire.
   _____

4. Le chien est dans son panier.
   _____

5. Elle est chez le dentiste pour une carie.
   _____

Y to Replace Things

AUDIO 33.3 ◀))

For things, we will mostly use **Y** to replace a noun introduced by: **à – au – aux – à l' – à la**

A few verbs taking Y:

Penser à   To think of
Je pense **à mes vacances.** *I am thinking of my vacation.*
J'**y** pense. *I am thinking of it.*

Réfléchir à   To think of
Je vais réfléchir **à cela.** *I am going to think of that.*
Je vais **y** réfléchir. *I am going to think of it.*

S'intéresser à   To be interested to
Je m'intéresse **à la peinture.** *I am interested in painting.*
Je m'**y** intéresse. *I am interested in it.*

Assister à   To attend
Elle a assisté **à cette réunion.** *She attended this meeting.*
Elle **y** a assisté. *She attended it.*

Participer à   To participate in / to
Nous avons participé **au concours.** *We participated to the contest.*
Nous **y** avons participé. *We participated to it.*

Jouer à   To play
Ils jouent **au football.** *They play soccer.*
Ils **y** jouent. *They play it.*

A few expressions with Y:

Il y a   There is / There are
Vas-y / Allons-y   Let's go

EX. 4.11 *Changez le groupe commençant par la préposition à par le pronom Y.*   AUDIO 33.4 ◀))

1.   Il réfléchit à cette solution.

_____

2.   J'ai goûté au gâteau mais il n'était pas bon.

_____

3.   Elle a cru à la blague.

_____

4.   Nous avons résisté au chocolat.

_____

5. Vous avez survécu à l'accident.

   _____

6. Tu as pensé à ta pauvre sœur ?

   _____

7. Il est important d'obéir aux ordres.

   _____

8. Elles ont participé au tournoi il y a quelques mois.

   _____

9. On a appris à jouer aux cartes.

   _____

10. Il ne pense pas à son futur.

    _____

The Pronoun EN

En is also a pronoun and is used to replace an object including the preposition **de** and **expressions of quantity**.
Expressions of quantity are likely to include a partitive article: **de, du, de la, des, etc.**
En is used to talk about **things** and **quantity**, not people. But in spoken French, you might hear **en** for people.
Even French speakers don't always have good grammar.

Just like other pronouns, **en** is placed before the verb.

> **Subject + EN + verb**
> **Subject + n' + EN + verb + pas**

AUDIO 33.5 ◄»)

Est-ce que tu as **du lait** ? *Do you have milk?*
Oui, j'**en** ai. *Yes, I have some.*

Elle boit **de l'eau**. *She is drinking water.*
Elle **en** boit. *She is drinking some.*

Tu as beaucoup **d'argent**. *You have a lot of money.*
Tu **en** as beaucoup. *You have a lot of it.*

J'ai **deux verres**. *I have two drinks.*
J'**en** ai deux. *I have two.*

On a **trois chiens**. *We have three dogs.*
On **en** a trois. *We have three.*

⇨ Here the number and quantity are repeated after the verb, but not de.

A few verbs taking EN:

AUDIO 33.6 ◄))

Avoir besoin de   To need
J'ai besoin **de temps.** *I need time.*
J'**en** ai besoin. *I need it.*

Avoir envie de   To want
Elle a envie **de chocolat.** *She wants some chocolate.*
Elle **en** a envie. *She want some.*

S'occuper de   To take care of
Il s'occupe **de ce problème.** *He is taking care of this problem.*
Il s'**en** occupe. *He is taking care of it.*

Parler de   To talk about
Elle parle **de ses recettes.** *She is talking about her recipes.*
Elle **en** parle. *She is talking about it.*

Manger de   To eat
Je ne mange pas **de viande.** *I don't eat meat.*
Je n'**en** mange pas. *I don't eat it.*

Sortir de   To leave
Ils sortent **de la maison.** *They are leaving the house.*
Ils **en** sortent. *They are leaving it.*

Donner de   To give
Il m'a donné **des tomates.** *He gave me some tomatoes.*
Il m'**en** a donné. *He gave me some.*

EX. 4.12 *Changez le groupe commençant par la préposition **de** par le pronom **EN**.* AUDIO 33.7 ◄))

1. Les patients ont besoin de médicaments.

   _____

2. Il s'est emparé du serpent avant l'attaque.

   _____

3. Nous parlons du problème avec les élèves.

   _____

4. C'est possible de se passer de produits laitiers.

   _____

5. Elle raffole de ces petits biscuits.

   _____

6. Nous venons juste de partir de notre maison

    _____

7. Son avenir dépend de ses notes.

    _____

8. Je doute de sa sincérité.

    _____

9. Il a appris à jouer du violon quand il était petit.

    _____

10. Les clients se servent de l'eau par eux-mêmes.

    _____

A few expressions with en: AUDIO 33.8 ◀))

J'en ai marre	I have enough
J'en ai assez	I have enough
J'en ai ras le bol	I have enough
Je m'en moque	I don't care
Je m'en fous	I don't care
Je m'en fiche	I don't care
Je m'en vais	I am leaving
Ne t'en fais pas	Don't worry
Je suis en route	I am on my way
Je suis en train de ...	I am in the process of ...

Qu'est-ce que tu en penses ?
What do you think of it?

EX. 4.13 *Ajoutez la bonne expression en réponse à la question - plusieurs possibilités possibles.*

AUDIO 33.9 ◀))

1. Tu pars ?

   Oui, _____

2. Qu'est-ce que tu fais ?

   _____

3. Qu'est-ce que tu en penses ?

   _____

4. Tu es déjà parti ?

   Oui, _____

5. Tu es de mauvaise humeur ?

   Oui, _____

*Remember to **download the audio** of the lists and to **watch the videos** – see Preface*

The Pronouns Together
Les Pronoms Ensemble

Direct and indirect object pronouns have a lot of similarities. Let's compare them: **AUDIO 34.1** 🔊

DOP		IOP	
me - m'	me	me - m'	me
te - t'	you	te - t'	you
le - l'	**him - it**	**lui**	**him - it**
la - l'	**her - it**	**lui**	**her - it**
nous	us	nous	us
vous	you	vous	you
les	**them**	**leur**	**them**

Only 3 of them are different. **Me, te, nous** and **vous** stay the same for both direct and indirect object pronouns.

In What Order to Use Them?

1st		2nd		3rd		4th	5th
me - m'	me	**le - l'**	him - it	**lui**	him - her – it	**y**	**en**
te - t'	you	**la - l'**	her - it	**leur**	them		
nous	us	**les**	them				
vous	you						

Since a lot of them are the same, knowing in what order to use them only requires 3 steps.
A good way to remember it is the **selfish rule.**

Me First
Object second
Other people third
Then Y and En

Elle lit une histoire à ... *She is reading a story to ...*   **AUDIO 34.2** 🔊

ME	Elle **me** lit une histoire	Elle **me la** lit
TE	Elle **te** lit une histoire	Elle **te la** lit
NOUS	Elle **nous** lit une histoire	Elle **nous la** lit
VOUS	Elle **vous** lit une histoire	Elle **vous la** lit
LUI	Elle **lui** lit une histoire	Elle **la lui** lit
LEUR	Elle **leur** lit une histoire	Elle **la leur** lit

Je donne des oranges à ... *I am giving oranges to ...*   **AUDIO 34.3** 🔊

TE	Je **te** donne des oranges	Je **t'en** donne
VOUS	Je **vous** donne des oranges	Je **vous en** donne
LUI	Je **lui** donne des oranges	Je **lui en** donne
LEUR	Je **leur** donne des oranges	Je **leur en** donne

Je rejoins ... à Londres *I join ... in London* AUDIO 34.4 🔊

TE	Je **te** rejoins à Londres	Je **t'y** rejoins
LE	Je **le** rejoins à Londres	Je **l'y** rejoins
LA	Je **la** rejoins à Londres	Je **l'y** rejoins
VOUS	Je **vous** rejoins à Londres	Je **vous** y rejoins
LES	Je **les** rejoins à Londres	Je **les** y rejoins

EX. 4.14 *Changez l'objet direct et l'objet indirect en pronoms.* AUDIO 34.5 🔊

1. Je prépare un café à mes amies.

    _____

2. Jeff envoie une lettre à sa femme.

    _____

3. Il a acheté un nouveau canapé à sa sœur.

    _____

4. Vous avez laissé votre chat au voisin ?

    _____

5. Tu as administré un médicament au patient.

    _____

6. Tu rends l'examen aux étudiants.

    _____

7. Il a expliqué le problème à son père.

    _____

8. Vous donnez un cadeau aux enfants.

    _____

9. L'infirmier écrit un compte-rendu à son chef.

    _____

10. Le policier lit ses droits au détenu.

    _____

EX. 4.15 *Changez le groupe de mots par EN ou par Y.*   **AUDIO 34.6** 🔊

1. Je pense avoir apporté assez de dossiers.

   _____

2. Elle a apporté une bouteille de Champagne.

   _____

3. Je ne veux pas aller aux courses.

   _____

4. Est-ce que vous participez à la course ?

   _____

5. Vous revenez du parc ?

   _____

6. Nous allons souvent au magasin.

   _____

7. Nous avons voyagé en Australie pendant 3 mois.

   _____

8. Je vais prendre un peu plus de soupe.

   _____

9. Mon oncle était à la maison quand c'est arrivé.

   _____

10. As-tu réfléchi à ma proposition ?

    _____

The Imperative – L'Impératif

> This is a review of "*The Complete French Conjugation Course*". The review includes only a part of what is taught in the conjugation course.

The **impératif** is the tense used to give **orders** and **advice**. It's used the same way as in English.

How to Conjugate Verbs in the Impératif

Verbs of the 1st group and 2nd group – regular verbs ending in -er and -ir:

To form the **impératif,** take the verb conjugated in the present tense with **tu, nous** and **vous,** and don't use the subject pronouns.

Verbs ending in **-er** and other verbs endings with **-es** with **tu,** only take **-e** with **tu, no s.**

AUDIO 34.1.1 🔊

Demander To ask

Present tense	Imperative	
Tu demandes	**Demande**	Ask
Nous demandons	**Demandons**	Let's ask
Vous demandez	**Demandez**	Ask

Choisir To choose

Present tense	Imperative	
Tu choisis	**Choisis**	Choose
Nous choisissons	**Choisissons**	Let's choose
Vous choisissez	**Choisissez**	Choose

Attendre To wait

Present tense	Imperative	
Tu attends	**Attends**	Wait
Nous attendons	**Attendons**	Let's wait
Vous attendez	**Attendez**	Wait

Only **avoir, être, savoir** and **vouloir** are irregular. The only form used for **vouloir** is **veuillez.**   **AUDIO 34.1.2** 🔊

Avoir To have	**Être** To be	**Savoir** To know	**Vouloir** To want
Aie	**Sois**	**Sache**	*Veuille*
Ayons	**Soyons**	**Sachons**	*Veuillons*
Ayez	**Soyez**	**Sachez**	**Veuillez**

EX. 4.16 *Conjuguez ces quatre verbes à l'impératif.*   AUDIO **34.1.3** ◀))

Garder	Finir	Aller	Être
_____	_____	_____	_____
_____	_____	_____	_____
_____	_____	_____	_____

EX. 4.17 *Conjuguez le verbe entre parenthèses à l'impératif avec le pronom donné.*   AUDIO **34.1.4** ◀))

1. (être – tu) à l'heure.

    _____

2. (aller – nous) à la boulangerie.

    _____

3. (regarder – tu) cet oiseau sur la branche.

    _____

4. (écouter – vous) le vent dans les arbres.

    _____

5. (garder – tu) ton argent.

    _____

6. (porter – vous) ce sac.

    _____

7. (donner – nous) un peu plus de notre temps.

    _____

8. (arrêter – tu) de fumer.

    _____

9. (monter – vous) cette valise à l'étage.

    _____

10. (démarrer – tu) la voiture.

    _____

The Imperative and Negation

The negation is added around the conjugated verb, **ne** is placed before the verb, and the second part of the negation (**pas, plus, rien, etc**) is placed after the verb.

> **ne + verb + pas**

AUDIO 34.1.5 🔊

Ne parlez pas. *Don't talk.*
N'attends pas. *Don't wait.*

EX. 4.18 *Utilisez les phrases de l'exercice 4.17 et transformez les phrases en phrases négatives.*
AUDIO 34.1.6 🔊

1. _____
2. _____
3. _____
4. _____
5. _____
6. _____
7. _____
8. _____
9. _____
10. _____

The Imperative and Object Pronouns

Object pronouns are placed right after the verb and are attached to the verb by a **hyphen**.

When the object pronouns are after the verb, **me** becomes **moi**, and **te** becomes **toi**. Other pronouns stay the same.

AUDIO 34.1.7 🔊

Regarde-moi quand je te parle. *Look at me when I talk to you.*
Tais-toi. *Be quiet.*
Rappelle-lui de prendre ses affaires. *Remind him to take his stuff.*
Mange-les. *Eat them.*
Réserve-nous une place. *Book us a spot.*
Allons-y. *Let's go.*
Prends-en. *Take some.*

But, when placed before the verb, **moi** and **toi** stay **me** and **te** in the negation:

> **Ne t'inquiète pas pour ça.** *Don't worry about that.*
> **Ne me compte pas dans la liste.** *Don't count me on the list.*

For verbs ending in **-er** and other verbs ending in **e** with **tu**, if the pronoun is **en** or **y**, we add an **s** as well as a liaison **[z]**.

> **Commandes-en.** *Order some.*
> **Restes-y.** *Stay there.*

EX. 4.19 *Traduisez les phrases ci-dessous.* AUDIO 34.1.8 ◄))

1. (tu) Talk to her.

   _____

2. (vous) Call me when you have time.

   _____

3. (tu) Buy them.

   _____

4. (vous) Listen to me when I speak.

   _____

5. (tu) Pay the bill.

   _____

6. (tu) Serve yourself some water.

   _____

7. (tu) Stay there, I am coming.

   _____

8. (vous) Don't talk to me.

   _____

9. (vous) Write down your name.

   _____

10. (nous) Let's sit down.

    _____

Chapter 4 – Review
Chapitre 4 – Révision

EX. 4.20 *Changez les objets par les pronoms directs, indirects, **Y** ou **EN**.* AUDIO 34.2.1 ◄ﴦ

1. Est-ce que tu as pris du vin ?

   _____

2. Nous sommes au parc depuis midi.

   _____

3. Je m'occupe de la plante.

   _____

4. On connaît bien le professeur.

   _____

5. Je vais réfléchir à cette idée.

   _____

6. J'ai parlé à mes parents de cette maison.

   _____

7. Elle va me prêter sa voiture.

   _____

8. Elle a laissé les clés à l'accueil.

   _____

9. Je mange de la banane à tous les repas.

   _____

10. Tu as téléphoné à l'avocat ?

   _____

Remember to **download the audio** of the lists and to **watch the videos** – see Preface

CHAPTER 5

Other Pronouns
Les Autres Pronoms

The Emphatic Pronouns
Les Pronoms Toniques

Emphatic pronouns, also called stressed pronouns, or **pronoms toniques** in French, are used to emphasize, to put the accent on a person. They are only used for people.

The emphatic pronouns: AUDIO 35.1 ◄))

Moi – me
Toi – you
Lui – him
Elle – her

Nous – us
Vous – you
Eux – them (m)
Elles – them (f)

Soi – oneself

Uses of the Emphatic Pronouns:

We use the emphatic pronouns:

* On their own or with an adverb: AUDIO 35.2 ◄))

Qui a les meilleurs points ?   **Moi**
Who has the best grades?   *Me*

Qui a tort ?   **Lui**
Who's is wrong?   *Him*

J'ai faim !   **Moi aussi**
I am hungry!   *Me too*

EX. 5.1 *Utilisez un des pronoms toniques de la liste pour répondre aux questions – plusieurs réponses possibles.*   AUDIO 35.3 ◄))

moi – toi – lui – elle – nous – eux – elles

1. Qui est arrivé premières ? _____

2. Qui s'occupe du repas ? _____

3. Qui a reçu une médaille ? _____

4. Qui a acheté la maison ? _____

5. Qui a organisé cette surprise ? _____

6. Qui a oublié d'éteindre la lumière ? _____

7. Qui a les plus beaux cheveux ? _____

- After prepositions such as **avec** (with), **pour** (for), **sans**, (without), **chez** (at someone's house)

  AUDIO 35.4 🔊

  Est-ce qu'il est <u>avec</u> **toi** ? *Is he with you?*
  C'est <u>pour</u> **elle.** *It's for her.*
  Je ne sais pas dormir <u>sans</u> **lui.** *I can't sleep without him.*
  On est <u>chez</u> **moi.** *We are at my house.*

- After **à** and **de**:

  On n'a pas besoin <u>de</u> **toi.** *We don't need you.*
  C'est <u>à</u> **lui.** *It's his.*

EX. 5.2 *Complétez les phrases en traduisant le pronom entre parenthèses.*   AUDIO 35.5 🔊

1. C'est pour qui ? C'est pour (them – m) _____.

2. C'est à elle ? Non, c'est à (me) _____.

3. Est-ce que tu as besoin d'elles ? Non, je n'ai pas besoin d'(them – f) _____.

4. Je suis perdue sans (you – sing) _____.

5. Nous sommes chez (us) _____.

AUDIO 35.6 🔊

- With comparisons:

  Elle est <u>plus</u> âgée que **nous.** *She is older than us.*
  Il a <u>plus</u> de chance qu'**elle.** *He is luckier than her.*
  On étudie <u>autant</u> qu'**eux.** *We study as much as them.*

- With **ne ... que** – the prepositions **à** and **de** might be after **que**, depending on the verb:

  Il ne pense <u>qu'à</u> **lui** ! *He thinks only about himself!*
  Je n'ai vu <u>qu'</u>**elle.** *I only saw her.*

- To emphasize:

  Toi, tu es grand, mais elle, elle est petite. (You) *You are tall, but (her) she is small.*
  Lui, on ne peut pas lui faire confiance. (Him) *We can't trust him.*

- To repeat the subject:

  Je n'ai pas envie d'y aller, **moi.** *I don't want to go (me).*
  Toi, tu ne l'as pas vu non plus ? (You) *You didn't see him either?*

- When the subject is made out of a pronoun and a noun, or two pronouns:

  <u>Mes parents et</u> **moi** habitons ensemble. *My parents and I live together.*
  <u>Marie et</u> **lui** étudient l'architecture. *Marie and he study architecture.*

- After **c'est** and **ce sont**:

  <u>C'est</u> **lui.** *It's him.*
  <u>Ce sont</u> **eux.** *It's them.*

*Remember to **download the audio** of the lists and to **watch the videos** – see Preface*

How to Use Soi

We use **soi** with words such as **tout le monde, chacun**, with **on**, or in **impersonal sentences**:

AUDIO 35.7 ◄))

Croire en **soi** est important. *Believing in yourself is important.*
Il est bon d'être chez **soi.** *It's good to be home.*
On ne peut compter que sur **soi.** *We can only count on ourselves.*

EX. 5.3 *Ajoutez un pronom tonique approprié.* AUDIO 35.8 ◄))

1. Elle ne pense qu'à _____.

2. _____ , il est arrivé premier cette année.

3. Elle a plus de succès que _____.

4. Je n'ai vu _____ à la réunion.

5. C'est mieux si tout le monde rentre chez _____.

6. Mon mari et _____ , nous nous sommes mariés en 2018.

Myself, Yourself, Himself, ...

If you want to emphasize even more who you are talking about, you can add **-même** or **-mêmes**:

AUDIO 35.8 ◄))

Moi-même – myself
Toi-même – yourself
Lui-même – himself
Elle-même – herself

Soi-même – oneself

Nous-mêmes – ourselves
Vous-même / Vous-mêmes – yourself / yourselves
Eux-mêmes – themselves (m)
Elles-mêmes – themselves (f)

C'est important de faire les choses **soi-même.** *It's important to do things by yourself.*
Ils ont fait ce gâteau **eux-mêmes.** *They made this cake themselves.*
Moi-même, je ne comprends pas très bien quand il parle. *I myself don't really understand when he speaks.*
Elle a choisi ce jouet **elle-même.** *She chose this toy herself.*

EX. 5.4 *Finissez les phrases avec **moi-même**, **lui-même**, etc.* AUDIO 35.10 🔊

1. Il a écrit ce roman _____.

2. Elle a réalisé ce film _____.

3. Vous avez pris cette décision _____.

4. Ils ont décidé cela d' _____.

5. Je gère mon business _____.

6. Nous avons compris cela de _____.

7. Tu as appris à conduire de _____.

8. Elles ont rénové cette maison _____.

The Possessive Pronouns
Les Pronoms Possessifs

Possessive pronouns, **pronoms possessifs** in French, are used to replace a previously mentioned noun in the conversation. In English, they are mine, yours, etc.
They always agree in gender and number with the noun that they replace.

They are very close to the possessive adjectives. The first letter is the same, sometimes the entire word:

AUDIO 36.1 ◀ﬞ))	Masc. Sing Or fem. starting with a vowel or a silent h	Fem. Sing.	Plural
My	**m**on	**m**a	**m**es
Your	**t**on	**t**a	**t**es
His / Her / Its	**s**on	**s**a	**s**es
Our	**notre**	**notre**	**nos**
Your	**votre**	**votre**	**vos**
Their	**leur**	**leur**	**leurs**

The French possessive pronouns always include a definite article (**le – la – les**). They replace a group of words made of a possessive adjective and a noun:

AUDIO 36.2 ◀ﬞ))	Masc. Sing	Fem. Sing.	Masc. Pl.	Fem. Pl
Mine	**le mien**	**la mienne**	**les miens**	**les miennes**
Yours	**le tien**	**la tienne**	**les tiens**	**les tiennes**
His / Hers / Its	**le sien**	**la sienne**	**les siens**	**les siennes**
Ours	**le nôtre**	**la nôtre**	**les nôtres**	
Yours	**le vôtre**	**la vôtre**	**les vôtres**	
Theirs	**le leur**	**la leur**	**les leurs**	

AUDIO 36.3 ◀ﬞ))

J'ai pris mon téléphone, tu as pris **le tien** ? *I took my phone; did you take yours?*
Ce n'est pas mon parapluie, c'est **le vôtre**. *It's not my umbrella, it's yours.*
Ce n'est pas **la mienne** ? *Isn't it mine?*

EX. 5.5 *Utilisez un des pronoms possessifs du tableau pour remplir les cases.* AUDIO 36.4 ◀ﬞ))

les nôtres – les vôtres – le tien – les siens – le leur

1. J'ai raté mon train, est-ce que tu as eu _____ .

2. _____ sont bien, mais _____ sont mieux.

3. Mes amis sont espagnols, _____ sont portugais.

4. Elle a perdu son téléphone, est-ce qu'elle peut emprunter _____ ?

Notes :

The Demonstrative Pronouns
Les Pronoms Démonstratifs

Demonstrative pronouns, **pronoms démonstratifs** in French, replace a noun and a demonstrative adjective previously mentioned in the conversation. In English, they are: this, that, these, and those. They can also be followed by **-ci** and **-là**.

They always agree in gender and number with the noun that they replace.

Review of the demonstrative adjectives: AUDIO 37.1 ◄))

Masc. Sing	**ce / cet**	this / that
Fem. Sing	**cette**	this / that
Plural	**ces**	these / those

The French demonstrative pronouns are: AUDIO 37.2 ◄))

Masc. Sing	**celui**	this / that
Fem. Sing	**celle**	this / that
Masc. Pl	**ceux**	these / those
Fem. Pl	**celles**	these / those

Before learning when to use them, you should know that French demonstrative pronouns can never be used alone, unlike in English. **They are always in a sentence or followed by -ci or -là.**

We use Demonstrative Pronouns:

- Followed by **-ci** and **-là** when answering a question or to point out a specific product. **-ci** usually refers to something close, when **-là** refers to something further. They translate to this one, that one, etc.

AUDIO 37.3 ◄))

Masc. Sing	**celui-ci**	this one	**celui-là**	that one
Fem. Sing	**celle-ci**	this one	**celle-là**	that one
Masc. Pl	**ceux-ci**	these ones	**ceux-là**	those ones
Fem. Pl	**celles-ci**	these ones	**celles-là**	those ones

AUDIO 37.4 ◄))

Lequel est-ce que tu veux ?
Which one do you want?

Celui-ci
This one

Lequel est-ce que tu veux ?
Which one do you want?

Celui-là
That one

Quelles fleurs préférez-vous ?
Which flowers do you prefer?

Celles-là
Those ones

Ceux-ci sont magnifiques !
Those are gorgeous!

EX. 5.6 *Utilisez un des **pronoms démonstratifs** de la liste pour répondre aux questions, Choisissez entre **-ci** et **-là** pour chaque pronom.* AUDIO 37.5 ◀))

1. Quel pantalon est-ce que tu veux ? _____

2. Quelle pizza est-ce que tu veux manger ? _____

3. Quelles vacances est-ce que tu as réservées ?_____

4. Quels champignons est-ce que tu manges ? _____

5. Quelle écharpe est-ce que tu préfères ? _____

6. Quel téléphone as-tu acheté ? _____

7. Quelles chaussures est-ce que tu as commandées ? _____

Sometimes we can find them in the same sentence. In this case, **-ci** will be first, and **-là** will be second. **-ci** and **-là** can be added to nouns to express a stronger opinion:

AUDIO 37.6 ◀))

Ces couleurs-ci sont plus vives que **celles-là**.
These colors are brighter than <u>those ones</u>.

J'aurais acheté **celui-ci** mais je préfère **celui-là**.
I would have bought <u>this one</u>, but I prefer <u>that one</u>.

EX. 5.7 *Utilisez un des éléments ci-dessous.* AUDIO 37.7 ◀))

celles-là – ce – -ci – celui-ci

1. Ces-chaussures _____ sont plus confortables que _____.

2. Elle a vu _____ manteau mais elle préfère _____.

AUDIO 37.8 ◀))

• Followed by a relative pronoun – translates to "the one(s)":

C'est **celui** que je t'ai donné. *It's <u>the one</u> I gave you.*
Voilà **celle** que je t'ai achetée. *Here is <u>the one</u> I bought you.*
Il est important de donner à **ceux** qui en ont besoin. *It's important to give to <u>the ones</u> who need it.*

• Before **de** in terms of possession – literally translate to "the one of":

Je préfère **celui** de Marie. *I prefer Marie's (the one of Marie).*
C'est **ceux** de mon frère. *They are my brother's.*
Celle de Jasmine est à droite. *Jasmin's is on the right.*

EX. 5.8 *Utilisez un des pronoms démonstratifs* **celui – celle – ceux – celles** *pour remplacer les noms entre parenthèses ou dans la phrase.* AUDIO 37.9 🔊

1. (les livres) _____ de Jules sont arrivés ce matin.

2. J'ai bien aimé (la jupe) _____ de Lucie.

3. Tu te rappelles de mes cousins, _____ qui habitent en Louisiane ?

4. Elle a acheté (le modèle) _____ en vitrine.

5. Mes réponses étaient fausses, mais _____ de Luc étaient correctes.

Notes :

The Indefinite Demonstrative Pronouns
Les Pronoms Démonstratifs Indéfinis

Indefinite demonstrative pronouns, **pronoms démonstratifs indéfinis** in French, are used to replace an abstract thing or concept or something unspecific.

AUDIO 38.1 ◄))

ce	it / this / that / these / those
ceci	this
cela	that
ça	this / that

AUDIO 38.2 ◄))

- **Ce** is commonly found with the verb **être** in the expressions **c'est** or **ce sont**:

  C'est mon anniversaire aujourd'hui. *It's my birthday today.*
  Ce sont ses chaussures. *These are his shoes.*
  Ce n'est pas le moment de lui demander quelque chose. *It's not the time to ask him something.*

- **Ceci** and **cela** with other verbs than **être**. **Ceci** referring to anything abstract but close, **cela** referring to anything further:

  Cela devrait être possible. *That should be possible.*
  Cela me semble curieux. *That seems curious to me (weird).*
  Ceci devrait fonctionner mieux. *This should work better.*

- **Ceci** and **cela** can also be **direct objects**:

  As-tu vu ceci ? *Did you see that?*
  Je me suis rappelé de cela hier. *I remembered that yesterday.*

- **Ça** is the abbreviation of **ceci** and **cela**. While **ceci** and **cela** are used more in written French and formal French, **ceci** and **cela** are replaced by **ça** in spoken French.

  Ça devrait être possible. *That should be possible.*
  Ça me semble curieux. *That seems curious to me (weird).*
  Ça devrait fonctionner mieux. *This should work better.*
  Tu as vu ça ? *Did you see that?*
  Je me suis rappelé de ça hier. *I remembered that yesterday.*

EX. 5.9 *Remettez les phrases dans l'ordre.* AUDIO 38.3 ◀))

1. que / je / devrait fonctionner / pense / cela

    _____

2. bizarre / ce / n' ... pas / est

    _____

3. et / il / prévu / ceci / cela / a

    _____

4. la / peine / ! / cela / vaut / en

    _____

5. ça / comment / va / ?

    _____

A few expressions avec ça: AUDIO 38.4 ◀))

Ça va ? Oui, ça va	*How are you? I am fine*
Ça me plaît	*I like it*
Ça y est	*Done / Finished*
Ça suffit	*Enough*
Ça craint	*It sucks*
Ça me saoule	*I don't want to do that, it sucks*
Ça marche	*Works (for me)*
Ça ne me regarde pas	*It's not my business*

EX. 5.10 *Traduisez les expressions suivantes.* AUDIO 38.5 ◀))

1. It sucks.

    _____

2. Enough.

    _____

3. It's not my business.

    _____

4. Works for me.

    _____

5. I like it.

    _____

*Remember to **download the audio** of the lists and to **watch the videos** – see Preface*

The Indefinite Pronouns
Les Pronoms Indéfinis

Indefinite pronouns, **pronoms indéfinis** in French, refer to people or things in a general way without saying exactly who or what they are. They are used in a very similar way to English.

AUDIO 39.1	Masc. Sing	Fem. Sing.	Masc. Pl.	Fem. Pl
Another one	un autre	une autre		
Others			d'autres	d'autres
Certain ones			certains	certaines
Each one	chacun	chacune		
Several			plusieurs	plusieurs
Something	quelque chose			
Someone	quelqu'un			
Some / A few			quelques-uns	quelques-unes
Anyone	quiconque			
Nobody	personne			
All	tout			
Everyone			tous	toutes
One	un	une		

As you can see, we already used some of them when we saw the indefinite adjectives. So why do we have both? The answer is easy. To sound less repetitive, that's all! When mentioning something for the first time, use an adjective and a noun, the second time, only use the pronoun.

AUDIO 39.1

- **Un autre - Une autre**   another

  Ce café est délicieux, je vais en prendre <u>un autre</u>.
  This coffee is delicious, I will have another one.

  Je t'en trouverai <u>un autre</u>.
  I will find you another one.

- **D'autres**   others

  Est-ce que tu en as d'autres ?
  Do you have others?

  Beaucoup d'employés arrivent à l'heure, d'autres arrivent en retard.
  A lot of employees arrive on time, others arrive late.

- **Certains - Certaines**   Certain ones

    Les enfants n'étaient pas prêts pour jouer dehors. <u>Certains</u> ont eu froid.
    The children weren't ready to play outside. Certain ones were cold.

    Ces peintures sont incroyables mais <u>certaines</u> sont un peu bizarres.
    These paintings are incredible, but certain ones are a little bit weird.

- **Chacun - Chacune**   each one

    <u>Chacun</u> prépare sa valise.
    Each one packs his luggage.

    <u>Chacune</u> a reçu une médaille.
    Each one got a medal.

- **Plusieurs**   several

    Les habitations ont été inondées. <u>Plusieurs</u> sont inhabitables.
    Houses have been flooded. Several are uninhabitable.

- **Quelque chose**   something

    <u>Quelque chose</u> me dit qu'il sera en retard.
    Something tells me that he will be late.

    <u>Quelque chose</u> est arrivé dans cette maison.
    Something happened in this house.

- **Quelqu'un**   someone

    <u>Quelqu'un</u> est venu à la porte.
    Someone came to the door.

    <u>Quelqu'un</u> lui a vendu cette voiture.
    Someone sold him this car.

- **Quelques-uns - Quelques-unes**   some, a few

    J'ai téléphoné à mes amis, <u>quelques-uns</u> ont répondu.
    I called my friends, a few answered.

    <u>Quelques-unes</u> des coiffeuses ne sont pas venues travailler.
    A few of the hairdressers didn't come to work.

- **Quiconque**   anyone

    <u>Quiconque</u> apprend le français sait que cela prend du temps.
    Anyone who is learning French knows that it takes time.

- **Personne**   nobody

    <u>Personne</u> ne connaît la réponse.
    Nobody knows the answer.

    Il n'y a <u>personne</u> ici.
    There is nobody here.

Personne can also be used alone or with **non** as an answer:

Quelqu'un est venu ? Non, personne.
Did someone come? No, nobody.

- **Tout**   everything

Tout va bien ?
Is everything ok?

Il vérifie tout.
He checks everything.

Tout a l'air en ordre.
Everything seems in order.

- **Tous - Toutes**   all

Je les ai tous vus.
I saw them all.

Toutes ont reçu un cadeau pour avoir participé.
All got a prize for participating.

- **Un - Une**   one

Can also be **L'un** or **L'une**

Un de mes amis est venu me voir.
One of my friends came to see me.

L'un d'entre vous devra arriver en avance.
One of you will have to be there earlier.

David est un de mes meilleurs amis.
David is one of my best friends.

EX. 5.11 *Utilisez un des **pronoms indéfinis** de la liste ci-dessous pour compléter la liste.*

AUDIO 39.3 ◀))

1. _____ sont rentrés après le travail mais _____ sont restés là-bas.

2. _____ n'est à l'abri d'un problème.

3. _____ s'est bien fini.

4. _____ a eu son mot à dire.

5. _____ ne sont pas venus, mais ce n'est pas grave.

6. _____ me dit que ce n'est pas vrai.

7. _____ a téléphoné mais je ne sais pas qui.

8. _____ ont finalement réussi leurs examens.

9. _____ est allé à l'université sait que c'est difficile.

Notes :

*Remember to **download the audio** of the lists and to **watch the videos** – see Preface*

Relative Pronouns – Les Pronoms Relatifs

Relative pronouns, **les pronoms relatifs** in French, link the main clause to the relative clause. They can also replace the subject, the direct object, or the indirect object. They usually represent a word from another clause, the **antecedent**.

French has 5 relative pronouns: **que – qui – dont –où – lequel.**   AUDIO 40.1 ◄))

In English, they can be translated to: who – which – that – whom – where. But the biggest difference between English and French is that in English, they can be skipped, but not in French!

Qui

Qui replaces the **subject** and can be translated to who, which, or that. The subject can be a person or a thing. **Qui** can <u>never be qu'</u> in front of a vowel.

AUDIO 40.2 ◄))

Le café a ouvert l'année dernière. Il a brûlé.
The cafe opened last year. It burned down.

Le café <u>qui</u> a ouvert l'année dernière, a brûlé.
The cafe that opened last year burned down.

J'ai vu un film. Ce film était romantique
I saw a movie. This movie was romantic.

J'ai vu un film <u>qui</u> était romantique
I saw a movie that was romantic.

EX. 5.12 *Joignez ces deux phrases ensemble avec le pronom relatif que.*   AUDIO 40.3 ◄))

1. Je connais une histoire. Cela va te faire peur.

    _____

2. Les touristes arrivent. Ils étaient perdus.

    _____

3. J'ai une tante. Elle est française.

    _____

4. C'est Marie. Elle a réussi son année.

    _____

5. Elle parle à une femme. Cette femme porte une robe rouge.

    _____

Qui can be used after the prepositions **à, de, pour, chez** and **avec**. The preposition goes with the verb.

AUDIO **40.4** 🔊

Mon ami à <u>qui</u> j'ai prêté un livre ne me l'a pas rendu. (prêter à)
My friend to whom I lent a book didn't give it back to me.

Le politicien <u>pour qui</u> j'ai voté, a perdu. (voter pour)
The politician who I voted for, lost.

L'homme <u>de qui</u> je parle. (parler de)
The man that I am talking about.

Le médecin <u>chez qui</u> je vais est en vacances. (aller chez)
The doctor to whom I am going is on vacation.

La personne <u>avec qui</u> je parle est ma cousine. (parler avec)
The person with whom I am talking is my cousin.

EX. 5.13 *Ajoutez* **à qui, pour quoi, de qui chez qui, ou avec qui***, ajoutez le verbe et la préposition entre parenthèses.*   AUDIO **40.5** 🔊

1. Le chat _____ elle joue, s'appelle Miko.
   (_____)

2. La personne _____ ma fille passe le week-end est ma mère.
   (_____)

3. Les personnes _____ je cuisine sont les clients.
   (_____)

4. La personne _____ je tiens mon caractère est mon père.
   (_____)

5. Le chien _____ je pense est décédé il y a peu.
   (_____)

Que

Que replaces the **direct object** and can be translated to who, whom, which, or that.
Que becomes **qu'** when placed before a word starting with a vowel or a silent h.
Que is always followed by a pronoun or a noun, but not a verb.

AUDIO **40.6** 🔊

J'ai vu un film. Le film était nul.
I saw a movie. The movie was bad.

Le film <u>que</u> j'ai vu, était nul.
The movie I saw was bad.

C'est l'homme que j'aime.
This is the man I love.

Le parfum que j'adore n'est plus en stock.
The perfume I love is out of stock.

When the following verb is conjugated in the **passé composé** with **avoir**, the **past participle agrees with the relative pronoun**:

Les vacances que j'ai réservées sont annulées.
The vacation I booked is canceled.

EX. 5.14 *Insérez que et réécrivez la phrase.* AUDIO_40.7 🔊

1. Je connais un restaurant tu vas adorer.

   _____

2. Voici le devoir je viens de finir.

   _____

3. C'est pour ça tu m'as fait venir ?

   _____

4. Le film je regarde est horrible.

   _____

5. Tu n'as pas ouvert la lettre je t'ai écrite.

   _____

6. La voiture j'ai achetée est déjà en panne.

   _____

7. Le champagne tu as acheté est bon ?

   _____

8. Le salon on a installé est confortable.

   _____

9. Le chapeau tu portais hier t'allait très bien.

   _____

10. Le couple j'ai rencontré est un peu bizarre.

    _____

Dont

Dont replaces **an object** or **a person** when it includes **de**. The preposition **de** goes with the verb.

AUDIO **40.8** 🔊

C'est la personne <u>dont</u> je t'ai parlé. (parler de)
This is the person that I talked to you about.

Le jardin <u>dont</u> je m'occupe est en mauvais état. (s'occuper de)
The yard I am taking care of is in a bad state.

Voici ce <u>dont</u> j'ai besoin ! (avoir besoin de)
Here is what I need!

EX. 5.15 *Insérez **dont** et réécrivez la phrase, ajoutez entre parenthèses le groupe de mots incluant de.* AUDIO **40.9** 🔊

1. C'est quelque chose il est fier. (_____)

   _____

2. La juridiction je dépends va bientôt changer. (_____)

   _____

3. C'est le résultat je suis heureuse. (_____)

   _____

4. Ce sont les photos je suis ravie. (_____)

   _____

5. La glace j'ai envie est en rupture de stock. (_____)

   _____

Où

The relative pronoun **où** refers to **a place,** but it can also refer to **a place in time**. It translates to where and when.

AUDIO **40.10** 🔊

Le jour <u>où</u> tu es né était merveilleux.
The day when you were born was wonderful.

C'est là <u>où</u> je travaille.
This is where I work.

Je ne sais pas <u>où</u> aller.
I don't know where to go.

EX. 5.16 *Insérez où et réécrivez la phrase.* AUDIO 40.11 ◄»

1. L'endroit je suis ne se trouve pas sur la carte.

   _____

2. La ville nous cherchons à déménager est pleine de vie.

   _____

3. C'est le moment j'ai su que c'était toi.

   _____

4. Elle ne sait pas il va.

   _____

5. Le parc est un bon endroit se reposer.

   _____

Lequel – Auquel - Duquel

Lequel is used **after a preposition other than de**. Such as: **sur, avec, dans, pour**, etc.
Auquel (à + lequel) is used when the verb in the sentence is followed by **the preposition à.**
Duquel (de + lequel) is used to replace a **preposition including de**, but not de alone: **près de, à côté de,
à gauche de**, etc.

AUDIO 40.12 ◄»

Masc. Sing	Fem. Sing.	Masc. Pl.	Fem. Pl
lequel	laquelle	lesquels	lesquelles
auquel	à laquelle	auxquels	auxquelles
duquel	de laquelle	desquels	desquelles

L'idée <u>à laquelle</u> je pense est risquée. (penser à)
The idea I am thinking about is risky.

Le client <u>auquel</u> je parle est impoli. (parler à)
The client to whom I am talking is rude.

C'est le bateau <u>au bord duquel</u> nous avons voyagé. (être à bord de)
This is the boat we traveled on.

C'est la robe avec <u>laquelle</u> je me suis mariée. (se marier avec – as to wear)
This is the dress in which I got married.

EX. 5.17 *Insérez **lequel, auquel, duquel** et variations.* AUDIO 40.13 ◄))

1. C'est la rais on **pour** _____ je ne suis pas venue.

2. La chaise **sur** _____ elle est assise est cassée.

3. Les chemins **au bord** _____ il y a des arbres sont les plus agréables.

4. C'est ne pas le problème _____ je pensais.

5. C'est l'avion **au bord** _____ je vais passer mon test.

6. Ce n'est pas l'ambiance **à** _____ je suis habitué.

7. Voici l'ordinateur **avec** _____ tu vas travailler.

*Remember to **download the audio** of the lists and to **watch the videos** – see Preface*

Ce qui – Ce que – Ce dont – Ce … quoi

French relative pronouns can also include **ce**, which is a **neutral pronoun**. Together, they mean what, which, or that, depending on the sentence.

The neutral pronoun **ce** can be replaced by **la chose** the thing. Remember that in French, a sentence can never end with a preposition. Let's see the list first with an example for each:

AUDIO 41.1 🔊

Ce qui	**Tu as vu <u>ce qui</u> s'est passé ?**
	Did you see what happened?
Ce que	**Tu comprends <u>ce que</u> je t'explique ?**
	Do you understand what I am explaining to you?
Ce dont	**Je sais <u>ce dont</u> tu as peur.** (avoir peur de)
	I know what you are afraid of.

Ce … quoi is built differently than others since we add the preposition from the verb between **ce** and **quoi** (more examples on this point later).

AUDIO 41.2 🔊

Ce à quoi	**Je veux savoir <u>ce à quoi</u> tu t'intéresses.** (s'intéresser à)
	I want to know what you are interested in.
Ce avec quoi	**Tu ne devineras jamais <u>ce avec quoi</u> le chien joue.** (jouer avec)
	You will never guess what the dog is playing with.
Ce en quoi	**Il parle de <u>ce en quoi</u> il croit.** (croire en)
	He is talking about what he believes in.
Ce pour quoi	**<u>Ce pour quoi</u> il travaille, c'est sa famille.** (travailler pour)
	What he is working for is his family.
Ce sur quoi	**<u>Ce sur quoi</u> je m'appuie, ce sont les lois.** (s'appuyer sur)
	What I am relying on, are the laws.

Now, if we replace **ce** with **la chose** (the thing) in the previous sentences.   **AUDIO 41.3** 🔊

Tu as vu <u>la chose</u> qui s'est passée ?
Tu comprends <u>la chose</u> que je t'explique ?
Je sais <u>la chose</u> dont tu as peur.

Je veux savoir <u>la chose</u> à quoi (laquelle) **tu t'intéresses.**
Tu ne devineras jamais <u>la chose</u> avec quoi (laquelle) **le chien joue.**
Il parle de <u>la chose</u> en quoi (laquelle) **il croit.**
<u>La chose</u> pour quoi (laquelle) **il travaille, c'est sa famille**

Ce qui

AUDIO 41.4 🔊

Ce qui is the **subject of the verb**:

<u>Ce qui</u> me fait peur, c'est le vide.
What scares me is the height.

Je pense que c'est <u>ce qui</u> lui plaît.
I think this is what he likes.

C'est <u>ce qui</u> me tracasse !
This is what worries me!

EX. 5.18 *Traduisez les phrases en français.*   AUDIO **41.5** ◀))

1. I can't read what is written.

   _____

2. Tell me what happened during class.

   _____

3. He didn't finish his homework, which is unusual.

   _____

4. After everything that happened in 2021, I hope 2022 will be better.

   _____

Ce que – qu'

Ce que is the **direct object**. There is no preposition involved with the verb. **Ce que** becomes **ce qu'** when followed by a vowel or a silent h.

AUDIO **41.6** ◀))

C'est <u>ce que</u> je veux dire.
This is what I mean.

Je ne sais pas encore <u>ce que</u> je vais acheter.
I don't know yet what I am going to buy.

Est-ce que tu sais <u>ce que</u> tu veux ?
Do you know what you want?

EX. 5.19 *Traduisez les phrases en français.*   AUDIO **41.7** ◀))

1. This is what we planned.

   _____

2. I don't know yet what I am going to sing.

   _____

*Remember to **download the audio** of the lists and to **watch the videos** – see Preface*

3. Think about what you wrote.

_____

4. What I want is a week without noise.

_____

5. Do you already know what you want?

_____

Ce dont

Ce dont is used when the verb is followed by the preposition **de**.

AUDIO 41.8 ◀)))

<u>Ce dont</u> elle rêve, c'est de devenir avocate. (rêver de)
What she dreams of is to become a lawyer.

<u>Ce dont</u> tu as honte n'est pas de ta faute. (avoir honte de)
What you are ashamed of is not your fault.

J'ignore <u>ce dont</u> tu parles. (parler de)
I don't know what you are talking about.

EX. 5.20 _Traduisez les phrases en français._ AUDIO 41.9 ◀)))

1. He talked to me about what he remembered.

_____

2. What I am sure about is that I have to go to work tomorrow.

_____

3. This is what they are talking (discuter) about.

_____

4. This is what I am responsible for.

_____

5. This trip, this is what he wanted for a long time.

_____

Ce ... quoi

Ce ... quoi is used with **all the other prepositions**, except **de** because it's used with **dont**.

AUDIO 41.10 ◀))

Ce à quoi

Ce à quoi je pense ne te regarde pas. (penser à)
What I am thinking about is not your business.

Ce n'est pas ce à quoi il s'attendait. (s'attendre à)
It's not what he was expecting.

Ce avec quoi

C'est différent de ce avec quoi je suis d'accord. (être d'accord avec)
It's different than what I agree with.

Ces matériaux, c'est ce avec quoi je dois travailler. (travailler avec)
These materials, there are what I have to work with.

Ce en quoi

Un dinosaure, c'est ce en quoi il va se déguiser. (se déguiser en)
A dinosaur, that's what he is going to dress up as.

Ce pour quoi

Je ne suis pas certaine de ce pour quoi il est venu. (venir pour)
I am not sure why he came.

C'est son travail, c'est ce pour quoi il est payé. (payer pour)
It's his job, this is what he is paid for.

Ce sur quoi

La maison était en feu, c'est ce sur quoi le chien essayait d'attirer l'attention. (attirer l'attention sur)
The house was on fire. This is what the dog was trying to bring attention to.

EX. 5.21 *Ajoutez* ***ce à quoi, ce avec quoi, ce en quoi, ce pour quoi, ce sur quoi*** *et réécrivez la phrase.*

AUDIO 41.11 ◀))

1. C'est _____ je m'attendais.

2. C'est _____ il travaille depuis l'année dernière.

3. C'est _____ il croit.

4. C'est _____ il a acheté cet instrument.

5. C'est _____ il compte depuis quelques temps.

*Remember to **download the audio** of the lists and to **watch the videos** – see Preface*

EX. 5.22 *Traduisez les phrases suivantes.*   AUDIO 41.12 ◄))

1. What hairdressers work with can be dangerous.

   _____

2. This is what I thought but I didn't want to say it.

   _____

3. It's his routine, this is what he is used to.

   _____

4. What bothers me is that he never takes news.

   _____

5. This is what the doctors are afraid of.

   _____

Notes :

The Present Conditional
Le Conditionnel présent

This is a review of "*The Complete French Conjugation Course*". The review includes only a part of what is taught in the conjugation course.

The present conditional, called **conditionnel présent** in French, is the equivalent of would + infinitive in English. When in English, you add would in front of the verb, for us, we add endings to the infinitive verb.

Uses of the Conditionnel

AUDIO 41.1.1 ◀))

- To talk about something that would happen "if", a possibility:

    Il pourrait venir avec nous. *He could come with us.*

- To ask something politely:

    Pourriez-vous me rappeler mon numéro de chambre ?
    Could you remind me of my room number?

- To express a wish:

    Je souhaiterais être plus grande. *I wish I were taller.*

How to Conjugation of Verbs Conditional

Verbs of the 1ˢᵗ group – regular verbs ending in -er:

To form the **conditionnel présent**, we are going to **add the endings of the imparfait to the stem used with the futur simple.**
The endings of the imparfait are: **-ais, -ais, -ait, -ions, iez and -aient.**

AUDIO 41.1.1 ◀))

Aimer To like / To love
Stem futur simple: aimer

J'**aimerais**
Tu **aimerais**
Il-Elle-On **aimerait**
Nous **aimerions**
Vous **aimeriez**
Ils-Elles **aimeraient**

Verbs of the 2nd group – regular verbs ending in -ir:

Agir To act
Stem futur simple: agir

J'**agirais**
Tu **agirais**
Il-Elle-On **agirait**
Nous **agirions**
Vous **agiriez**
Ils-Elles **agiraient**

Verbs of the 3rd group – regular verbs ending in -re:

Descendre To go down
Stem futur simple: descendr

Je **descendrais**
Tu **descendrais**
Il-Elle-On **descendrait**
Nous **descendrions**
Vous **descendriez**
Ils-Elles **descendraient**

Other irregular verbs: AUDIO 41.1.3 ◄»

Verb	Futur simple	Conditionnel
Aller To go	Nous **ir**ons	J'**irais**
Avoir To have	Nous **aur**ons	J'**aurais**
Connaître To know	Nous **connaitr**ons	Je **connaitrais**
Devoir To have to	Nous **devr**ons	Je **devrais**
Dire To tell	Nous **dir**ons	Je **dirais**
Être To be	Nous **ser**ons	Je **serais**
Faire To do / To make	Nous **fer**ons	Je **ferais**
Mettre To put	Nous **mettr**ons	Je **mettrais**
Pouvoir To be able to	Nous **pourr**ons	Je **pourrais**
Prendre To take	Nous **prendr**ons	Je **prendrais**
Savoir To know	Nous **saur**ons	Je **saurais**
Tenir To hold	Nous **tiendr**ons	Je **tiendrais**
Venir To come	Nous **viendr**ons	Je **viendrais**
Vouloir To want	Nous **voudr**ons	Je **voudrais**

*Remember to **download the audio** of the lists and to **watch the videos** – see Preface*

EX. 5.23 *Conjuguez les verbes suivants au conditionnel présent.*　AUDIO **41.1.4** ◄))

1. **Chercher**

   Je _____

   Tu _____

   On _____

   Nous _____

   Vous _____

   Elles _____

2. **Réfléchir**

   Je _____

   Tu _____

   Il _____

   Nous _____

   Vous _____

   Ils _____

3. **Mordre**

   Je _____

   Tu _____

   Elle _____

   Nous _____

   Vous _____

   Elles _____

EX. 5.24 *Ajoutez un de ces verbes au conditionnel.* AUDIO 41.1.5 ◀))

faire – aimer – dormir – pouvoir – apprendre – aller – vouloir – avoir – être

1. J'_____ être en vacances !

2. Il m'a dit qu'il _____ là à 15 heures.

3. Elle _____ toute la journée si elle pouvait !

4. Il y _____ plus de monde s'il faisait moins froid.

5. On _____ voyager plus.

6. Nous _____ vous envoyer de l'argent.

7. Si tu marchais plus peut-être que tu _____ mieux ?

8. Si elle avait plus de patience, elle _____ à cuisiner.

9. Nous _____ au marché si nous avions plus de temps.

10. Qu'est-ce que tu _____ si tu gagnais un million ?

Chapter 5 – Review
Chapitre 5 – Révision

EX. 5.25 *Ajoutez un de ces pronoms.* **AUDIO 41.2.1** 🔊

plusieurs – lequel – que – qui – à qui – dont – ce qui – pour laquelle – toi – celui-ci –
celle – ce – le mien – moi-même – ça

1. C'est le numéro de téléphone _____ je t'ai donné.

2. C'est _____ m'intéresse.

3. Je préfère _____ mais je l'ai laissé à la maison.

4. _____ marche pour moi.

5. L'histoire _____ je t'ai parlé est une histoire vraie.

6. _____ n'est pas ce que j'ai dit.

7. Tu as choisi _____ de ces appartements ?

8. C'est la raison _____ j'ai introduit un dossier.

9. Est-ce que c'est _____ de Marie ?

10. _____ , tu peux toujours y aller si tu veux.

11. _____ des coureurs ont abandonné la course.

12. C'est la personne _____ je m'intéresse.

13. C'est _____ qu'elle veut.

14. Ne t'inquiète pas, je vais le faire _____ .

15. Le restaurant _____ a ouvert appartient à un ami.

CHAPTER 6

Adverbs & Conjunctions
Les Adverbes & Les Conjonctions

Adverbs – Les Adverbes

What is in an adverb?

Adverbs help describe words such as verbs, adjectives, or other adverbs.
They give us more information such as **quantity**, **time**, **manner**, and more.

A few things to know about French adverbs:

- They can consist of one word (**beaucoup, très, bientôt,** etc.) or a group of words (**aujourd'hui, jusqu'ici, tout de suite,** etc.) or words ending in **-ment** (**heureusement, chaudement,** etc.)
- They don't agree in gender and number, unlike adjectives. They are **invariable.**
- Their place in a French sentence is very similar to their place in an English sentence.

> **Adverbs are invariable. They don't change with gender and number.**

How to Form French Adverbs?

Many adverbs in English end with **-ly,** the equivalent in French is **-ment.**
A lot of them are formed using their adjectives.

- When an adjective **ends with a vowel,** simply add **-ment** at the end to form the adverb: AUDIO 42.1 ◄))

Adjective	Adverb
Autre Other	**Autrement** Otherwise
Bizarre Strange	**Bizarrement** Strangely
Calme Calm	**Calmement** Calmly
Drôle Funny	**Drôlement** Funnily
Étrange Strange	**Étrangement** Strangely
Facile Easy	**Facilement** Easily
Faible Weak	**Faiblement** Weakly
Grave Serious	**Gravement** Seriously
Honnête Honest	**Honnêtement** Honestly
Juste Just	**Justement** Justly, rightly
Lâche Coward	**Lâchement** Cowardly
Libre Free	**Librement** Freely
Malhonnête Dishonest	**Malhonnêtement** Dishonestly
Pauvre Poor	**Pauvrement** Poorly
Poli Polite	**Poliment** Politely
Possible Possible	**Possiblement** Possibly
Propre Neat	**Proprement** Neatly
Rapide Fast, quick	**Rapidement** Quickly
Rare Rare	**Rarement** Rarely

Sage Wise	**Sagement** Wisely
Simple Simple	**Simplement** Simply
Stupide Stupid	**Stupidement** Stupidly
Timide Shy	**Timidement** Shyly
Tranquille Calm	**Tranquillement** Calmly
Triste Sad	**Tristement** Sadly
Utile Useful	**Utilement** Usefully
Vrai True	**Vraiment** Really / Truly

- When an adjective **ends with a consonant**, use the **feminine adjective** and add **-ment** at the end to form the adverb: AUDIO 42.2 ◀))

Adjective	Adverb
Amical - Amicale Friendly	**Amicalement** Friendly
Ancien - Ancienne Former	**Anciennement** Formerly
Certain - Certaine Certain	**Certainement** Certainly
Chaud - Chaude Warm	**Chaudement** Warmly
Clair - Claire Clear	**Clairement** Clearly
Courageux - Courageuse Brave	**Courageusement** Bravely
Dernier - Dernière Last	**Dernièrement** Lastly
Doux - Douce Soft	**Doucement** Softely
Dur - Dure Hard	**Durement** Hardly
Entier - Entière Full	**Entièrement** Fully
Faux - Fausse Wrong	**Faussement** Falsely
Fort - Forte Strong	**Fortement** Strongly
Frais - Fraîche Fresh	**Fraîchement** Freshly
Froid - Froide Cold	**Froidement** Coldly
Généreux - Généreuse Generous	**Généreusement** Generously
Haut - Haute High	**Hautement** Highly
Heureux - Heureuse Happy	**Heureusement** Happily / Fortunately
Humain - Humaine Human	**Humainement** Humanly
Léger - Légère Light	**Légèrement** Lightly
Lent - Lente Slow	**Lentement** Slowly
Lourd - Lourde Heavy	**Lourdement** Heavily
Naïf - Naïve Naive	**Naïvement** Naively
Ouvert - Ouverte Open	**Ouvertement** Openly
Plein - Pleine Full	**Pleinement** Fully
Premier - Première First	**Premièrement** Firstly
Prochain - Prochaine Next	**Prochainement** *Shortly*
Sérieux - Sérieuse Serious	**Sérieusement** Seriously
Seul - Seule Alone	**Seulement** Only

*Exceptions:

Gentil - Gentille Nice	**Gentiment** Nicely
Bref - Brève Brief	**Brièvement** Briefly

- For a few adjectives **ending in E**, the adverb form will change the **E** into **É** before **-ment**: AUDIO 42.3 ◀))

Adjective   Adverb

Aveugle Blind   **Aveuglément** Blindly
Énorme Enormous   **Énormément** Very much
Intense Intense   **Intensément** Intensely
Précis - Précise Precise   **Précisément** Precisely
Profond - Profonde Deep   **Profondément** Deeply

- Adjectives ending in **-ant** and **-ent** will become **-amment** and **-emment** when adverbs: AUDIO 42.4 ◀))

Adjective   Adverb

Bruyant Loud   **Bruyamment** Loudly
Constant Constant   **Constamment** Constantly
Courant Current   **Couramment** Fluently
Différent Different   **Différemment** Differently
Évident Obvious   **Évidemment** Obviously
Impatient Impatient   **Impatiemment** Impatiently
Méchant Bad   **Méchamment** Badly
Patient Patient   **Patiemment** Patiently
Précédent Previous   **Précédemment** Previously
Récent Recent   **Récemment** Recently

⇨ **-amment** and **-emment** have the same pronunciation.

- A short list of adverbs has a different form than the adjectives: AUDIO 42.5 ◀))

Adjective   Adverb

Bon Good   **Bien** Well
Mauvais Bad   **Mal** Badly
Meilleur Best   **Mieux** Better
Petit Small   **Peu** Little

EX. 6.1 *Changez ces adjectifs en adverbes.* AUDIO 42.6 ◀))

1. Léger _____
2. Malhonnête _____
3. Énorme _____
4. Courant _____
5. Patient _____
6. Évident _____
7. Méchant _____
8. Intense _____
9. Sérieux _____
10. Précis _____

11. Timide _____
12. Propre _____
13. Gentil _____
14. Profond _____
15. Récent _____
16. Amicale _____
17. Bon _____
18. Premier _____
19. Mauvais _____
20. Petit _____

*Remember to **download the audio** of the lists and to **watch the videos** – see Preface*

French Adverbs by Type

- **Adverbs of place** – To explain where something happens: AUDIO 42.7 ◄))

À côté de Next to

À droite de On the right of

À gauche de On the left of

À l'intérieur Inside of

Ailleurs Somewhere else

Autour Around

Dedans Inside

Dehors Outside

Derrière Behind

Dessous Under

Dessus On top

Devant In front of

En bas Downstairs

En face In front of

En haut Upstairs

Ici Here

Là There

Là-bas Over there

Loin Far

Nulle part Nowhere

Partout Allover

Près Near

Quelque part Somewhere

Tout droit Straight

- **Adverbs of time and frequency** – To explain when and how many times something happens: AUDIO 42.8 ◄))

Actuellement Currently

Aujourd'hui Today

Après After

Aussitôt As soon as

Autrefois Formerly

Avant Before

Bientôt Soon

Brièvement Briefly

D'abord First

Déjà Already

Demain Tomorrow

Dernièrement Lately

Encore Again /Still

Enfin Finally

En même temps At the same time

Ensuite Then

Fréquemment Frequently

Généralement Generally / Usually

Habituellement Usually

Hier Yesterday

Jamais Never

Longtemps Long time

Longuement At length

Maintenant Now

Quelquefois Sometimes

Quotidiennement Daily

Précédemment Previously

Parfois Sometimes

Puis Then

Rarement Rarely

Soudain Suddenly

Souvent Often

Tard Late

Toujours Always

Tôt Early

Tout à coup All of a sudden

Tout de suite Right away

Tout le temps Always

Trop Too much / Too many

- **Adverbs of quantity** - To explain how much or how many there is: AUDIO 42.9 ◄))

Assez Enough
Aussi Also
Autant As much
Beaucoup A lot
Davantage Further
Encore Again
Environ Around
Moins Less
Peu Little

Plus More
Presque Almost
Seulement Only
Tant So much
Tellement So much
Tout All
Très Very
Trop Too much / Too many
Un peu A little

- Adverbs of reason – To explain for what reason something happens: AUDIO 42.10 ◄))

Aussi Also
Cependant However
Donc So
En revanche In contrast
Encore Again
Même Even
Par ailleurs Moreover

Par conséquent Consequently
Pourtant Yet
Quand même Even though
Seulement Only
Tout de même Even so
Toutefois Nevertheless

- **Adverbs of manner** – To explain how something happens: AUDIO 42.11 ◄))

Ainsi Thus
Bien Well
Brusquement Suddenly
Calmement Calmly
Debout Standing
D'habitude Usually
Doucement Slowly
Ensemble Together
Facilement Easily
Fort Strong
Gentiment Nicely
Heureusement Luckily
Joyeusement Happily

Lentement Slowly
Mal Badly
Mieux Better
Naturellement Naturally
Parfaitement Perfectly
Poliment Politely
Précisément Precisely
Plutôt Rather
Sérieusement Seriously
Simplement Simply
Surtout Mostly
Rapidement Fast / Quickly
Vite Fast

- **Adverbs of affirmation** – To confirm in a positive way that something happens: AUDIO 42.12 ◄))

Assurément Certainly
Certainement Certainly
Oui Yes
Peut-être Maybe
Précisément Precisely

Probablement Probably
Sans doute Without a doubt
Volontiers Gladly
Vraiment Really
Aussi Also

- **Adverbs of negation** – To turn the sentence into a negative sentence: AUDIO 42.13 🔊

  Ne … jamais Never
  Ne … pas Not
  Ne … plus No longer / Not anymore
  Ne … rien Nothing

  Non No
  Pas du tout Not at all
  Non plus Neither

- **Adverbs of interrogation** – To ask a question: AUDIO 42.14 🔊

  Combien How much / How many
  Comment How
  Pourquoi Why
  Quand When
  Où Where

- **Adverbs of conjunction** – To link two clauses: AUDIO 42.15 🔊

  Ainsi Thus
  Alors Then
  Certes Certainly
  Donc So
  En effet In effect
  Ensuite Then

  Enfin Finally
  Néanmoins However
  Par contre On the other side
  Pourtant Yet
  Puis Then

EX. 6.2 *Choisissez parmi les adverbes ci-dessous.* AUDIO 42.16 🔊

aussi – pourtant – seulement – beaucoup – aussitôt – jamais
bruyamment – aveuglément – doucement – faiblement

1. _____ que la maison est vendue, nous partons au Mexique.

2. Le chien respire _____.

3. _____ il est arrivé tôt.

4. Il a _____ exprimé ses derniers vœux.

5. Il a _____ reçu une partie du remboursement.

6. Elle l'aime _____.

7. Il est chanteur mais il est _____ auteur.

8. La tortue est arrivée tout _____.

9. Nous avons _____ de choses en commun.

10. Il n'est _____ à l'heure !

Where to Place the Adverbs
Où Placer les Adverbes

French adverbs are usually placed **right after the verb**, especially in sentences when the verb is not a compound tense, which is similar to English:

Subject + verb + adverb

Il est <u>toujours</u> en retard. *He is always late.*
Les enfants jouent <u>calmement</u>. *Children play calmly.*
Je suis <u>ici</u>. *I am here.*

Longer adverbs are placed at the beginning of the sentence or the end, not in the middle. Once again, this is similar to English:

<u>En général</u>, il a de bonnes notes. *Usually, he has good grades.*
Il a de bonnes notes <u>en général</u>. *He has good grades usually.*

In compounds tenses such as the **passé composé, passé récent, futur proche**, etc, some short adverbs are placed before the past participle.

Subject + avoir / être + adverb + past participle

Here is the list of the most common ones for you to remember:

Assez Enough	**Mal** Badly
Bien Well	**Mieux** Better
Beaucoup A lot	**Moins** Less
Bientôt Soon	**Souvent** Often
Déjà Already	**Toujours** Always
Encore Again / Still	**Trop** Too much / Too many
Enfin Finally	**Vite** Fast
Jamais Never	

Note that **trop** can be followed by another adverb: **trop souvent, trop vite, trop mal**, etc.

Nous avons <u>beaucoup</u> aimé ce film. *We really liked this movie.*
Il a <u>mal</u> réagi aux médicaments. *He reacted badly to the medicine.*
Le gouvernement n'a <u>jamais</u> promis ça. *The government never promised that.*
Elle est <u>trop souvent</u> partie. *She is gone too often.*

Note that if an adverb of quantity is followed by **de**, it will be placed after the verb:

J'ai eu <u>assez d'</u>argent pour acheter une voiture. *I got enough money to buy a car.*

*Remember to **download the audio** of the lists and to **watch the videos** – see Preface*

Some adverbs that qualify the whole sentence can be placed **at the beginning, middle, or end.**

Hier j'ai reçu mon diplôme par la poste. *Yesterday I got my degree by mail.*
J'ai reçu mon diplôme par la poste hier. *I got my degree by mail yesterday.*
J'ai reçu hier mon diplôme par la poste. *I got my degree yesterday by mail.*

The last sentence sounds a little bit less natural. To make the sentence lighter, I would personally turn **mon diplôme** into a direct object pronoun:

Je l'ai reçu hier par la poste. *I got it yesterday by mail.*

EX. 6.3 *Traduisez les phrases suivantes.*

1. Has he arrived yet?

   _____

2. She complains less than usual.

   _____

3. There are too many flies here.

   _____

4. Is it better to leave now?

   _____

5. Did you eat enough?

   _____

6. They had so much to see!

   _____

7. Is he there?

   _____

8. He is often called to the principal's office.

   _____

9. Fortunately, she likes her new job.

   _____

10. I read the newspapers daily.

    _____

EX. 6.4 *Conjuguez le verbe au passé composé et ajoutez l'adverbe.*

1. (enfin – comprendre) Il _____ comment opérer cette machine.

2. (vite – partir) Après avoir découvert cela, nous _____.

3. (souvent – parler) Elle _____ de cette possibilité.

4. (encore – manquer) On _____ le train !

5. (déjà – partir) Il _____ mais il va bientôt revenir.

6. (jamais – tomber) Nous ne _____ en manque de riz.

7. (bien – finir) Cette pièce de théâtre _____.

8. (beaucoup – apprendre) Vous _____ durant l'année.

9. (jamais – dire) Il n' _____ ça.

10. (assez – manger) Est-ce que vous _____ ?

Notes :

Remember to **download the audio** of the lists and to **watch the videos** – see Preface

Bon vs Bien

Bon and **bien** both mean good in French. Both can also be adjectives, adverbs, or nouns. They can seem confusing, but they have very specific uses. Let's start with **bon**:

Bon can be an adjective, an adverb or, a noun.
Bon as an adjective agrees in gender and number with the noun that it describes: **AUDIO 44.1** ◀))

	Masculine	Feminine
Singular	**Bon**	**Bonne**
Plural	**Bons**	**Bonnes**

Bon

The adjective **bon** can have 3 different translations in English: good – nice – right. **AUDIO 44.2** ◀))

- **Bon** – good

  C'est un <u>bon</u> plan. *It's a good plan.*
  C'est une <u>bonne</u> idée. *It's a good idea.*

- **Bon** – nice

  Nous avons passé un <u>bon</u> moment. *We had a nice moment.*
  Nous avons passé une <u>bonne</u> journée. *We had a nice day.*

- **Bon** – right

  Ce n'est pas le <u>bon</u> ticket. *It's not the right receipt.*
  Ce n'est pas la <u>bonne</u> rue. *It's not the right street.*

Bon as an adverb doesn't agree in gender and number. It always stays bon.

Il fait bon aujourd'hui. *It's nice today.*
Ce parfum sent bon. *This perfume smells nice.*

Bon as a noun:

Un bon (d'achat) – A coupon, a voucher
J'ai un bon (d'achat) de 5 dollars. *I have a 5-dollar voucher.*

Bon in expressions:

Pour de bon – For good
Il est parti pour de bon. *He is gone for good.*

Bon marché – Cheap
Ce pull est bon marché. *This sweater is cheap.*

Ah bon ? – Really?

Bon in greetings and wishes: AUDIO **44.3** 🔊

Bonne année – Happy New Year
Bon anniversaire – Happy birthday
Bonne journée – Have a good day
Bon après-midi – Have a good afternoon
Bonne soirée – Have a good evening
Bonne nuit – Have a good night
Bon week-end – Have a good weekend
Bon samedi – Have a good Saturday

Bonne chance – Good luck
Bonne route – Have a safe trip
Bon séjour – Have a nice stay
Bonnes vacances – Have a good vacation
Bon voyage – Have a good trip
Bon courage – Hang in there
Bon appétit – Enjoy your meal
Bon rétablissement – Get well soon

EX. 6.5 *Ajoutez **bon – bonne – bons – bonnes**.*   AUDIO **44.4** 🔊

1. Ce n'est pas la _____ adresse.

2. Je te souhaite un _____ rétablissement.

3. Il devrait faire _____ ce week-end.

4. On a passé une _____ soirée avec nos amis.

5. C'est une _____ idée mais je ne sais pas si ça va marcher.

6. Est-ce que ce plat est _____ ?

7. J'espère que nous aurons des _____ notes.

8. On a reçu des _____ d'achat pour ce magasin.

9. _____ appétit !

10. C'est vraiment _____ marché !

Bien

Bien can be an adjective, an adverb, or a noun. **Bien** never agrees in gender and number unless it's a noun.

AUDIO **44.5** 🔊

	Masculine	Feminine
Singular	**Bien**	**Bien**
Plural	**Bien**	**Bien**

The difference between the adjective and the adverb is hard to understand, especially since bien doesn't agree in gender and number. So, let's see it by translation: 44.6

- **Bien** – Good

  C'est bien. *It's good.*
  Très bien ! *Very good!*
  Ça a l'air bien. *It seems good.*

- **Bien** – well   **verb + bien**

    Tu vas bien ? *How are you doing?*
    Je vais bien, merci. *I am doing well, thanks.*
    Je sais bien. *I know, I am well aware of it.*
    Le wifi ne fonctionne pas bien. *The WiFi doesn't work well.*

- **Bien** – well   **auxiliary + bien + verb**

    Nous avons bien mangé. *We ate well.*
    Nous avons bien étudié. *We studied well.*
    Nous avons bien travaillé. *We worked well.*
    Nous avons bien dormi. *We slept well.*

Bien as a noun:

    Un bien (immobilier) – Real estate

Bien in expressions:

    Aller bien – To be well
    Je vais très bien aujourd'hui.
    I am doing very well today.

Bien entendu – Of course / Obviously

    Bien entendu, nous serons là pour Noël.
    Of course, we will be there for Christmas.

Bien sûr – Of course

    Bien sûr je peux te conduire à l'aéroport.
    Of course, I can drive you to the airport.

Bien sûr que – Of course

    Bien sûr que non – Of course not
    Bien sûr que oui – Yes of course

Dire du bien de – To speak well of

    Elle dit toujours du bien de toi.
    She always speaks well of you.

On verra bien – We will see

    On verra bien si on a le temps.
    We will see if we have time.

Bien prendre – To take (something) well

    Il a bien pris la nouvelle.
    He took the news well.

*Remember to **download the audio** of the lists and to **watch the videos** – see Preface*

Bien souvent – Very often

Bien souvent, j'ai encore faim après le petit déjeuner.
Very often, I am still hungry after breakfast.

Faire bien de – To do the good thing, the right thing

Tu fais bien de me le dire !
It's a good thing you told me!

Être bien / se sentir bien dans sa peau – To feel comfortable in one's skin

Elle est bien dans sa peau.
She feels comfortable in her own skin.

Être bien arrivé(e) – To arrive safely

Tu es bien arrivé ?
Did you arrive safely?

EX. 6.6 *Traduisez les phrases suivantes.*   AUDIO 44.7 ◄ᴺ

1. I don't know yet, we will see.

    _____

2. Of course not!

    _____

3. Are you feeling well / ok?

    _____

4. She studied well, I think.

    _____

5. How are you doing? (sing)

    _____

C'est bien or **c'est bon**?   AUDIO 44.8 ◄ᴺ

The biggest struggle I see among French learners is when to use correctly **c'est bien** ou **c'est bon**, since they both mean it's good / that's good.

We use **c'est bon** for a physical sensation, a taste:
C'est vraiment bon ! *It's really good!*

We use **c'est bien** for judgment, opinion:
Tu as réussi, c'est bien ! *You made it, that's good!*

EX. 6.7 *Répondez aux commentaires avec **c'est bon** ! ou **c'est bien** !.* AUDIO **44.9** ◀))

1. Tu as réussi ?

   _____

2. Ce vin est délicieux !

   _____

3. Elle est bien arrivée ?

   _____

4. Regarde ce qu'il a fait !

   _____

5. C'est toi qui as cuisiné ce plat ?

   _____

*Remember to **download the audio** of the lists and to **watch the videos** – see Preface*

Notes :

Encore, Toujours & Déjà, Jamais

Encore & Toujours

Encore and **toujours** are adverbs of frequency with similar meanings and many exceptions!

AUDIO **45.1** ◀)

The basic rule is that **encore** means again and **toujours** means always:

- **Encore** – Again
  Il a encore téléphoné. *He called again.*

- **Toujours** – Always
  Il est toujours fatigué. *He is always tired.*

It gets a little bit more complicated when talking about the translations still and yet because both can be translated this way:

Elle est <u>encore</u> étudiante. *She is still a student.*
Elle est <u>toujours</u> étudiante. *She is still a student.*

Il n'a pas <u>encore</u> fini. *He isn't done yet.*
Il n'a <u>toujours</u> pas fini. *He isn't done yet.*

Other uses of toujours:

- **Toujours** – Anyhow / Anyway
  C'est difficile, mais c'est <u>toujours</u> bon à savoir. *It's difficult but it's good to know anyway.*

Other uses of encore:

- **Encore** – More
  C'est délicieux, est-ce que je peux en avoir <u>encore</u> ? *It's delicious, can I have more?*

- **Encore** - Another
  Il veut <u>encore</u> du thé. *He wants another cup of tea.*

- **Encore** - Even
  C'était <u>encore</u> mieux que ce que je pensais. *It was even better that what I thought.*

EX. 6.8 *Ajoutez **encore** ou **toujours**, parfois les deux peuvent fonctionner.*   AUDIO 45.2 ◄⑴

1. Tu n'es pas _____ partie ? (Change the position of pas if needed)

2. Il a _____ cette couverture avec lui.

3. Vous jouez _____ à ce jeu ?

4. Est-ce que tu en veux _____ ?

5. Honnêtement, c'était _____ mieux que sur la brochure.

6. Tu espères _____ voir un koala ?

7. Nous sommes _____ ensemble.

8. Il reste _____ du café ?

9. C'est _____ bon à savoir.

10. Est-ce qu'ils veulent _____ faire une offre ?

Déjà & Jamais

But if you want to use yet in a positive question, you can use **déjà**.

AUDIO 45.3 ◄⑴

Tu as <u>déjà</u> appris ça ? *Have you learned that yet?*
Il est <u>déjà</u> parti ? *Is he gone yet?*

Déjà also means ever in sentences such as have you ever:

Tu as déjà vu ce film ? *Have you ever seen this movie?*
Tu as déjà été en Italie ? *Have you ever been to Italy?*

However, if we change these 2 sentences into negative sentences, we will use **jamais** instead of **déjà**:

Tu n'as <u>jamais</u> vu ce film ? *You have never seen this movie?*
Tu n'as <u>jamais</u> été en Italie ? *You have never been to Italy?*

EX. 6.9 *Ajoutez **jamais** ou **déjà**.*   AUDIO 45.4 ◄⑴

1. Avez-vous _____ visité ce musée ?

2. Non, nous ne l'avons _____ visité.

3. C'est difficile à croire que tu n'as _____ vu ce film.

4. Je l'ai _____ vu mais je ne m'en souviens plus.

5. Est-ce que l'avion a _____ décollé ?

The Subjonctive – Le Subjonctif

This is a review of "*The Complete French Conjugation Course*". The review includes only a part of what is taught in the conjugation course.

The **subjonctif** is used after **que**, mostly in subordinate clauses and indicates a **wish, a regret, an emotion, an opinion, or a doubt.**

Uses of the Subjonctif

AUDIO 45.1.1 ◀))

- To express a **wish**:
  Je tiens à ce que tu viennes. *I want you to come.*

- To express an e**motion**:
  Elle est triste qu'il soit parti si tôt. *She is sad that he left so early.*

- For **impersonal expressions**:
  Il faut que tu dormes. *You must sleep.*

- To express **regret or a recommendation**:
  Je regrette que ce soit là fin. *I regret that it's the end.*

- To express a **doubt** :
  Il est impossible qu'il soit ici. *It's impossible that he is here.*

- To express an **opinion**:
  Il est rare qu'il soit d'accord. *It's unusual that he agrees.*

How to Conjugation of Verbs Subjonctif

Verbs of the 1st group – regular verbs ending in -er:

The **subjonctif présent** is formed by taking the verb conjugated in the **present tense** with **ils** and removing the **-ent.** That gives us the stem.

Then we add the endings for the **subjonctif présent**: **-e, -es, -e, -ions, iez** and **-ent.**

AUDIO 45.1.2 ◀⁙

Changer To change
Stem présent: chang

Que je **change**
Que tu **changes**
Qu'il **change**
Qu'elle **change**
Qu'on **change**
Que nous **changions**
Que vous **changiez**
Qu'ils **changent**
Qu'elles **changent**

Verbs of the 2nd group – regular verbs ending in -ir:

Finir To finish
Stem présent: finiss

Que je **finisse**
Que tu **finisses**
Qu'il **finisse**
Qu'elle **finisse**
Qu'on **finisse**
Que nous **finissions**
Que vous **finissiez**
Qu'ils **finissent**
Qu'elles **finissent**

Verbs of the 3rd group – regular verbs ending in -re:

Attendre To wait
Stem présent: attend

Que j'**attende**
Que tu **attendes**
Qu'il **attende**
Qu'elle **attende**
Qu'on **attende**
Que nous **attendions**
Que vous **attendiez**
Qu'ils **attendent**
Qu'elles **attendent**

Irregular verbs: AUDIO 45.1.3 ◀))

Battre (Ils **batt**ent)	Que je **batte** – Que nous **battions** – Qu'ils **battent**
Conduire (Ils **conduis**ent)	Que je **conduise** – Que nous **conduisions** – Qu'ils **conduisent**
Connaître (Ils **connaiss**ent)	Que je **connaisse** – Que nous **connaissions** – Qu'ils **connaissent**
Courir (Ils **cour**ent)	Que je **coure** – Que nous **courions** – Qu'ils **courent**
Craindre (Ils **craign**ent)	Que je **craigne** – Que nous **craignions** – Qu'ils **craignent**
Dire (Ils **dis**ent)	Que je **dise** – Que nous **disions** – Qu'ils **disent**
Écrire (Ils **écriv**ent)	Que j'**écrive** – Que nous **écrivions** – Qu'ils **écrivent**
Lire (Ils **lis**ent)	Que je **lise** – Que nous **lisions** – Qu'ils **lisent**
Mettre (Ils **mett**ent)	Que je **mette** – Que nous **mettions** – Qu'ils **mettent**
Ouvrir (Ils **ouvr**ent)	Que j'**ouvre** – Que nous **ouvrions** – Qu'ils **ouvrent**
Partir (Ils **part**ent)	Que je **parte** – Que nous **partions** – Qu'ils **partent**
Plaire (Ils **plais**ent)	Que je **plaise** – Que nous **plaisions** – Qu'ils **plaisent**
Rire (Ils **ri**ent)	Que je **rie** – Que nous **riions** – Qu'ils **rient**
Suivre (Ils **suiv**ent)	Que je **suive** – Que nous **suivions** – Qu'ils **suivent**
Vivre (Ils **viv**ent)	Que je **vive** – Que nous **vivions** – Qu'ils **vivent**

Irregular verbs with 2 different stems:

Some verbs (and compounds) have two different stems in the **subjonctif présent**.
The first one will be used for: **je, tu, il, elle, on, ils, elles**.
The second one will be used for: **nous, vous**.

Memorize one of each to be more efficient. Here we are going to see **je** and **nous**: AUDIO 45.1.4 ◀))

Boire	Que je **boive**	Que nous **buv**ions
Devoir	Que je **doive**	Que nous **dev**ions
Envoyer	Que j'**envoie**	Que nous **envoy**ions
Mourir	Que je **meure**	Que nous **mourr**ions
Recevoir	Que je **reçoive**	Que nous **recev**ions
Tenir	Que je **tienne**	Que nous **ten**ions
Venir	Que je **vienne**	Que nous **ven**ions
Voir	Que je **voie**	Que nous **voy**ions

Être and **avoir** are fully irregular. They are also used to form the subjunctive past. Therefore they must be learned by heart.

AUDIO 45.1.5 ◀))

Être To be	**Avoir** To have
Que je **sois**	Que j'**aie**
Que tu **sois**	Que tu **aies**
Qu'il **soit**	Qu'il **ait**
Qu'elle **soit**	Qu'elle **ait**
Qu'on **soit**	Qu'on **ait**
Que nous **soyons**	Que nous **ayons**
Que vous **soyez**	Que vous **ayez**
Qu'ils **soient**	Qu'ils **aient**
Qu'elles **soient**	Qu'elles **aient**

EX. 6.10 *Conjuguez les verbes suivants au subjonctif présent.*   AUDIO **45.1.6** ◀))

1. **Visiter**

   Que je _____

   Que tu _____

   Qu'on _____

   Que nous _____

   Que vous _____

   Qu'elles _____

2. **Nourrir**

   Que je _____

   Que tu _____

   Qu'il _____

   Que nous _____

   Que vous _____

   Qu'ils _____

3. **Descendre**

   Que je _____

   Que tu _____

   Qu'elle _____

   Que nous _____

   Que vous _____

   Qu'elles _____

EX. 6.11 *Conjuguez le verbe entre parenthèses au subjonctif.* AUDIO 45.1.7 ◀))

1. **(partir)** Il faut que je _____.

2. **(arriver)** Ce n'est pas normal qu'il _____ à cette heure !

3. **(pouvoir)** On a cet appareil pour qu'il _____ se lever tout seul.

4. **(se décider)** On joue aux cartes en attendant qu'il _____.

5. **(être)** Prends une décision avant qu'il ne _____ trop tard.

6. **(travailler)** C'est dommage qu'elle _____ autant.

7. **(mettre)** Il faut que tu _____ ton manteau.

8. **(boire)** Il faut que je _____ plus d'eau.

9. **(finir)** J'exige que tu _____ ton repas.

10. **(savoir)** Il ne faut pas qu'ils _____ la vérité.

Notes :

Conjunctions – Les Conjonctions

What is a conjunction?

A conjunction is a word (or a few) used to connect sentences, words, or clauses.

In French, just like in English, we have a few different types of conjunctions. The most common ones are the **coordinating conjunctions**:

Coordinating Conjunctions

There are 7 coordinating conjunctions in French: **mais – ou – et – donc – or – ni – car**
Remember it as: **Mais ou est donc Ornicar?**

AUDIO 46.1 ◀))

- **Mais** – but
  C'est difficile mais tu peux y arriver. *It's difficult but you can do it.*

- **Ou** – or
  Tu veux un café ou un thé ? *Do you want a coffee or a tea?*

- **Et** – and
  J'ai acheté des champignons et des tomates. *I bought mushrooms and tomatoes.*

- **Donc** – so / therefore
  Il a raté le bus donc il sera en retard. *He missed the bus, so he will be late.*

- **Or** – now / yet
  On est partis tôt, or, il y avait des travaux sur la route. *We left early, yet there was construction on the road.*

- **Ni** – neither /nor
  Je n'ai ni argent ni travail. *I have neither money nor a job.*

- **Car** – for / because
  On a accepté car il n'y avait pas d'autres choix. *We accepted because there was no other choice.*

EX. 6.12 *Ajoutez une des conjonctions ci-dessus.*   **AUDIO 46.2** ◀))

1. Ce sont mes frères _____ mes sœurs.

2. On n'a trouvé _____ trésor _____ indices.

3. Cela prendra du temps _____ tu seras content quand tu auras fini.

4. Nous nous sommes disputés, _____ pour une fois j'avais raison.

*Remember to **download the audio** of the lists and to **watch the videos** – see Preface*

5. Je vais pendre le canard _____ pas trop cuit.

6. Il a accepté _____ il avait le temps.

7. Est-ce que tu prends du sucre _____ du lait dans ton café ?

8. C'est _____ lui dont tu me parlais ?

9. Je suis professeur _____ je connais la réponse.

10. Je vais étudier ce matin _____ cet après-midi.

Subordinating Conjunctions

The second type of conjunctions is called **subordinating conjunctions**:

AUDIO 46.3 ◄))

- **Comme** – as / since   To compare or indicate a cause

  Comme on ne peut pas compter sur lui, je vais demander à quelqu'un d'autre.
  Since we can't count on him, I will ask someone else.

- **Puisque** – as / since   To indicate a subordinate clause

  Faisons ça maintenant puisqu'on est là.
  Let's do that now since we are here.

- **Quand** – when   To indicate a cause or a condition

  Je serai prête quand tu arrives.
  I will be ready when you get here.

- **Lorsque** – when   To indicate a cause

  Lorsqu'il a vu les preuves, il a tout de suite compris.
  When he saw the evidence, he understood right away.

- **Que** – that   To indicate another subordinating clause

  Il pense qu'il sera élu président.
  He thinks he will be elected president.

- **Quoique** – even though   To indicate two opposite ideas

  C'est son rêve, quoique cela coûtera beaucoup d'argent.
  It's his dream, even though it will cost a lot of money.

- **Si** – if   To indicate a condition

  Tu le vendras si tu diminues le prix.
  You will sell it if you lower the price.

EX. 6.13 *Ajoutez une des conjonctions ci-dessus.* AUDIO 46.4 🔊

1. _____ c'est comme ça, autant ne pas y aller.
2. _____ tu arrives, nous en discuterons.
3. _____ malade, il est tout de même venu.
4. Il est vrai _____ ce n'est pas facile.
5. _____ tu arrives, est-ce que tu peux commencer le ménage ?
6. _____ je ne suis pas revenu dans une heure, appelle la police.
7. _____ je n'ai pas été choisie, je suis rentrée à la maison.
8. J'espère _____ tu vas bien.
9. Je me demande toujours _____ tu es sincère.
10. _____ tu es là, est-ce que tu peux m'aider ?

Other Conjunctions

The two lists that we just saw are the most common. Other conjunctions are ones made of 2 words or more and usually, but not always, include **que**: AUDIO 46.5 🔊

À condition que – On the condition that
À moins que – Unless that
Afin que – So that
Au cas où – In case
Aussitôt que – As soon as
Bien que – Although
Dans la mesure où – Givent that
D'autant plus que – Especially given that
De peur que – For fear that
Depuis que – Since
Dès que – As soon as
Encore que – Although
Étant donné que – Given that
Jusqu'à ce que – Until
Maintenant que – Now that

Malgré que – Despite that
Même si – Even if
Parce que – Because
Pendant que – While
Pour autant que – Provided that
Pour que – So that
Pourvu que – Provided that
Quand bien même que – Even if
Si bien que – So much that
Si jamais – If ever
Si tant est que – Supposing that
Tandis que – Whereas
Une fois que – As soon as
Vu que – Seeing that

<u>**À moins que**</u> **tu paies plus cher, tu n'auras pas le même service.**
Unless you pay more, you won't have the same service.

Il apportera un dessert <u>**de peur qu'**</u>**il n'y ait pas assez à manger.**
He will bring a dessert for fear that it won't be enough to eat.

<u>**Même si**</u> **j'avais envie de venir, je n'ai pas le temps.**
Even if I wanted to come, I don't have enough time.

Elle a fait une sieste <u>parce qu</u>'elle était fatiguée.
She took a nap because she was tired.

Tiens-moi au courant <u>si jamais</u> tu entends quelque chose.
Let me know if you ever hear something.

Mangeons à la maison <u>vu que</u> le restaurant est fermé.
Let's eat at home, seeing that the restaurant is closed.

EX. 6.14 *Ajoutez une des conjonctions ci-dessus.*   AUDIO 46.6 ◀))

1. _____ vous arrivez avant moi, appelez la réception pour ouvrir la porte.

2. Il peut rester _____ il soit calme.

3. Elle a préparé assez à manger _____ tout le monde mange.

4. Reste ici _____ elle arrive.

5. _____ tu disais la vérité, ils ne te croiraient pas.

6. Il dort _____ tout le monde travaille.

7. _____ tu es là, est-ce que tu peux regarder à l'imprimante ?

8. _____ tu n'aurais pas compris, c'est non.

9. Il fouille son téléphone _____ il ne le trompe.

10. _____ tu le commandes maintenant, il ne sera pas livré.

EX. 6.15 *Ajoutez une des conjonctions de ce chapitre.*   AUDIO 46.7 ◀))

1. Elle a étudié à New York _____ à Los Angeles.

2. Il était là _____ tu as téléphoné.

3. _____ tu le dis !

4. Il ne s'est pas arrêté après sa blessure, _____ il a besoin de rééducation.

5. Tu es à l'hôtel _____ à la plage ?

6. Je vais le jeter _____ tu ne le veuilles ?

7. Ils sauront _____ il sera prêt.

8. Elle est habituée à nager _____ elle a grandi près de la mer.

9. _____ je l'ai vu, je ne vois plus que ça.

10. _____ j'avais le temps, je n'ai pas envie de venir.

---

11. Ils ne savent pas ce que c'est _____ ils ont fait des tests.

12. On va rester ici _____ la tempête passe.

13. _____ le client ne vient pas chercher sa commande, elle sera annulée.

14. Appelle-moi _____ tu arrives.

15. On est en retard _____ il y a des travaux.

CHAPTER 7

Review
Révision

Review

EX. 7.1 *Choisissez un nom pour chaque phrase et ajoutez l'**article** si besoin.*   AUDIO **46.1.1** ◄))

arbre – professeur – pont – docteur – voiture – bagages – temps – glace – biscuit – avertissement – courses – nouvelles – agent immobilier – passager – train – tempête – mariés – rendez-vous.

1. Il est parti sans _____.
2. _____ risque de tomber sur la maison.
3. Il a reçu _____ à son travail.
4. Est-ce que tu as vu _____ ce matin ?
5. _____ traverse _____ à toute vitesse.
6. Elle n'a pas besoin de _____.
7. Il est devenu _____ il y a quelques mois.
8. _____ a arrangé _____.
9. _____ (jeunes) ont fait le tour du monde.
10. J'ai acheté _____ et _____.
11. _____ est demandé à l'accueil.
12. _____ s'approche rapidement.
13. _____ est encore en retard.
14. Est-ce que tu as fait _____ ?
15. C'est _____ (incroyable).

EX. 7.2 *Changez ces phrases du **singulier** au **pluriel**, Changez tout ce qui est possible (pas le lever du soleil par exemple).*   AUDIO **46.1.2** ◄))

1. L'oiseau est sur la branche.

   _____

2. Elle est partie ce matin avant le lever du soleil.

   _____

3. Tu l'as reçu ?

   _____

4. Il s'est marié il y a quelques mois.

   _____

5. Tu es au courant de cette histoire ?

   _____

6. Cette pâtisserie coûte seulement 3 dollars.

   _____

7. C'est le mien.

   _____

8. Je me suis dépêché de partir. (on)

   _____

9. L'assistant regarde l'opération de loin.

   _____

10. Finis ton assiette.

   _____

EX. 7.3 *Complétez les phrases avec **c'est - ce sont - Il est - Il y a**.*   AUDIO **46.1.3** 🔊

1. _____ parti de bonne heure.
2. _____ mon petit frère, Jules.
3. _____ 3 heures que je travaille sur ce projet.
4. _____ moi.
5. _____ une mauvaise idée !
6. _____ courageux de travailler autant.
7. Est-ce que _____ ton tour ?
8. _____ ses parents, Marc et Julie.
9. Tu penses que _____ bien comme ça ?
10. _____ du fromage dans le frigo si tu veux.

EX. 7.4 *Ajoutez les adjectifs possessifs entre parenthèses.*   AUDIO **46.1.4** 🔊

1. J'ai reçu _____ courrier par erreur. (his)
2. _____ voiture a été emboutie dans l'accident. (your – pl)
3. _____ parents ont déménagé en Espagne. (my)
4. Tu as oublié _____ affaires à la salle de sport. (your – sing)
5. _____ lettre est arrivée après quelques mois. (his / her)

6. _____ portefeuille est tombé de _____ poche.
   (your – sing)

7. _____ réception est prévue pour décembre. (their)

8. _____ grands-parents viennent dîner ce week-end. (my)

9. _____ maison a été détruite à cause des feux de forêt. (his / her)

10. _____ symptômes se sont aggravés ces derniers jours. (his / her)

EX. 7.5 *Complétez les phrases avec votre date d'anniversaire, l'étage où vous vivez. etc. (si cela ne s'applique pas, inventez). Écrivez les dates en toutes lettres.*

1. J'habite au (étage)

   _____

2. J'ai (âge)

   _____

3. J'ai (dogs, brothers, sisters, etc)

   _____

4. Je suis né(e) le (jour – mois)

   _____

5. Je gagne (argent) par mois

   _____

6. J'habite au (numéro)

   _____

7. J'ai eu fini l'école en (année)

   _____

8. Je suis né(e) en (année)

   _____

9. Ce cours de grammaire dure ... jours

   _____

10. Mon appartement, ma maison fait ... mètres carrés

    _____

EX. 7.6 *Changez ces phrases en phrases négatives.* AUDIO 46.1.5 ◀»

1. Je suis déjà là.

   _____

2. Ma mère me laisse sortir tard le soir.

   _____

3. On a assez de nourriture pour la semaine.

   _____

4. Elle prend toujours ses médicaments régulièrement.

   _____

5. Il travaillait ce jour-là.

   _____

6. Elle consomme trop de boissons sucrées.

   _____

7. Il a enfoncé le clou trop loin.

   _____

8. Il veut un vélo électrique pour son anniversaire.

   _____

9. Nous avons cueilli plus de 3 kilos de pommes.

   _____

10. Elle a trouvé son sac à main dans la poubelle.

    _____

EX. 7.7 *Ajoutez les propositions **à** ou **de** aux phrases suivantes.* AUDIO 46.1.6 ◀»

1. Je suis _____ accord avec toi.

2. Ce tableau vient _____ Maroc.

3. Tu as beaucoup _____ devoirs aujourd'hui ?

4. Nous sommes prêts _____ partir.

5. J'ai mal _____ la tête depuis ce matin.

6. L'avion décolle _____ Paris et sera là dans une heure ou deux.

7. Est-ce que tu as acheté un cadeau _____ tes parents ?

8. Le design _____ cette bouteille _____ vin est parfait.

9. Il faut boire 3 litres _____ eau par jour.

10. C'est difficile _____ dire.

EX. 7.8 *Conjuguez le verbe aller au temps indiqué et ajouter la préposition et un lieu de votre choix.*

Exemple : Hier, j'étais chez le docteur.

1. (passé composé) Hier, je _____

2. (futur simple) Demain, j' _____

3. (passé récent) Je _____

4. (imparfait) En 2015, j' _____

5. (présent – habits) En général, je _____

EX. 7.9 *Ajoutez la préposition manquante.*   AUDIO 46.1.7 ◀))

1. Je suis arrivée _____ heure.

2. Ils sont partis en week-end _____ les enfants.

3. Elle aime bien se regarder _____ le miroir.

4. Tu as pris rendez-vous _____ le dermatologue ?

5. Le voyage _____ États-Unis semble incroyable !

6. Nous serons _____ Paris _____ lundi.

7. Il est assis _____ son père.

8. Je suis _____ la gare mais je ne te vois pas.

9. Elle est arrivée _____ les 3 premières finalistes.

10. Il a été renvoyé _____ son erreur.

EX. 7.10 *Formez une question avec les éléments donnés. Ajoutez les articles, les prépositions, et la conjugaison, nécessaires. Le type de question est donné à la fin ainsi que la conjugaison.* AUDIO 46.1.8 ◄))

1. Tu / décharger / voiture (Est-ce que – passé composé)

   _____

2. Ça / faire / longtemps / que / tu / fumer (? – présent)

   _____

3. Il / se préparer / déjà / pour / aller / lit (Est-ce que – passé composé)

   _____

4. Voiture / s'arrêter / ne pas (? – présent)

   _____

5. Tu / penser / que / ça / marcher (Est-ce que – présent / futur proche)

   _____

6. Tu / savoir / jouer / cartes (inversion – présent)

   _____

7. Vous / pouvez / répéter / s'il vous plaît (inversion – présent)

   _____

8. Il / ne jamais / revoir / femme (Est-ce que – passé composé)

   _____

9. Qui / vaincre / dernier / niveau (? – passé composé)

   _____

10. Tu / avoir / temps (Est-ce que – présent)

    _____

EX. 7.11 *Ajoutez les adjectifs et accordez le nom en fonction.* AUDIO 46.1.9 ◄))

1. Gentil – Un homme _____
2. Original – Une chanson _____
3. Bleu – Des oiseaux _____
4. Grand – Une communauté _____
5. Vieux – Une église _____

---

6. Blanc – Une voiture _____

7. Dangereux – Une idée _____

8. Étroit – Une route _____

9. Chaud – Un repas _____

10. Froid – Une douche _____

11. Méchant – Un chien _____

12. Rapide – Une voiture _____

13. Gros – Un chien _____

14. Délicieux – Des friandises _____

15. Bruyant – Une moto _____

16. Énorme – Un terrain _____

17. Marron – De l'eau _____

18. Sec – La peau _____

19. Affamé – Un chat _____

20. Cassé – Une jambe _____

EX. 7.12 *Changez les objets en pronoms directs et indirects. Changez le participe passé si besoin.*

AUDIO 46.1.10 ◀》

1. Elle a offert une voiture à son amie.

   _____

2. Tu ne regardes pas le film ?

   _____

3. Le policier ordonne au conducteur de s'arrêter.

   _____

4. Elle a fait mal au patient en faisant la prise de sang.

   _____

5. Est-ce que cela convient à tous les invités ?

   _____

6. J'ai cassé la tasse en vidant le lave-vaisselle.

   _____

7. Elle a transmis tous les dossiers à son avocat.

_____

8. Ils ont promis une augmentation aux employés.

_____

9. Tu m'as donné un chat.

_____

10. Nous avons dit à Paul que le professeur est absent.

_____

EX. 7.13 *Changez le groupe de noms par **en** ou **y**.*   AUDIO 46.1.11 ◄))

1. Il est mort de la tuberculose.

_____

2. Est-ce que tu restes à Paris ce week-end ?

_____

3. Tu prends de la crème dans ton café ?

_____

4. Il est toujours dans le bus.

_____

5. Vous voulez des cacahuètes ?

_____

6. Est-ce que tu es déjà allée en Thaïlande ?

_____

7. Nous avons apporté une bouteille de champagne.

_____

8. Le docteur est satisfait de ses progrès.

_____

9. La voiture est au garage.

_____

10. Elle n'est pas allée à la cafétéria.

_____

EX. 7.14 *Ajoutez* **qui** *ou* **que**.   AUDIO 46.1.12 ◄))

1. C'est le chien _____ j'ai adopté.

2. C'est le chien _____ a été adopté.

3. C'est toi _____ lui as dit ça ?

4. Je dois refaire le test _____ j'ai raté.

5. Les chaussures _____ tu as achetées sont magnifiques.

6. C'est une blague _____ je ne trouve pas drôle.

7. C'est une blague _____ est drôle.

8. La dame _____ tu vois est célèbre.

9. Tu peux prendre le plat _____ est dans le frigo.

10. C'est lui _____ a demandé le divorce.

EX. 7.15 *Ajoutez* **ce qui – ce que – ce dont – ce ... quoi**   AUDIO 46.1.13 ◄))

1. Elle ne comprend pas _____ lui a pris.

2. Après tout _____ elle t'a fait !

3. Ce n'est pas _____ nous avons payé.

4. Je ne comprends pas _____ tu parles.

5. _____ tu as besoin, c'est de plus de repos.

6. _____ est bizarre, c'est qu'elle a disparu sans une trace.

7. J'ignore _____ elle pense.

8. _____ il travaille c'est sa famille.

9. C'est _____ je t'ai dit !

10. Je ne sais pas _____ tu joues mais je n'aime pas ça.

EX. 7.16 *Ajoutez les adverbes donnés dans la phrase.*   AUDIO 46.1.14 ◄))

1. Rapidement - C'est arrivé.

   _____

2. Passionnément - Ils s'aiment.

   _____

3. Vers / Déjà - Ils sont arrivés 15 heures mais ils sont partis.

   _____

4.   Lentement / Sûrement – Mais.

   _____

5.   Depuis - Cette route est fermée des mois.

   _____

6.   Facilement – Il a trouvé une maison.

   _____

7.   Ouvertement – Elle a annoncé son divorce.

   _____

8.   Ici – Je vais rester quelques semaines de plus.

   _____

9.   Toujours – Tu es là ?

   _____

10. Enfin – Il a compris ce que j'essayais de lui expliquer.

   _____

EX. 7.17 *remplissez les phrases avec **toujours – encore – déjà – bon – bien** (plusieurs possibilités possibles).*   AUDIO 46.1.15 ◄))

1.   Est-ce qu'il vit _____ en Espagne ?
2.   Qu'est-ce que tu fais _____ là ?
3.   C'est _____ pour la santé.
4.   Je vais reprendre _____ un peu de café.
5.   Est-ce que tu t'es _____ reposé ?
6.   Il fait du _____ travail.
7.   Les enfants ne sont pas _____ faciles.
8.   Il a _____ 10 ans ?
9.   Il a _____ compris ce que je lui ai dit.
10. Je ne l'avais pas _____ à ce moment-là.

EX. 7.18 *Ajoutez une des conjonctions de la liste ci-dessous.*   AUDIO 46.1.16 ◀))

ou – puis – si – mais – alors – puisque – ensuite – comme – parce que – à condition que

1. Il a dit oui _____ il a dit non.

2. Cela ne sert à rien _____ c'est fini.

3. Tu préfères le jaune _____ l'orange ?

4. Je suis d'accord _____ tu rentres tôt.

5. Allons au magasin et _____ au garage.

6. Est-ce que ça va _____ je viens maintenant ?

7. _____ je t'ai dit, l'appartement est déjà loué.

8. Elle était en vacances _____ je travaillais.

9. Il est indécis _____ son budget est serré.

10. Ils pensaient pouvoir venir _____ il a eu un empêchement.

EX. 7.19 *Traduisez les phrases suivantes.*   AUDIO 46.1.17 ◀))

1. I hope you will find a job. (sing)

    _____

2. How much does he earn?

    _____

3. I didn't notice anything.

    _____

4. We painted the walls white.

    _____

5. The teacher isn't always right.

    _____

6. What movie did you see recently?

    _____

7. The elevator is out of order.

    _____

8. You are walking too fast for me!

_____

9. This family lost everything.

_____

10. The dishwasher uses less water.

_____

EX. 7.20 _Trouvez l'erreur et réécrivez la phrase._ 　AUDIO 46.1.18 ◄))

1. Tu te rappelles de me ?

_____

2. Est-ce que c'est la mien que tu as dans ton sac ?

_____

3. Les fleurs que j'ai acheté sont déjà mortes.

_____

4. L'hamburger est fait de viande.

_____

5. Ce sont des nouveaus rideaus.

_____

6. Qu'est-ce que tu regardes en télévision ?

_____

7. Je ne sais pas que est cette personne.

_____

8. Nous avons parti tôt pour aller à l'aéroport.

_____

9. Tu veux du café oú du thé ?

_____

10. J'y ai besoin !

_____

Notes :

10 Main Verbs Solutions

Aller – To go

Participe présent	allant

Présent de l'indicatif

Je vais	Nous allons
Tu vas	Vous allez
Il va	Ils vont
Elle va	Elles vont
On va	

Imparfait

J'allais	Nous allions
Tu allais	Vous alliez
Il allait	Ils allaient
Elle allait	Elles allaient
On allait	

Futur simple

J'irai	Nous irons
Tu iras	Vous irez
Il ira	Ils iront
Elle ira	Elles iront
On ira	

Conditionnel présent

J'irais	Nous irions
Tu irais	Vous iriez
Il irait	Ils iraient
Elle irait	Elles iraient
On irait	

Impératif

Va !
Allons !
Allez !

Participe passé	allé

Passé composé

Je suis allé(e)	Nous sommes allé(e)s
Tu es allé(e)	Vous êtes allé(e)s
Il est allé	Ils sont allés
Elle est allée	Elles sont allées
On est allé(e)s	

Plus-que-parfait

J'étais allé(e)	Nous étions allé(e)s
Tu étais allé(e)	Vous étiez allé(e)s
Il était allé	Ils étaient allés
Elle était allée	Elles étaient allées
On était allé(e)s	

Futur antérieur

Je serai allé(e)	Nous serons allé(e)s
Tu seras allé(e)	Vous serez allé(e)s
Il sera allé	Ils seront allés
Elle sera allée	Elles seront allées
On sera allé(e)s	

Conditionnel passé

Je serais allé(e)	Nous serions allé(e)s
Tu serais allé(e)	Vous seriez allé(e)s
Il serait allé	Ils seraient allés
Elle serait allée	Elles seraient allées
On serait allé(e)s	

Subjonctif présent

Que j'aille	Que nous allions
Que tu ailles	Que vous alliez
Qu'il aille	Qu'ils aillent
Qu'elle aille	Qu'elles aillent
Qu'on aille	

*Remember to **download the audio** of the lists and to **watch the videos** – see Preface*

Avoir – To have

Participe présent	ayant	**Participe passé**	eu

Présent de l'indicatif

J'ai	Nous avons
Tu as	Vous avez
Il a	Ils ont
Elle a	Elles ont
On a	

Passé composé

J'ai eu	Nous avons eu
Tu as eu	Vous avez eu
Il a eu	Ils ont eu
Elle a eu	Elles ont eu
On a eu	

Imparfait

J'avais	Nous avions
Tu avais	Vous aviez
Il avait	Ils avaient
Elle avait	Elles avaient
On avait	

Plus-que-parfait

J'avais eu	Nous avions eu
Tu avais eu	Vous aviez eu
Il avait eu	Ils avaient eu
Elle avait eu	Elles avaient eu
On avait eu	

Futur simple

J'aurai	Nous aurons
Tu auras	Vous aurez
Il aura	Ils auront
Elle aura	Elles auront
On aura	

Futur antérieur

J'aurai eu	Nous aurons eu
Tu auras eu	Vous aurez eu
Il aura eu	Ils auront eu
Elle aura eu	Elles auront eu
On aura eu	

Conditionnel présent

J'aurais	Nous aurions
Tu aurais	Vous auriez
Il aurait	Ils auraient
Elle aurait	Elles auraient
On aurait	

Conditionnel passé

J'aurais eu	Nous aurions eu
Tu aurais eu	Vous auriez eu
Il aurait eu	Ils auraient eu
Elle aurait eu	Elles auraient eu
On aurait eu	

Impératif

Aie !
Ayez !
Ayons !

Subjonctif présent

Que j'aie	Que nous ayons
Que tu aies	Que vous ayez
Qu'il ait	Qu'ils aient
Qu'elle ait	Qu'elles aient
Qu'on ait	

Donner – To give

Participe présent   donnant

Participe passé   donné

Présent de l'indicatif

Je donne	Nous donnons
Tu donnes	Vous donnez
Il donne	Ils donnent
Elle donne	Elles donnent
On donne	

Passé composé

J'ai donné	Nous avons donné
Tu as donné	Vous avez donné
Il a donné	Ils ont donné
Elle a donné	Elles ont donné
On a donné	

Imparfait

Je donnais	Nous donnions
Tu donnais	Vous donniez
Il donnait	Ils donnaient
Elle donnait	Elles donnaient
On donnait	

Plus-que-parfait

J'avais donné	Nous avions donné
Tu avais donné	Vous aviez donné
Il avait donné	Ils avaient donné
Elle avait donné	Elles avaient donné
On avait donné	

Futur simple

Je donnerai	Nous donnerons
Tu donneras	Vous donnerez
Il donnera	Ils donneront
Elle donnera	Elles donneront
On donnera	

Futur antérieur

J'aurai donné	Nous aurons donné
Tu auras donné	Vous aurez donné
Il aura donné	Ils auront donné
Elle aura donné	Elles auront donné
On aura donné	

Conditionnel présent

Je donnerais	Nous donnerions
Tu donnerais	Vous donneriez
Il donnerait	Ils donneraient
Elle donnerait	Elles donneraient
On donnerait	

Conditionnel passé

J'aurais donné	Nous aurions donné
Tu aurais donné	Vous auriez donné
Il aurait donné	Ils auraient donné
Elle aurait donné	Elles auraient donné
On aurait donné	

Impératif

Donne !
Donnez !
Donnons !

Subjonctif présent

Que je donne	Que nous donnions
Que tu donnes	Que vous donniez
Qu'il donne	Qu'ils donnent
Qu'elle donne	Qu'elles donnent
Qu'on donne	

Entendre – To hear

Participe présent   entendant

Participe passé   entendu

Présent de l'indicatif

J'entends	Nous entendons
Tu entends	Vous entendez
Il entend	Ils entendent
Elle entend	Elles entendent
On entend	

Passé composé

J'ai entendu	Nous avons entendu
Tu as entendu	Vous avez entendu
Il a entendu	Ils ont entendu
Elle a entendu	Elles ont entendu
On a entendu	

Imparfait

J'entendais	Nous entendions
Tu entendais	Vous entendiez
Il entendait	Ils entendaient
Elle entendait	Elles entendaient
On entendait	

Plus-que-parfait

J'avais entendu	Nous avions entendu
Tu avais entendu	Vous aviez entendu
Il avait entendu	Ils avaient entendu
Elle avait entendu	Elles avaient entendu
On avait entendu	

Futur simple

J'entendrai	Nous entendrons
Tu entendras	Vous entendrez
Il entendra	Ils entendront
Elle entendra	Elles entendront
On entendra	

Futur antérieur

J'aurai entendu	Nous aurons entendu
Tu auras entendu	Vous aurez entendu
Il aura entendu	Ils auront entendu
Elle aura entendu	Elles auront entendu
On aura entendu	

Conditionnel présent

J'entendrais	Nous entendrions
Tu entendrais	Vous entendriez
Il entendrait	Ils entendraient
Elle entendrait	Elles entendraient
On entendrait	

Conditionnel passé

J'aurais entendu	Nous aurions entendu
Tu aurais entendu	Vous auriez entendu
Il aurait entendu	Ils auraient entendu
Elle aurait entendu	Elles auraient entendu
On aurait entendu	

Impératif

Entends !
Entendons !
Entendez !

Subjonctif présent

Que j'entende	Que nous entendions
Que tu entendes	Que vous entendiez
Qu'il entende	Qu'ils entendent
Qu'elle entende	Qu'elles entendent
Qu'on entende	

Être – To be

Participe présent   étant

Présent de l'indicatif

Je suis	Nous sommes
Tu es	Vous êtes
Il est	Ils sont
Elle est	Elles sont
On est	

Imparfait

J'étais	Nous étions
Tu étais	Vous étiez
Il était	Ils étaient
Elle était	Elles étaient
On était	

Futur simple

Je serai	Nous serons
Tu seras	Vous serez
Il sera	Ils seront
Elle sera	Elles seront
On sera	

Conditionnel présent

Je serais	Nous serions
Tu serais	Vous seriez
Il serait	Ils seraient
Elle serait	Elles seraient
On serait	

Impératif

Sois !
Soyons !
Soyez !

Participe passé   été

Passé composé

J'ai été	Nous avons été
Tu as été	Vous avez été
Il a été	Ils ont été
Elle a été	Elles ont été
On a été	

Plus-que-parfait

J'avais été	Nous avions été
Tu avais été	Vous aviez été
Il avait été	Ils avaient été
Elle avait été	Elles avaient été
On avait été	

Futur antérieur

J'aurai été	Nous aurons été
Tu auras été	Vous aurez été
Il aura été	Ils auront été
Elle aura été	Elles auront été
On aura été	

Conditionnel passé

J'aurais été	Nous aurions été
Tu aurais été	Vous auriez été
Il aurait été	Ils auraient été
Elle aurait été	Elles auraient été
On aurait été	

Subjonctif présent

Que je sois	Que nous soyons
Que tu sois	Que vous soyez
Qu'il soit	Qu'ils soient
Qu'elle soit	Qu'elles soient
Qu'on soit	

Faire – To do / To make

Participe présent	faisant	**Participe passé**	fait

Présent de l'indicatif

Je fais	Nous faisons
Tu fais	Vous faites
Il fait	Ils font
Elle fait	Elles font
On fait	

Passé composé

J'ai fait	Nous avons fait
Tu as fait	Vous avez fait
Il a fait	Ils ont fait
Elle a fait	Elles ont fait
On a fait	

Imparfait

Je faisais	Nous faisions
Tu faisais	Vous faisiez
Il faisait	Ils faisaient
Elle faisait	Elles faisaient
On faisait	

Plus-que-parfait

J'avais fait	Nous avions fait
Tu avais fait	Vous aviez fait
Il avait fait	Ils avaient fait
Elle avait fait	Elles avaient fait
On avait fait	

Futur simple

Je ferai	Nous ferons
Tu feras	Vous ferez
Il fera	Ils feront
Elle fera	Elles feront
On fera	

Futur antérieur

J'aurai fait	Nous aurons fait
Tu auras fait	Vous aurez fait
Il aura fait	Ils auront fait
Elle aura fait	Elles auront fait
On aura fait	

Conditionnel présent

Je ferais	Nous ferions
Tu ferais	Vous feriez
Il ferait	Ils feraient
Elle ferait	Elles feraient
On ferait	

Conditionnel passé

J'aurais fait	Nous aurions fait
Tu aurais fait	Vous auriez fait
Il aurait fait	Ils auraient fait
Elle aurait fait	Elles auraient fait
On aurait fait	

Impératif

Fais !
Faisons !
Faites !

Subjonctif présent

Que je fasse	Que nous fassions
Que tu fasses	Que vous fassiez
Qu'il fasse	Qu'ils fassent
Qu'elle fasse	Qu'elles fassent
Qu'on fasse	

Finir – To finish

Participe présent   finissant

Présent de l'indicatif

Je finis	Nous finissons
Tu finis	Vous finissez
Il finit	Ils finissent
Elle finit	Elles finissent
On finit	

Imparfait

Je finissais	Nous finissions
Tu finissais	Vous finissiez
Il finissait	Ils finissaient
Elle finissait	Elles finissaient
On finissait	

Futur simple

Je finirai	Nous finirons
Tu finiras	Vous finirez
Il finira	Ils finiront
Elle finira	Elles finiront
On finira	

Conditionnel présent

Je finirais	Nous finirions
Tu finirais	Vous finiriez
Il finirait	Ils finiraient
Elle finirait	Elles finiraient
On finirait	

Impératif

Finis !
Finissons !
Finissez !

Participe passé   fini

Passé composé

J'ai fini	Nous avons fini
Tu as fini	Vous avez fini
Il a fini	Ils ont fini
Elle a fini	Elles ont fini
On a fini	

Plus-que-parfait

J'avais fini	Nous avions fini
Tu avais fini	Vous aviez fini
Il avait fini	Ils avaient fini
Elle avait fini	Elles avaient fini
On avait fini	

Futur antérieur

J'aurai fini	Nous aurons fini
Tu auras fini	Vous aurez fini
Il aura fini	Ils auront fini
Elle aura fini	Elles auront fini
On aura fini	

Conditionnel passé

J'aurais fini	Nous aurions fini
Tu aurais fini	Vous auriez fini
Il aurait fini	Ils auraient fini
Elle aurait fini	Elles auraient fini
On aurait fini	

Subjonctif présent

Que je finisse	Que nous finissions
Que tu finisses	Que vous finissiez
Qu'il finisse	Qu'ils finissent
Qu'elle finisse	Qu'elles finissent
Qu'on finisse	

Pouvoir – To be able to - Must

Participe présent   pouvant

Présent de l'indicatif

Je peux	Nous pouvons
Tu peux	Vous pouvez
Il peut	Ils peuvent
Elle peut	Elles peuvent
On peut	

Imparfait

Je pouvais	Nous pouvions
Tu pouvais	Vous pouviez
Il pouvait	Ils pouvaient
Elle pouvait	Elles pouvaient
On pouvait	

Futur simple

Je pourrai	Nous pourrons
Tu pourras	Vous pourrez
Il pourra	Ils pourront
Elle pourra	Elles pourront
On pourra	

Conditionnel présent

Je pourrais	Nous pourrions
Tu pourrais	Vous pourriez
Il pourrait	Ils pourraient
Elle pourrait	Elles pourraient
On pourrait	

Impératif

/
/
/

Participe passé   pu

Passé composé

J'ai pu	Nous avons pu
Tu as pu	Vous avez pu
Il a pu	Ils ont pu
Elle a pu	Elles ont pu
On a pu	

Plus-que-parfait

J'avais pu	Nous avions pu
Tu avais pu	Vous aviez pu
Il avait pu	Ils avaient pu
Elle avait pu	Elles avaient pu
On avait pu	

Futur antérieur

J'aurai pu	Nous aurons pu
Tu auras pu	Vous aurez pu
Il aura pu	Ils auront pu
Elle aura pu	Elles auront pu
On aura pu	

Conditionnel passé

J'aurais pu	Nous aurions pu
Tu aurais pu	Vous auriez pu
Il aurait pu	Ils auraient pu
Elle aurait pu	Elles auraient pu
On aurait pu	

Subjonctif présent

Que je puisse	Que nous puissions
Que tu puisses	Que vous puissiez
Qu'il puisse	Qu'ils puissent
Qu'elle puisse	Qu'elles puissent
Qu'on puisse	

Savoir - To know

Participe présent   sachant

Participe passé   su

Présent de l'indicatif

Je sais	Nous savons
Tu sais	Vous savez
Il sait	Ils savent
Elle sait	Elles savent
On sait	

Passé composé

J'ai su	Nous avons su
Tu as su	Vous avez su
Il a su	Ils ont su
Elle a su	Elles ont su
On a su	

Imparfait

Je savais	Nous savions
Tu savais	Vous saviez
Il savait	Ils savaient
Elle savait	Elles savaient
On savait	

Plus-que-parfait

J'avais su	Nous avions su
Tu avais su	Vous aviez su
Il avait su	Ils avaient su
Elle avait su	Elles avaient su
On avait su	

Futur simple

Je saurai	Nous saurons
Tu sauras	Vous saurez
Il saura	Ils sauront
Elle saura	Elles sauront
On saura	

Futur antérieur

J'aurai su	Nous aurons su
Tu auras su	Vous aurez su
Il aura su	Ils auront su
Elle aura su	Elles auront su
On aura su	

Conditionnel présent

Je saurais	Nous saurions
Tu saurais	Vous sauriez
Il saurait	Ils sauraient
Elle saurait	Elles sauraient
On saurait	

Conditionnel passé

J'aurais su	Nous aurions su
Tu aurais su	Vous auriez su
Il aurait su	Ils auraient su
Elle aurait su	Elles auraient su
On aurait su	

Impératif

Sache !
Sachons !
Sachez !

Subjonctif présent

Que je sache	Que nous sachions
Que tu saches	Que vous sachiez
Qu'il sache	Qu'ils sachent
Qu'elle sache	Qu'elles sachent
Qu'on sache	

Venir – To come

Participe présent	venant		**Participe passé**	venu

Présent de l'indicatif

Je viens	Nous venons
Tu viens	Vous venez
Il vient	Ils viennent
Elle vient	Elles viennent
On vient	

Passé composé

Je suis venu(e)	Nous sommes venu(e)s
Tu es venu(e)	Vous êtes venu(e)s
Il est venu	Ils sont venus
Elle est venue	Elles sont venues
On est venu(e)s	

Imparfait

Je venais	Nous venions
Tu venais	Vous veniez
Il venait	Ils venaient
Elle venait	Elles venaient
On venait	

Plus-que-parfait

J'étais venu(e)	Nous étions venu(e)s
Tu étais venu(e)	Vous étiez venu(e)s
Il était venu	Ils étaient venus
Elle était venue	Elles étaient venues
On était venu(e)s	

Futur simple

Je viendrai	Nous viendrons
Tu viendras	Vous viendrez
Il viendra	Ils viendront
Elle viendra	Elles viendront
On viendra	

Futur antérieur

Je serai venu(e)	Nous serons venu(e)s
Tu seras venu(e)	Vous serez venu(e)s
Il sera venu	Ils seront venus
Elle sera venue	Elles seront venues
On sera venu(e)s	

Conditionnel présent

Je viendrais	Nous viendrions
Tu viendrais	Vous viendriez
Il viendrait	Ils viendraient
Elle viendrait	Elles viendraient
On viendrait	

Conditionnel passé

Je serais venu(e)	Nous serions venu(e)s
Tu serais venu(e)	Vous seriez venu(e)s
Il serait venu	Ils seraient venus
Elle serait venue	Elles seraient venues
On serait venu(e)s	

Impératif

Viens !
Venons !
Venez !

Subjonctif présent

Que je vienne	Que nous venions
Que tu viennes	Que vous veniez
Qu'il vienne	Qu'ils viennent
Qu'elle vienne	Qu'elles viennent
Qu'on vienne	

Solutions – La Phrase Simple

EX. 1.1

1. Il regarde un film.
   Sujet : **Il**
   Verbe : **regarde**
   Article : **un**
   Nom : **film**

2. Elle chante une chanson.
   Sujet : **Elle**
   Verbe : **chante**
   Article : **une**
   Nom : **chanson**

3. Nous achetons une maison.
   Sujet : **Nous**
   Verbe : **achetons**
   Article : **une**
   Nom : **maison**

4. Je conduis une voiture.
   Sujet : **Je**
   Verbe : **conduis**
   Article : **une**
   Nom : **voiture**

5. Tu entends un oiseau.
   Sujet : **Tu**
   Verbe : **entends**
   Article : **un**
   Nom : **oiseau**

6. Ils font un vœu.
   Sujet : **Ils**
   Verbe : **font**
   Article : **un**
   Nom : **vœu**

EX. 1.2

1. Elle offre une rose.
2. J'ai un rhume.
3. Tu prends un bain.
4. Nous apportons un cadeau.
5. Vous adoptez un chien.
6. Elles ont un enfant.
7. Tu photographies une famille.
8. Je regarde une série télé.
9. Tu as un accent.
10. Elle achète un sac à main.

EX. 1.3

1. Rasoir – **M**
2. Printemps – **M**
3. Voiture – **F**
4. Mètre – **M**
5. Couteau – **M**
6. Histoire – **F**
7. Raison – **F**
8. Chinois – **M**
9. Été – **M**
10. Limonade – **F**
11. Chapeau – **M**
12. Devoir – **M**
13. Couverture – **F**
14. Télévision – **F**
15. Chance – **F**
16. Mercredi – **M**
17. Skateboard – **M**
18. Hibou – **M**
19. Bleu – **M**
20. Crayon – **M**

EX. 1.4

Masculin : fauteuil – ordinateur – t-shirt – film – livre – bureau – micro – ananas – tiroir
Féminin : tante – eau – souris – tasse – orange – carte – ligne – crème – baignoire – lampe – chaussure

---

EX. 1.5

1. Un acteur – Une **actrice**
2. Un ami – Une **amie**
3. Un cousin – Une **cousine**
4. Un coiffeur – Une **coiffeuse**
5. Un veuf – Une **veuve**
6. Un Australien – Une **Australienne**
7. Un infirmier – Une **infirmière**
8. Un étudiant – Une **étudiante**
9. Un Américain – Une **Américaine**
10. Un patron – Une **patronne**

EX. 1.6

1. Inde – **F**
2. Algérie – **F**
3. Danemark – **M**
4. Japon – **M**
5. Canada – **M**
6. Vietnam – **M**
7. Portugal – **M**
8. Bénin – **M**
9. Italie – **F**
10. France – **F**

EX. 1.7

1. Une année – Des **années**
2. Une personne – Des **personnes**
3. Un insecte – Des **insectes**
4. Une ligne – Des **lignes**
5. Une image – Des **images**
6. Une femme – Des **femmes**
7. Une robe – Des **robes**
8. Un frère – Des **frères**
9. Un élève – Des **élèves**
10. Une chemise – Des **chemises**
11. Une faute – Des **fautes**
12. Un verre – Des **verres**
13. Un rhume – Des **rhumes**
14. Une ville – Des **villes**
15. Une peinture – Des **peintures**
16. Une balle – Des **balles**
17. Une histoire – Des **histoires**
18. Une brosse – Des **brosses**
19. Une jambe – Des **jambes**
20. Une fille – Des **filles**

EX. 1.8

1. Une souris – Des **souris**
2. Un bus – Des **bus**
3. Une croix – Des **croix**
4. Un bras – Des **bras**
5. Un tapis – Des **tapis**
6. Un gaz – Des **gaz**
7. Une noix – Des **noix**
8. Un choix – Des **choix**
9. Un pays – Des **pays**
10. Un repas – Des **repas**

EX. 1.9

1. Un cheveu – Des **cheveux**
2. Un voyou – Des **voyous**
3. Un feu – Des **feux**
4. Un chou – Des **choux**
5. Un tuyau – Des **tuyaux**
6. Un bateau – Des **bateaux**
7. Un genou – Des **genoux**
8. Un bleu – Des **bleus**
9. Un pou – Des **poux**
10. Un caillou – Des **cailloux**

EX. 1.10

1. Un journal – Des **journaux**
2. Un rail – Des **rails**
3. Un détail – Des **détails**
4. Un total – Des **totaux**
5. Un vitrail – Des **vitraux**
6. Un travail – Des **travaux**
7. Un récital – Des **récitals**
8. Un hôpital – Des **hôpitaux**
9. Un bal – Des **bals**
10. Un bocal – Des **bocaux**

EX. 1.11

1. Une sœur – Des **sœurs**
2. Un aéroport – Des **aéroports**
3. Un œil – Des **yeux**
4. Un coussin – Des **coussins**
5. Un éclair – Des **éclairs**
6. Un lit – Des **lits**
7. Un toit – Des **toits**
8. Un parfum – Des **parfums**
9. Un chat – Des **chats**
10. Madame – **Mesdames**
11. Un citron – Des **citrons**
12. Un écran – Des **écrans**
13. Un escalier – Des **escaliers**
14. Un avocat – Des **avocats**
15. Un fil – Des **fils**
16. Un professeur – Des **professeurs**
17. Un écouteur – Des **écouteurs**
18. Un bain – Des **bains**
19. Un habit – Des **habits**
20. Monsieur – **Messieurs**

EX. 1.12

1. **Elles**
2. **Nous**
3. **Je / J'**
4. **Vous**
5. **Il**
6. **On**
7. **Tu**
8. **Elle**
9. **Ils**

EX. 1.13

1. **Elle**
2. **Il**
3. **Elle**
4. **Il**
5. **Elle**
6. **Il**
7. **Elle**
8. **Il**
9. **Elle**
10. **Il**
11. **Elle**
12. **Il**
13. **Elle**
14. **Il**
15. **Il**
16. **Il**
17. **Elle**
18. **Il**
19. **Elle**
20. **Il**

EX. 1.14

1. **Ils**
2. **Elles**
3. **Ils**
4. **Elles**
5. **Elles**
6. **Ils**
7. **Elles**
8. **Ils**
9. **Elles**
10. **Elles**
11. **Elles**
12. **Ils**
13. **Elles**
14. **Elles**
15. **Ils**
16. **Ils**
17. **Ils / Elles**
18. **Elles**
19. **Elles**
20. **Elles**

EX. 1.15

1. **Ils** aiment voler des bananes.
2. **Elle** est brûlée par le soleil.
3. **Elle** n'est pas droite.
4. **Ils** sont en retard.
5. **Ils** vont au parc.
6. **Il** dort sur le lit.
7. **Ils** sont fermés aujourd'hui.
8. **Elle** s'intéresse à la peinture.
9. **Ils** discutent du meurtre.
10. **Elle** est arrivée ce matin.

EX. 1.16

1. **L'**anglais
2. **La** photo
3. **La** mère
4. **Le** pays
5. **Le** sang
6. **La** bague
7. **Le** téléphone
8. **Le** travail
9. **L'**erreur
10. **La** soupe
11. **La** carotte
12. **Le** moulin
13. **La** donnée
14. **La** tâche
15. **La** guerre
16. **Le** contenu
17. **Le** muscle
18. **Le** bruit
19. **La** table
20. **La** chance

EX. 1.17

1. **L'**incendie a brûlé la maison.
2. **La** Nouvelle-Zélande est divisée en deux îles.
3. Il a réservé **les** chambres d'hôtel.
4. Mes parents font **la** cuisine à tour de rôle.
5. Tu as reçu **la** carte que je t'ai envoyée ?
6. J'ai imprimé **le** document pour toi.
7. **Le** plafond est peint en blanc.
8. Ils rénovent **la** cuisine cet été.
9. **Les** courses sont livrées tous les samedis.
10. **La** soupe est trop chaude.

EX. 1.18

1. **La** hauteur
2. **L'**habit
3. **Le** haricot
4. **L'**histoire
5. **L'**horreur
6. **Le** héros
7. **Le** hérisson
8. **La** Hongrie
9. **L'**herbe
10. **L'**humain
11. **L'**hiver
12. **L'**horloge
13. **La** haine
14. **L'**hôpital
15. **L'**haleine
16. **Le** hasard
17. **L'**hélicoptère
18. **L'**horoscope
19. **Le** hibou
20. **Le** hamburger

EX. 1.19

1. **De la** chance
2. **Du** temps
3. **Des** bébés
4. **De l'**énergie
5. **Du** lait
6. **De l'**abricot
7. **De la** cannelle
8. **Du** courage
9. **Des** chips
10. **De la** vie
11. **De la** crème
12. **De l'**espoir
13. **Du** yaourt
14. **Des** vacances
15. **Du** shampoing
16. **De la** graisse
17. **Du** vin
18. **De l'**inspiration
19. **Des** nouvelles
20. **Du** pain

EX. 1.20

1. Les Belges mangent **du** chocolat.
2. Je vais prendre **de la** salade et **du** fromage.
3. Elle a fait pousser **des** tomates.
4. Nous mangeons **des** pâtisseries tous les dimanches.
5. J'achète **de la** glace.
6. Elle prendra **des** frites avec le hamburger.
7. Il a **des** chiens et **des** chats.
8. Elle a volé **de l'**argent.
9. Ma grand-mère ajoute **de la** farine.
10. Mon mari mange **des** flocons d'avoine tous les matins.

EX. 1.21

1. Chanter
   Je **chante**
   Tu **chantes**
   On **chante**
   Nous **chantons**
   Vous **chantez**
   Elles **chantent**

2. Grandir
   Je **grandis**
   Tu **grandis**
   Il **grandit**
   Nous **grandissons**
   Vous **grandissez**
   Ils **grandissent**

3. Pendre
   Je **pends**
   Tu **pends**
   Il **pend**
   Nous **pendons**
   Vous **pendez**
   Ils **pendent**

EX. 1.22

1. Le banquier **vérifie** le numéro de compte.
2. L'entreprise **finit** de construire la maison.
3. J'**entends** les oiseaux depuis le balcon.
4. Nous **marchons** dans la forêt.
5. L'enfant **cherche** son jouet.
6. Les hommes **vieillissent** moins vite que les femmes.
7. L'armée **défend** le pays.
8. Le magasin **vend** du vin d'Espagne.
9. L'entreprise **bâtit** les appartements.
10. Il **porte** des lunettes.

EX. 1.23

1. Il **fait** chaud aujourd'hui.
2. Elle **a** peur des araignées.
3. Ce sac **est** à ma mère.
4. Mes parents **vont** au magasin à pied.
5. J'**ai** de la chance.
6. La tempête **est** de retour.
7. Tu **fais** des progrès à l'école ?
8. Nous **faisons** du vélo ensemble.
9. Comment ça **va** ?
10. L'ouvrier **a** mal au dos.

EX. 1.24

1. Les hommes **se rasent** le matin.
2. Je **me demande** si je vais y arriver.
3. Le garçon **s'habille** tout seul.
4. Il **se passe** beaucoup de choses.
5. Je **m'excuse**, je suis en retard.

EX. 1.25

1. Il **reste** du café.
2. Il **fait** 3 degrés.
3. Il y **a** des chats sur la table.
4. Il **est** midi.
5. Il **est** temps de partir.
6. Il **faut** se décider.
7. Il **pleut** depuis ce matin.
8. Il **gèle**, les routes sont glissantes.
9. Il y **a** trop de personnes ici.
10. Il **est** triste.

EX. 1.26

1. **Ce sont** des ours.
2. **C'est** bon.
3. **C'est** un verre d'eau.
4. **C'est** une pilote.
5. **C'est** génial.
6. **Ce sont** des Américaines.
7. **C'est** Pâques.
8. **C'est** super.
9. **Ce sont** des bonnes idées.
10. **C'est** un Canadien.

EX. 1.27

1. **Il est** beau / **C'est** beau.
2. **Il est** Français.
3. **C'est** génial !
4. **C'est** un livre.
5. **Il est** midi.
6. **C'est** une surprise.
7. **C'est** un professeur.
8. **C'est** une femme.
9. **Ce sont** des photos.
10. **Il est / C'est** tard.

EX. 1.28

1. **Ce** magasin
2. **Cette** coiffeuse
3. **Cet** avion
4. **Ces** olives
5. **Cette** vue
6. **Ces** haricots
7. **Ce** héros
8. **Ces** enquêteurs
9. **Ce** lit
10. **Ces** fauteuils
11. **Cette** laine
12. **Ce** chemin
13. **Ce** singe
14. **Cet** exemple
15. **Cet** aéroport
16. **Cette** idée
17. **Ce** buisson
18. **Cette** table
19. **Ces** envies
20. **Cette** maison

EX. 1.29

1. J'aime **cet** acteur.
2. Mes parents veulent **cette** télévision.
3. **Cet** homme est mon oncle.
4. **Ce** bureau est son bureau.
5. La couleur de **ce** tableau est magnifique.
6. Elle a **cette** idée depuis des semaines.
7. **Cet** ordinateur est cassé.
8. **Ces** oiseaux font leur nid.
9. **Ce** petit chat est perdu.
10. **Cette** forêt est sombre.

EX. 1.30

1. Elle répète **son** discours.
2. C'est **leur** maison.
3. **Leurs** commandes sont arrivées.
4. C'est **ton** tour.
5. **Mon** idée n'est pas bonne.
6. Le chat est dans **ta** chambre.
7. Ce sont **ses** livres.
8. **Mon** camion ne démarre plus.
9. **Vos** valises sont ici.
10. Est-ce que tu as vu **leurs** portefeuilles ?

EX. 1.31

1. Cinquante-trois
2. Quatre-vingt-quinze
3. Cent
4. Dix-neuf
5. Vingt-six
6. Quatre-vingt-huit
7. Quarante-neuf
8. Soixante-douze
9. Trente-quatre
10. Cinquante-sept

EX. 1.32

1. 1849
2. 289
3. 777
4. 121
5. 1524

EX. 1.33

1. Cinquante-septième
2. Douzième
3. Soixante-troisième
4. Soixante-quinzième
5. Centième

EX. 1.34

1. Je **n'**aime **pas** cette couleur.
2. Mon père **ne** fume **plus** tous les jours.
3. Il **n'**est **pas encore** arrivé.
4. Ce **n'**est **pas** le bon moment pour lui dire.
5. Tu **ne** travailles **plus** au même endroit ?
6. Le bus **n'**est **jamais** en retard.
7. Elle **ne** mange **que** bio.
8. Tu **n'**habites **pas** près de chez moi.
9. Il **ne** dit **rien.**
10. Ce **n'**est **pas** ma faute.

EX. 1.35

1. Elle n'a pas **d'**argent.
2. Ce n'est pas **une** bonne idée.
3. Elle ne veut plus **de** viande.
4. Nous faisons **du** basketball.
5. Tu ne portes jamais **d'**écharpe.
6. Il ne joue plus **de** guitare.
7. Vous ne faites pas **d'**études.
8. Elle ne prend pas **de** rendez-vous pour le moment.
9. Tu ne poses jamais **de** questions.
10. Ce n'est pas **un** bon jeu.

EX. 1.36

1. Il **ne** mange **jamais** <u>de</u> pain à midi.
   Il mange **jamais** <u>de</u> pain à midi.
2. Ses blagues **ne** sont **pas** drôles !
   Ses blagues sont **pas** drôles !
3. Les acheteurs **n'**ont **plus** le choix entre plusieurs maisons.
   Les acheteurs ont **plus** le choix entre plusieurs maisons.
4. Est-ce que tu **ne** peux **pas** te taire ?
   Est-ce que tu peux **pas** te taire ?
5. Vous **n'**avez **pas** entendu ce bruit.
   Vous avez **pas** entendu ce bruit.
6. Il **ne** reste **plus** <u>de</u> fromage du repas d'hier.
   Il reste **plus** <u>de</u> fromage du repas d'hier.
7. Je **ne** suis **pas du tout** impressionnée par ce spectacle.
   Je suis **pas** du tout impressionnée par ce spectacle.
8. Elle **ne** veut **rien** apprendre !
   Elle veut **rien** apprendre !
9. Nous **ne** préparons **pas encore** les cadeaux pour Noël.
   Nous préparons **pas** encore les cadeaux pour Noël.
10. Elle **n'**étudie **pas** tous les jours.
    Elle étudie **pas** tous les jours.

EX. 1.37

1. Merci de **ne pas** fermer la porte.
2. **Ne pas** ouvrir.
3. **Ne pas** toucher.
4. Merci de **ne pas** fumer.
5. Merci de **ne pas** utiliser votre téléphone.

EX. 1.38

1. **Connu**
2. **Regardé**
3. **Été**
4. **Choisi**
5. **Dormi**
6. **Eu**
7. **Pris**
8. **Mis**
9. **Allé**
10. **Pu**
11. **Entendu**
12. **Lancé**
13. **Vu**
14. **Fait**
15. **Dit**
16. **Grandi**
17. **Tenu**
18. **Su**
19. **Parlé**
20. **Appris**

EX. 1.39

1. <u>Jouer</u>
   J'**ai joué**
   Tu **as joué**
   On **a joué**
   Nous **avons joué**
   Vous **avez joué**
   Elles **ont joué**

2. <u>Faire</u>
   J'**ai fait**
   Tu **as fait**
   Il **a fait**
   Nous **avons fait**
   Vous **avez fait**
   Ils **ont fait**

3. <u>Conduire</u>
   J'**ai conduit**
   Tu **as conduit**
   Elle **a conduit**
   Nous **avons conduit**
   Vous **avez conduit**
   Elles **ont conduit**

EX. 1.40

1. Elles **sont devenues** célèbres l'année dernière.
2. Le valet **est descendu** avec les clients.
3. Les jumeaux **sont nés** lundi.
4. Les clients **sont arrivés** il y a quelques heures.
5. Le patron **est passé** au bureau ce matin.
6. Nous **sommes tombés** dans le lac.
7. Le courrier **est revenu** car l'adresse était fausse.
8. Elles **sont parties** aux alentours de 19 heures.
9. Jeff **est retourné** au bureau car il avait oublié ses clés.
10. Mes parents **sont montés** se coucher.

EX. 1.41

1. Elle **s'est brossée** les dents ce matin.
2. Je **me suis changé(e)** après l'entrainement.
3. Nous **nous sommes imaginé(e)s** quelque chose de différent.
4. Il **s'est rappelé** de cette histoire hier.
5. On n'a rien fait ce week-end, on **s'est reposés**.
6. Les enfants **se sont cachés** sous le lit.
7. Ils **se sont amusés** avec la voiture électrique dans le jardin.
8. Tu **t'es excusé(e)** auprès de ton ami ?
9. L'enfant **s'est adapté** en quelques semaines après l'adoption.
10. Vous **vous êtes couché(e)s** à quelle heure ?

EX. 1.42

1. Il **s'est rappelé** de Marc.
   Il **ne** s'est **pas** rappelé de Marc.
2. Les ouvriers **se sont faits** des sandwichs pour midi.
   Les ouvriers **ne** se sont **pas** faits de sandwichs pour midi.
3. Tu **t'es séché(e)** les cheveux ?
   Tu **ne** t'es **pas** séché(e) les cheveux ?
4. Elle **s'est levée** de mauvaise humeur.
   Elle **ne** s'est **pas** levée de mauvaise humeur.
5. On **s'est dépêchés** et on est arrivés à temps.
   On **ne** s'est **pas** dépêchés et on est arrivés à temps.
6. Sa femme **s'est précipitée** quand elle l'a vu.
   Sa femme **ne** s'est **pas** précipitée quand elle l'a vu.
7. Mon oncle **s'est occupé** du jardin cet été.
   Mon oncle **ne** s'est **pas** occupé du jardin cet été.
8. Tout le monde **s'est tu** quand il est entré.
   Personne ne s'est tu quand il est entré.
9. Je **me suis trompé(e)** dans la date.
   Je **ne** me suis **pas** trompé(e) dans la date.
10. Tu **t'es souvenu** de moi ?
    Tu **ne** t'es **pas** souvenu de moi ?

EX. 1.43

1. **Il y a** une bouteille dans ma voiture.
2. Il est arrivé **il y a** deux heures.
3. **Il n'y a** pas assez de place.
4. **Il y a** un lit et un bureau.
5. Elle est née **il y a** quelques heures.

EX. 1.44

1. **Elle a payé** les salaires la semaine dernière.
2. **Ils se précipitent** pour l'aider.
3. **Elle ralentit** avant le feu rouge.
4. **Ils ont joué** tout l'après-midi.
5. **Elles louent** depuis quelques années.
6. **Ils ont quitté** le restaurant à 21 heures.
7. **Il sent** bizarre.
8. **Elle tremble** de froid.
9. **Il s'est coupé** le doigt en travaillant.
10. **Elle a laissé** partir le suspect.

EX. 1.45

1. **Ils ont quitté leurs femmes** après 3 ans de mariage.
2. **Les patients guérissent** très vite avec ce nouveau traitement.
3. **Les fleurs ne poussent** pas comme **elles devraient.**
4. **Vous vous êtes réveillées** de mauvaise humeur ?
5. **Les piétons traversent** la rue quand le feu est vert.
6. **Les juges déduisent** que cette histoire est fausse.
7. **Les victimes** ont pardonné **leur agresseur.**
8. **Les oies protègent leurs œufs.**
9. **Les immigrants espèrent** trouver un travail assez vite.
10. **Les élèves ont oublié** de faire **leurs devoirs.**

EX. 1.46

1. Il est mexicain, il vient **du Mexique.**
2. Elle est australienne, elle vient **de l'Australie.**
3. Il est chinois, il vient **de la Chine.**
4. Elle est espagnole, elle vient **de l'Espagne.**
5. Il est suisse, il vient **de la Suisse.**
6. Elle est indienne, elle vient **de l'Inde.**
7. Il est luxembourgeois, il vient **du Luxembourg.**
8. Elle est thaïlandaise, elle vient **de la Thaïlande.**
9. Il est anglais, il vient **de l'Angleterre.**
10. Elle est coréenne, elle vient **de la Corée.**

EX. 1.47

1. Tu **n'**as **pas de** chance.
2. Elle est toujours en retard.
3. Ce **n'**est **pas** bien de manger du sucre.
4. Il y a assez de farine dans ce gâteau.
5. Les Jeux Olympiques **ne** sont **pas** annulés.
6. Le bébé **ne** mange **pas** de fruits tous les jours.
7. La barrière est assez haute pour protéger le jardin.
8. Le centre commercial **n'**est **pas** construit depuis janvier.
9. Je **n'**ai **pas** hâte d'être samedi !
10. Cette clé **n'**ouvre **pas** cette porte.

EX. 1.48

1. Ils ont réussi **leurs** examens.
2. C'est le chien de ma voisine. C'est **son** chien.
3. Elle a laissé **ses** affaires dans le casier.
4. **Cette** idée est géniale !
5. J'ai oublié **mon** parapluie.
6. Tu as vu **cet** ours dans le jardin ?
7. C'est **sa** voiture je crois.
8. **Ces** soldats reviennent de l'entrainement.
9. Ce n'est pas ton problème, c'est **son** problème.
10. J'ai reçu **son** invitation par courrier.

EX. 1.49

1. C'est possible.
2. Nous buvons du vin.
3. Le chat mange du poisson.
4. Le Luxembourg est un pays.
5. Nous avons accepté l'offre.
6. Il est deux heures.
7. Le petit déjeuner est délicieux.
8. Je ne me souviens pas de ce film.
9. J'ai faim, j'ai soif.
10. Il y a un cerf dans le jardin.

EX. 1.50 Personnel.

Solutions – Les Prépositions

EX. 2.1

1. Le rendez-vous est **à** 16 heures.
2. **À** tout de suite !
3. Nous habitons **au** Portugal.
4. Je suis **à la** librairie.
5. Cet enfant **aux** cheveux roux.
6. Tu as mal **à la** tête ?
7. Est-ce que c'est **à** Nicole ?
8. C'est bon **à** savoir !
9. Veux-tu un thé **à la** framboise ?
10. Est-ce qu'il est **au** courant ?

EX. 2.2

1. Elle **a acheté** un collier **à** sa mère.
2. Cet outil **a servi à la** construction.
3. Le commerçant **a parlé au** policier.
4. Tu **as dit à** ton frère de fermer la porter ?
5. Les enfants **ont écrit** une lettre **au** Père Noël.
6. L'agresseur **a demandé** pardon **à la** victime.
7. Est-ce que tu **as goûté au** dessert ?
8. J'**ai interdit au** chien de dormir sur le lit.
9. Il **a raconté** une histoire **aux** enfants.
10. Elle **a répondu au** téléphone.

EX. 2.3

1. Il **s'est décidé à** appeler pour un rendez-vous.
2. Nous **avons appris à** changer un peu.
3. Les parents **obligent** les enfants **à** finir leurs assiettes.
4. Il **a tenu à** acheter le cadeau tout seul.
5. On **réfléchit à** changer de voiture.
6. Ma famille **a invité** les voisins **à** dîner.
7. J'**encourage** mon petit frère **à** nager.
8. Tu **hésites à** partir plus tôt ?
9. Il **a aidé** ses parents **à** déménager.
10. Elle **aspire à** devenir scientifique.

EX. 2.4

1. Nous **sommes occupés à** lire un livre.
2. Tu **es prête à** te marier ?
3. Elle **est déterminée à** réussir.
4. Vous **êtes habitués à** voyager avec Air Canada.
5. Il **est autorisé à** retirer de l'argent.

EX. 2.5

1. Elle ne veut pas être **la seule à** aller à la plage.
2. Ce ne sont pas **les seuls à** créer ces produits.
3. Les femmes sont **nombreuses à** faire attention à leur apparence.
4. Il est **le seul à** connaître le secret.
5. Les oiseaux **sont nombreux à** passer l'hiver ici.

EX. 2.6

1. Le **dernier à** arriver a perdu !
2. C'est **la deuxième à** me dire ça.
3. Il est **le premier à** aller aux Jeux Olympiques.
4. Je suis **la première à** aller à l'université.
5. Ils sont toujours **les premiers à** se lever.

EX. 2.7

1. Je suis **d'**accord avec toi !
2. Ce train va **de** New York à Montréal.
3. Moins **de la** moitié des étudiants réussissent.
4. Je suis la plus chanceuse **du** monde !
5. Pour une fois, il est **de** bonne humeur.
6. C'est la maison **de** ma tante.
7. Cet avion arrive **de** Madrid.
8. J'ai regardé ce film **du** début à la fin.
9. Ce sac **de** couchage est confortable.
10. Est-ce que tu veux aller à la plaine **de** jeux ?

EX. 2.8

1. Il **joue du** violon depuis des années.
2. Nous **rêvons d'**une année sans problèmes.
3. Je **me suis trompé de** numéro.
4. Il **a changé de** carrière il y a quelques années.
5. Vous **avez besoin de** toutes ces affaires ?
6. Il **doute de** sa volonté.
7. Elle **s'occupe des** enfants tous les jours.
8. On **se passe de** viande depuis quelques années déjà.
9. Tu **as envie d'**une glace ?
10. Je **raffole des** brownies !

EX. 2.9

1. Je **me suis souvenu de** vider le lave-vaisselle.
2. Elle **évite de** s'exposer au soleil sans crème solaire.
3. Les employés **se plaignent de** rester tard au travail.
4. Elle **a supplié** le docteur **de** sauver la vie de son fils.
5. Il **risque de** faire un infarctus.
6. Il **a raison de** demander une augmentation.
7. La banque **a accepté de** débloquer les fonds.
8. J'**ai décidé de** déménager.
9. On **se dépêche de** manger avant de partir.
10. Je **viens de** recevoir une augmentation !

EX. 2.10 Personnel.

EX. 2.11

1. Il **est** ravi **du** résultat.
2. Tu **es** sûr **de** ton choix ?
3. Je **suis** heureux **du** choix que j'ai fait.
4. Nous **sommes** impatients **de** te voir !
5. Elle **est** enchantée **de** te rencontrer.

EX. 2.12

1. C'est **interdit** de déposer des ordures ici.
2. C'est **difficile** de se détendre après le travail.
3. Il est **possible** d'apprendre la méditation.
4. C'est **impossible** de se téléporter.
5. Il est **dangereux** de traverser la rue sans regarder.
6. C'est **défendu** de vendre de la drogue.
7. Il est **nécessaire** d'aider la planète.
8. C'est **dommage** de jeter ces légumes.
9. C'est **inutile** de se lever tôt.
10. Il est **bon** de prendre l'air.

EX. 2.13

1. Mon anniversaire est **en** novembre.
2. Il a déménagé **en** Colombie.
3. Je peux être prête **en** 5 minutes.
4. Elle veut cette veste **en** cuir.
5. C'est arrivé **en** 1990.

EX. 2.14

1. Elle a de la chance d'**être en vie**.
2. On **est en vacances** à partir de ce samedi.
3. Tu **es en avance** aujourd'hui !
4. Il **est en forme** depuis qu'il prend soin de lui.
5. Cette voiture **est en panne**.

EX. 2.15

1. Je **vais au** marché demain matin.
2. Il **va au** cinéma avec ses amis.
3. Tu **vas à la** bibliothèque ce matin ?
4. Nous **allons chez** le docteur.
5. Ils **vont aux** États-Unis pour le documentaire.
6. On **va à** Londres pour le week-end.
7. Est-ce que tu **vas à l'**épicerie ?
8. Mes amis et moi **allons au** Japon en mai.
9. Je **vais chez** le dentiste ce soir.
10. Tu **vas en** Australie en décembre ?

EX. 2.16

1. Le chat dort **sur** le lit.
2. Le train est arrêté **entre** deux villes.
3. Je t'attends **devant** le magasin.
4. Est-ce que tu as regardé **sous** le meuble ?
5. Il est appuyé **contre** la porte.
6. J'ai mis des serviettes propres **dans** la salle de bain.
7. Le garage est **derrière** la maison.

EX. 2.17

1. La maison est **à gauche du** magasin.
2. Je range toujours les biscuits **au-dessus de l'**armoire.
3. Nous étions **à droite du** monument.
4. Le lac est **au milieu du** pays.
5. Je suis **à côté de** toi.
6. L'appartement a été vendu **au-dessous du** prix demandé.
7. Elle habite **en face de** ce restaurant.
8. Est-ce que l'appartement **est loin de la** plage ?
9. Ils sont **au bord de la** rupture.
10. L'avion s'est posé **près de chez** mes grands-parents.

EX. 2.18

1. Je travaille ici **depuis** plusieurs mois.
2. Il n'est jamais **à l'**heure.
3. **Avant** que tu ne partes, est-ce que tu peux m'aider ?
4. Nous nous reposons **dans** la chambre.
5. Vous étiez **avant** moi.
6. La ville était détruite **après** la tempête.
7. Je suis **au** marché, tu veux me rejoindre ?
8. On se verra **après** le travail.
9. Ce document est **à** moi.
10. Mon voyage **en** Allemagne était incroyable.

EX. 2.19

1. Il est allé **jusqu'où** ?
2. **Jusqu'en** Amérique.
3. On a **jusqu'à** dimanche pour faire une offre.
4. Il restera là-bas **jusqu'à** Noël.
5. Cette réservation est valide **jusqu'au** premier janvier.

EX. 2.20

1. Ce chien sera en traitement **pour** quelques semaines.
2. Il est venu **pendant** que tu étais parti.
3. J'ai paniqué **durant** l'examen.
4. On a étudié **pendant** des semaines pour cet examen !
5. Elle jouait avec son téléphone **durant** le speech.

EX. 2.21

1. Nous prévoyons d'aller **en** Espagne cet été.
2. Le livre est **sur** la table, tu ne l'as pas trouvé.
3. Le train est parti **avant** l'heure prévue.
4. Nous sommes en manque d'eau **à cause de la** canicule.
5. Je suis restée **après** toi au travail.
6. Il y a un moustique **dans** la tente.
7. Nous avons beaucoup de choses à faire **durant** le week-end.
8. Est-ce que tu peux attendre **jusqu'à la** semaine prochaine ?
9. Nous restons toujours **au bord de la** plage.
10. J'ai laissé le sachet **devant** la porte.

EX. 2.22

1. Elle a répondu **par** hasard.
2. Est-ce que tu habites **par** ici ?
3. Nous sommes venus **par** la vieille route.
4. Ils ont obtenu l'argent **par** la force.
5. Il est entré **par** la porte.

EX. 2.23

1. J'**ai acheté** les cadeaux **pour** les enfants.
2. Nous **sommes pour** l'avortement.
3. Est-ce que tu **as remercié** Julie **pour** son aide ?
4. Elle **est partie pour** Barcelone.
5. Toute la province **a voté pour** la gauche.

EX. 2.24

1. Il a réalisé le film **selon** les directions.
2. J'ai tout acheté **sauf** les bananes.
3. On prendra une pizza **avec** du jambon.
4. **Malgré** leurs efforts, ils n'ont pas réussi.
5. **D'après** la météo, il va faire beau toute la semaine.
6. Elle gagne **environ** 3000 dollars.
7. C'est possible de vivre **sans** manger de viande.
8. Cette attaque était dirigée **envers** les diplomates.
9. Je rêve d'une semaine **sans** travailler.
10. J'ai grandi **parmi** des garçons.

EX. 2.25

1. Le mariage était magnifique **malgré** la pluie.
2. **Selon** l'article, le politicien a démissionné.
3. Elle est arrivée **aux environs de** minuit.
4. J'écris toujours **avec** ma main droite.
5. Est-ce que tu as entendu quelque chose **à propos de** cette histoire ?
6. Le contrat est signé **par** tous les participants.
7. Ce n'est pas **pour** toi.
8. Qu'est-ce qu'on mange **pour** le déjeuner ?
9. La plupart des élèves réussissent **sans** difficulté.
10. La souris est passé **par** le trou pour rentrer.

EX. 2.26

1. J'apprends **le** chinois depuis janvier.
2. Il parle / luxembourgeois et / allemand.
3. **Les** commandes sont arrivées.
4. C'est **un** docteur incroyable !

5. Elle s'est mariée par / obligation.
6. Elle a gagné **le** gros lot !
7. Tu manges beaucoup trop de / sel.
8. Elle a acheté plusieurs / chapeaux.

EX. 2.27

1. Il va finir **par** se faire arrêter.
2. Le balcon donne **sur** la mer.
3. C'est **pour** moi.
4. J'ai appris **à** peindre très tôt.
5. Elle tient son caractère **de** son père.

EX. 2.28

1. Elle **vient de chanter** une chanson au concert.
2. On **vient juste de se promener** au parc.
3. Il **vient de réaliser** son erreur.
4. Nous **venons de finir** le travail.
5. Le bébé **vient de boire** son biberon.
6. Le passager **vient de manquer** son train.
7. Les chercheurs **viennent de découvrir** une planète.
8. Les parents **viennent de signer** le contrat.
9. Elle **vient de préparer** la valise.
10. L'administration **vient de soumettre** le dossier.

EX. 2.29

1. Est-ce qu'elles ont vu le papier sur la table ?
   Ont-elles vu le papier sur la table ?
2. Est-ce que tu as gagné à la loterie ?
   As-tu gagné à la loterie ?
3. Est-ce que vous êtes arrivés à temps ?
   Êtes-vous arrivés à temps ?
4. Est-ce qu'ils ont déjà signé le contrat ?
   Ont-ils déjà signé le contrat ?
5. Est-ce que vous économisez assez d'argent ?
   Économisez-vous assez d'argent ?
6. Est-ce que tu as accordé la bourse aux familles ?
   As-tu accordé la bourse aux familles ?
7. Est-ce que vous avez gardé cette vieille valise ?
   Avez-vous gardé cette vieille valise ?
8. Est-ce qu'ils ont quitté la maison il y a une heure ?
   Ont-ils quitté la maison il y a une heure ?
9. Est-ce que vous avez visité ce château ?
   Avez-vous visité ce château ?
10. Est-ce que tu as répondu à la question correctement ?
    As-tu répondu à la question correctement ?

EX. 2.30

1. **Est-ce que** tu as vu ce film ?
2. **Est-ce qu'**il a répondu au téléphone ?
3. **Est-ce que** la police a prévenu ses parents ?
4. **Est-ce qu'**ils ont remercié les invités ?
5. **Est-ce que** vous avez marché toute la journée ?

EX. 2.31

1. **Est-il arrivé** dans la soirée ?
2. **A-t-elle établi** un plan pour réussir ses études ?
3. **A-t-il laissé** le chien dehors ?
4. **A-t-elle donné** son salaire à une association ?
5. **A-t-il essayé** de se faire pardonner ?

EX. 2.32

1. Quand **est-ce que** tu vas au magasin ?
   Tu vas au magasin **quand** ?
2. **Comment est-ce qu'**il étudie ?
   Il étudie **comment** ?
3. **Pourquoi est-ce que** tu es en retard ?
   Tu es en retard **pourquoi** ?
4. **Combien de** maisons **est-ce qu'**il possède ?
   Il possède **combien de** maisons ?
5. **Où est-ce qu'**elle va ?
   Elle va **où** ?
6. **Où est-ce que** tu travailles ?
   Tu travailles **où** ?
7. **Combien de** chiens **est-ce qu'**elle a ?
   Elle a **combien de** chiens ?
8. **Où est-ce que** tes parents vivent ?
   Tes parents vivent **où** ?
9. **Combien de** mois **est-ce que** tu travailles durant l'année ?
   Tu travailles **combien de** mois durant l'année ?
10. **Quand est-ce que** ton frère revient ?
    Ton frère revient **quand** ?

EX. 2.33

1. **Qui est-ce qui** est là ?
2. **Qui est-ce que** tu vas voir ?
3. **Qui est-ce que** le chien a mordu ?
4. **Qui est-ce qui** a adopté un enfant ?
5. **Qui est-ce que** vous aimez voir le week-end ?
6. **Qui est-ce qui** a téléphoné ce matin ?
7. **Qui est-ce qui** a mangé mon plat ?
8. **Qui est-ce que** tu as appelé ?
9. **Qui est-ce qui** est arrivée la première ?
10. **Qui est-ce que** vous avez vu ?

EX. 2.34

1. **À qui** est-ce que tu as donné l'enveloppe ?
2. **Avec qui** est-ce que vous êtes au cinéma ?
3. **De qui** est-ce qu'il s'agit ?
4. **À qui** est-ce que vous avez téléphoné ?
5. **Avec qui** est-ce qu'il est parti ?
6. **À qui** est-ce que vous avez fait mal ?
7. **De qui** est-ce que tu as rêvé ?
8. **À qui** est-ce que cet argent a servi ?
9. **Avec qui** est-ce que tu as mangé ?
10. **De qui** est-ce qu'elle a profité ?

EX. 2.35

1. **Qu'est-ce que** tu as reçu pour Noël ?
2. **Qu'est-ce qui** pèse 10 kilos ?
3. **Qu'est-ce qu'**il aime faire le week-end ?
4. **Qu'est-ce qui** arrivera si elle ne vient pas ?
5. **Qu'est-ce que** tu attends ?
6. **Qu'est-ce qui** t'arrive ?
7. **Qu'est-ce qui** lui a plu ?
8. **Qu'est-ce que** vous faites ce soir ?
9. **Qu'est-ce qui** est arrivé à la voiture ?
10. **Qu'est-ce que** tu écoutes ?

EX. 2.36

1. **À quoi** est-ce que ce monument ressemble ?
2. **De quoi** est-ce que vous avez hérité ?
3. **Avec quoi** est-ce que tu veux jouer ?
4. **De quoi** est-ce que tu parles ?
5. **Avec quoi** est-ce que tu cuisines ?
6. **De quoi** est-ce que tu as peur ?
7. **À quoi** est-ce que vous pensez ?
8. **De quoi** est-ce qu'il se sert pour travailler ?
9. **Avec quoi** est-ce qu'elle nourrit les chevaux ?
10. **À quoi** est-ce que tu penses ?

EX. 2.37

1. **Quel** est votre nom ?
2. **Quelle** idée est la meilleure ?
3. **De quel** film est-ce que tu parles ?
4. **Quel** est votre chanteur préféré ?
5. J'ai reçu un appel de l'avocat. **Quel** avocat ?
6. **Quelle** heure est-il ?
7. **Quelles** sont les meilleures fraises ?
8. **De quelle** personne es-tu responsable ?
9. **Quel** temps fait-il aujourd'hui ?
10. **Quels** livres est-ce que vous avez lu ?

EX. 2.38

1. **Lequel** est-ce que tu as commandé ?
2. **Laquelle de** vous est responsable ?
3. **Lesquelles** est-ce que tu as visitées ?
4. **Lesquels** sont à toi ?
5. **Lequel** est-ce que vous avez acheté ?
6. **Laquelle** est-ce que tu as choisie ?
7. **Lesquelles** sont les plus confortables ?
8. **Lequel** est-ce que tu préfères ?
9. **Lesquelles** sont les meilleures ?
10. **Laquelle** est-ce que le patron a aimée le plus ?

EX. 2.39

1. **Si,** je parle espagnol.
2. **Si,** je suis mariée.
3. **Si,** je travaille encore.
4. **Si,** j'habite toujours en ville.
5. **Si,** j'ai fait les courses ce matin.

EX. 2.40

1. Est-ce que tu as essayé cette robe ?
   Non, je n'ai pas essayé cette robe.
2. Avez-vous réservé vos vacances d'été ?
   Oui, nous avons réservé nos vacances d'été.
3. Est-ce qu'elle aime cueillir les fruits de son jardin ?
   Oui, elle aime cueillir les fruits de son jardin.
4. A-t-il forcé l'homme à rentrer dans la voiture ?
   Non, il n'a pas forcé l'homme à rentrer dans la voiture.
5. Est-ce que tu vas bien ?
   Oui, je vais bien.
6. Est-ce que ton grand-père a fondé l'entreprise en 1990 ?
   Non, il n'a pas fondé l'entreprise en 1990.
7. A-t-il descendu la poubelle ?
   Oui, il a descendu la poubelle.
8. Est-ce que tu dors tard tous les samedis ?
   Non, je ne dors pas tard tous les samedis.
9. As-tu menti aux enquêteurs ?
   Oui, j'ai menti aux enquêteurs.
10. Est-ce que cette route mène à la vieille ville ?
    Non, cette route ne mène pas à la vieille ville.

Solutions – Les Adjectifs

EX. 3.1

Masc. Sing	Fem. Sing.	Masc. Pl.	Fem. Pl
Lâche	Lâche	Lâches	Lâches
Désolé	Désolée	Désolés	Désolées
Grand	Grande	Grands	Grandes
Bleu	Bleue	Bleus	Bleues
Brun	Brune	Bruns	Brunes
Doré	Dorée	Dorés	Dorées
Gris	Grise	Gris	Grises
Suivant	Suivante	Suivants	Suivantes
Ravi	Ravie	Ravis	Ravies
Vivant	Vivante	Vivants	Vivantes

EX. 3.2

1. **Gentille**
2. **Naïve**
3. **Grosse**
4. **Entière**
5. **Pareille**
6. **Première**
7. **Banale**
8. **Chère**
9. **Grosse**
10. **Ancienne**

EX. 3.3

1. Quelle **belle** maison !
2. Mes petits-enfants sont **roux**.
3. Ce **vieux** château doit être rénové.
4. Sa couleur préférée est le **marron**.
5. Les matins sont **frais** au Canada.
6. Les températures sont **douces** aujourd'hui.
7. Ce fleuve est **long** de 10 kilomètres.
8. Elle a reçu des **nouvelles** informations.
9. C'est **fou** !
10. Je pense que cette réponse est **fausse**.

EX. 3.4

1. C'est un **vieil** ami.
2. Elle a des **beaux** yeux.
3. Le **nouvel** employé est malade.
4. Quel **bel** endroit !
5. Ces papiers sont **vieux** et fragiles.

EX. 3.5

1. Cette chienne est tellement **mignonne** !
2. Tu es (m) **léger** comme une plume.
3. Les couvertures sont déjà **sèches**.
4. Mon père est un homme **patient**.
5. Nous (f) sommes très **heureuses** pour toi.
6. Ma **nouvelle** voiture n'est pas encore arrivée.
7. Tu as vu ce **bel** homme ?
8. Pourquoi est-ce que tu gardes cette **vieille** chemise ?
9. C'est le **meilleur** athlète dans sa catégorie.
10. Les fleurs roses sont les plus **belles**.
11. C'est mon opinion mais ces chaussures sont **laides**.
12. Il fait **orageux** aujourd'hui.
13. Ma grand-mère est **inquiète** quand je ne donne pas de nouvelles.
14. Cette pâtisserie est trop **dure** à manger.
15. C'est une histoire **étrange**.
16. Je (f) préfère étudier **seule** dans ma chambre.
17. Le **prochain** train est à 10 heures.
18. On a acheté de la peinture **noire** pour la buanderie.
19. Je préfère les matelas **mous**.
20. Elle a acheté une **jolie** robe pour le mariage.

EX. 3.6

1. C'est un **nouveau** manteau.
2. Il a raconté une blague **amusante**.
3. Je cherche le **meilleur** restaurant de la ville.
4. C'est un problème **impossible** à résoudre.
5. Le **dernier** survivant de l'accident est décédé récemment.
6. La porte **ouverte** laisse entrer de l'air frais.
7. Elle a les cheveux **longs** pour son âge.
8. Fais attention c'est un colis **lourd**.
9. Les pompiers sont des personnes **courageuses**.
10. C'est une **bonne** idée.

EX. 3.7

1. C'est un colis **important et prioritaire**.
2. C'est une femme **gentille et patiente**.
3. C'est une journée **froide et nuageuse**.
4. C'est un **bon gros** gâteau.
5. C'est une histoire **longue et stupide**.

EX. 3.8

1. <u>Écouter</u>
   J'**écoutais**
   Tu **écoutais**
   On **écoutait**
   Nous **écoutions**
   Vous **écoutiez**
   Elles **écoutaient**

2. <u>Choisir</u>
   Je **choisissais**
   Tu **choisissais**
   Il **choisissait**
   Nous **choisissions**
   Vous **choisissiez**
   Ils **choisissaient**

3. <u>Vendre</u>
   Je **vendais**
   Tu **vendais**
   Il **vendait**
   Nous **vendions**
   Vous **vendiez**
   Ils **vendaient**

EX. 3.9

1. Il connaissait la bonne réponse.
2. Cet homme était grand et mince / maigre.
3. Il tenait le livre dans ses mains.
4. Elle achetait toujours de beaux habits.
5. Cet homme croyait à des histoires étranges / bizarres.
6. On habitait au Canada entre 1995 et 2005.
7. Je ne comprenais pas les problèmes difficiles.
8. Le jardinier arrosait les plantes sèches.
9. Tu buvais un chocolat chaud.
10. Le bébé semblait fatigué.

EX. 3.10

1. Elle **peignait** des tableaux **magnifiques**.
2. Ta grand-mère **était** une très **jolie jeune** fille.
3. La fenêtre **donnait** sur un **petit** jardin.
4. Il **mettait** la vaisselle **sale** dans le lave-vaisselle.
5. Tu ne **portais** jamais de lunettes **rondes**.
6. On **aimait** les films **romantiques**.
7. Le panneau **signalait** des **gros** travaux.
8. Elle **faisait** toujours des gâteaux **délicieux**.
9. Il **finissait** son petit déjeuner quand le bus **rouge** est arrivé.
10. Le clown **rendait** les enfants **joyeux**.

EX. 3.11

1. L'avion est **plus rapide que** le train.
2. Le bus est **plus confortable que** le train.
3. Les singes sont **plus intelligents que** les cochons.
4. Ce matelas est **aussi mou que** celui-là.
5. Elle est **moins douée que** sa compétitrice.
6. Les vraies fleurs sont **plus jolies que** les fausses.
7. Je gagne **autant que** mon collègue.
8. Cette maison est **moins grande que** la maison où j'habitais avant.
9. J'étais **plus heureuse que** l'année dernière.
10. Elle est **aussi grande que** toi.

EX. 3.12

1. Il a **plus de cheveux que** son frère.
2. J'ai besoin de **moins de sommeil que** mon mari.
3. Elle porte **plus de maquillage qu'**avant.
4. Nous avons **autant d'opportunités que** les autres.
5. Elle a **plus de ressources que** sa sœur.

*Remember to **download the audio** of the lists and to **watch the videos** – see Preface*

EX. 3.13

1. Cette voiture est **la plus abordable du** magasin.
2. C'est **la plus jolie des** princesses.
3. Ma grand-mère est **la plus sociable de la** famille.
4. C'est le voyage **le plus long du** monde.
5. Elle est **la moins chanceuse du** groupe.

EX. 3.14

1. Ce sont les **meilleurs** croissants de la ville.
2. Sa participation était **moindre**.
3. Marc a les **pires** notes de la classe. Quelle honte.
4. Il est le **meilleur** chef de l'hôtel.
5. C'est **pire** que ce que je ne pensais.

EX. 3.15

1. **Tous** les élèves participeront au spectacle.
2. J'ai **quelques** idées si tu veux les entendre.
3. Il a réussi **chaque** test depuis le début de l'année.
4. Nous avons **divers** projets pour le mois de décembre.
5. Il reste **plusieurs** macarons si tu veux.
6. On risque d'avoir une **autre** tornade ce week-end.
7. Elle était **certaine** de l'avoir pris.
8. Il y a **telle** personne à la porte.

EX. 3.16

1. Parler
   Je **parlerai**
   Tu **parleras**
   On **parlera**
   Nous **parlerons**
   Vous **parlerez**
   Elles **parleront**

2. Choisir
   Je **choisirai**
   Tu **choisiras**
   Il **choisira**
   Nous **choisirons**
   Vous **choisirez**
   Ils **choisiront**

3. Perdre
   Je **perdrai**
   Tu **perdras**
   Il **perdra**
   Nous **perdrons**
   Vous **perdrez**
   Ils **perdront**

EX. 3.17

1. Je **serai** là 15 heures.
2. On **verra** si on peut partir demain.
3. On **mangera** une lasagne ce week-end.
4. Il **pleuvra** ce soir.
5. À ce moment lundi prochain, nous **serons** au Mexique.
6. Mon ami **promènera** le chien quand nous serons partis.
7. Ils se **marieront** l'année prochaine.
8. Je **ferai** le ménage plus tard.
9. J'espère qu'il **neigera** cet hiver.
10. Il **sera** tard quand on arrivera.

EX. 3.18

1. Il **va lire** un livre passionnant.
2. Je **vais réfléchir** à cette proposition.
3. Tu **vas tomber** de la branche.
4. On **va mange**r au restaurant ce soir.
5. Toute la famille **va se coucher**.
6. Nous **allons être** en retard à cause du trafic.
7. Il **va se faire** mal s'il continue.
8. Ils **vont partir** dans quelques minutes si tu n'arrives pas.
9. L'avion **va arriver** bientôt.
10. Est-ce que tu **vas aller** à l'université ?

EX. 3.19

1. Est-ce que tu es **prête** ?
2. Les voitures **blanches** deviennent **sales** plus vite.
3. L'eau du lac est **claire**.
4. Ce n'est pas **drôle**.
5. La réponse que tu as donnée est **fausse**.
6. Cette crème au chocolat est **légère**.
7. Ils sont **heureux** d'être arrivés.
8. Les voitures **électriques** sont une invention **incroyable**.
9. Je suis **paresseuse**, je n'ai envie de ne rien faire.
10. Tu penses qu'elle était **sérieuse** ?

EX. 3.20 Personnel.

Solutions – Les Pronoms

EX. 4.1

1. J'aime **la vanille**.
2. On voit **la mer**.
3. J'appelais **Paul et Marc** tous les jours.
4. Nous achetons **un pain**.
5. Tu remplis **le dossier**.
6. Est-ce que tu entends **la chanson** ?
7. Je dessine **une tortue**.
8. Il donne **ses vieux habits**.
9. Elle prépare **le petit déjeuner**.
10. Tu connais **les résultats** ?

EX. 4.2

1. Je **l'**aime.
2. On **la** voit.
3. Je **les** appelais tous les jours.
4. Nous **l'**achetons.
5. Tu **le** remplis.
6. Est-ce que tu **l'**entends ?
7. Je **la** dessine.
8. Il **les** donne.
9. Elle **le** prépare.
10. Tu **les** connais ?

EX. 4.3

1. Est-ce que tu **le** connais ?
   Est-ce que tu **ne** le connais **pas** ?
2. Le chien **les** mange.
   Le chien **ne** les mange **pas**.
3. Vous **les** dégustez.
   Vous **ne** les dégustez **pas**.
4. L'étudiant **les** finit.
   L'étudiant **ne** les finit **pas**.
5. Je **le** lis tranquillement.
   Je **ne** le lis **pas** tranquillement.
6. Toute la famille **la** regarde.
   Personne ne la regarde.
7. Les passagers **l'**attendent.
   Les passagers **ne** l'attendent **pas**.
8. Il **la** pose au professeur.
   Il **ne** la pose **pas** au professeur.
9. Tu **la** termines.
   Tu **ne** la termines **pas**.
10. Je **le** vois cet après-midi.
    Je **ne** le vois **pas** cet après-midi.

EX. 4.4

1. J'ai acheté une rose.
   La rose **que** j'ai achet**ée**.
2. J'ai vu les filles au magasin.
   Les filles **que** j'ai v**ues** au magasin.
3. Luc a gagné sa course.
   La course **que** Luc a gagn**ée**.
4. Michel a commandé les t-shirts.
   Les t-shirts **que** Michel a command**és**.
5. Ils ont gagné le match.
   Le match **qu'**ils ont gagné.
6. Elle a reçu la balle sur la tête.
   La balle **qu'**elle a reç**ue** sur la tête.
7. Nous avons mangé une tarte en famille.
   La tarte **que** nous avons mang**ée** en famille.
8. L'avocat a signé les papiers.
   Les papiers **que** l'avocat a sign**és**.
9. J'ai invité Marie à manger.
   C'est Marie **que** j'ai invit**ée** à manger.
10. Il a acheté la voiture.
    La voiture **qu'**il a achet**ée**.

EX. 4.5

1. Oui, je **les** ai achet**ées**.
2. Oui, nous **l'**avons compris**e**.
3. Oui, je **les** ai fini**s**.
4. Oui, nous **l'**avons suivi**e**.
5. Oui, je **les** ai accept**ées**.
6. Oui, nous **l'**avons appelé**e**.
7. Oui, je **l'**ai perdu.
8. Oui, nous **l'**avons mangé**e**.
9. Oui, je **les** ai invité**s**.
10. Oui, nous **les** avons aim**ées**.

EX. 4.6

1. J'ai acheté un bouquet de fleurs **à mes parents**.
2. Le juge ordonne **à l'avocat** de se taire.
3. On fait confiance **à nos amis**.
4. Elle sourit **aux passants** dans la rue.
5. Elle a promis **aux élèves** de trouver une solution.
6. Il interdit **à ses enfants** de manger du sucre.
7. Tu as téléphoné **à tes parents**.
8. J'ai répondu **au client** par email.
9. Elle donne des conseils **aux personnes âgées**.
10. Je conseille **à mes voisins** de prendre soin de leur pelouse.

EX. 4.7

1. Je **leur** ai acheté un bouquet de fleurs.
2. Le juge **lui** ordonne de se taire.
3. On **leur** fait confiance.
4. Elle **leur** sourit dans la rue.
5. Elle **leur** a promis de trouver une solution.
6. Il **leur** interdit de manger du sucre.
7. Tu **leur** as téléphoné.
8. Je **lui** ai répondu par email.
9. Elle **leur** donne des conseils.
10. Je **leur** conseille de prendre soin de leur pelouse.

EX. 4.8

1. Elle **m'**a appelé hier.
   Elle **ne** m'a **pas** appelé hier.
2. Cela **te** plaît beaucoup.
   Cela **ne** te plaît **pas** beaucoup.
3. Cette robe **lui** va très bien.
   Cette robe **ne** lui va **pas** très bien.
4. Il **nous** a apporté un cadeau.
   Il **ne** nous a **pas** apporté de cadeau.
5. L'hôtesse **vous** a servi un café.
   L'hôtesse **ne** vous a **pas** servi de café.
6. Il **lui** succède bientôt.
   Il **ne** lui succède **pas** bientôt.
7. Il **me** rappelle ça tous les jours.
   Il ne **me** rappelle pas ça tous les jours.
8. Tu **leur** as volé cette bouteille de vin ?
   Tu **ne** leur as **pas** volé cette bouteille de vin ?
9. Elle **t'**a envoyé un paquet pour Noël.
   Elle **ne** t'a **pas** envoyé un paquet pour Noël.
10. C'est fou comme tu **lui** ressembles.
    C'est fou comme tu **ne** lui ressembles **pas**.

EX. 4.9

1. Tu es en train de parler à l'employé ?
   Oui, je suis en train de **lui** parler.
2. Vous avez envoyé la facture au fournisseur ?
   Oui, nous **lui** avons envoyé la facture.
3. Tu as offert des fleurs à ta femme ?
   Oui, je **lui** ai offert des fleurs.
4. Il a écrit une lettre à ses parents ?
   Oui, il **leur** a écrit une lettre.
5. Est-ce que les voisines ont rendu les clés au propriétaire ?
   Oui, les voisines **lui** ont rendu les clés.

EX. 4.10

1. J'**y** vais ce samedi.
2. Tu **y** vas dans quelques semaines.
3. Elle **y** va pour son anniversaire.
4. Le chien **y** est.
5. Elle **y** est pour une carie.

EX. 4.11

1. Il **y** réfléchit.
2. J'**y** ai goûté mais il n'était pas bon.
3. Elle **y** a cru.
4. Nous **y** avons résisté
5. Vous **y** avez survécu.
6. Tu **y** as pensé ?
7. Il est important d'**y** obéir.
8. Elles **y** ont participé il y a quelques mois.
9. On a appris à **y** jouer.
10. Il n'**y** pense pas.

EX. 4.12

1. Les patients **en** ont besoin.
2. Il s'**en** est emparé avant l'attaque.
3. Nous **en** parlons avec les élèves.
4. C'est possible de s'**en** passer.
5. Elle **en** raffole.
6. Nous venons juste d'**en** partir.
7. Son avenir **en** dépend.
8. J'**en** doute.
9. Il a appris à **en** jouer quand il était petit.
10. Les clients s'**en** servent par eux-mêmes.

EX. 4.13

1. Oui, je m'en vais.
2. Je suis en train de cuisinier.
3. Je m'en fiche.
4. Oui, je suis en route.
5. Oui, j'en ai assez.

EX. 4.14

1. Je **le leur** prépare.
2. Jeff **la lui** envoie.
3. Il **le lui** a acheté.
4. Vous **le lui** avez laissé ?
5. Tu **le lui** as administré.
6. Tu **le leur** rends.
7. Il **le lui** a expliqué.
8. Vous **le leur** donnez.
9. L'infirmier **le lui** écrit.
10. Le policier **les lui** lit.

EX. 4.15

1. Je pense **en** avoir apporté assez.
2. Elle **en** a apporté une.
3. Je ne veux pas **y** aller.
4. Est-ce que vous **y** participez ?
5. Vous **en** revenez ?
6. Nous **y** allons souvent.
7. Nous **y** avons voyagé pendant 3 mois.
8. Je vais **en** prendre un peu plus.
9. Mon oncle **y** était quand c'est arrivé.
10. **Y** as-tu réfléchi ?

EX. 4.16

1. **Garder**	2. **Finir**	3. **Aller**	4. **Être**
Garde	Finis	Va	Sois
Gardons	Finissons	Allons	Soyons
Gardez	Finissez	Allez	Soyez

EX. 4.17

1. **Sois** à l'heure.
2. **Allons** à la boulangerie.
3. **Regarde** cet oiseau sur la branche.
4. **Écoutez** le vent dans les arbres.
5. **Garde** ton argent.
6. **Portez** ce sac.
7. **Donnons** un peu plus de notre temps.
8. **Arrête** de fumer.
9. **Montez** cette valise à l'étage.
10. **Démarrez** la voiture.

EX. 4.18

1. **Ne** sois **pas** à l'heure.
2. **N'**allons **pas** à la boulangerie.
3. **Ne** regarde **pas** cet oiseau sur la branche.
4. **N'**écoutez **pas** le vent dans les arbres.
5. **Ne** garde **pas** ton argent.
6. **Ne** portez **pas** ce sac.
7. **Ne** donnons **pas** un peu plus de notre temps.
8. **N'**arrête **pas** de fumer.
9. **Ne** montez **pas** cette valise à l'étage.
10. **Ne** démarrez **pas** la voiture.

EX. 4.19

1. Parle-lui.
2. Appelez-moi quand vous avez le temps.
3. Achète-les.
4. Écoutez-moi quand je parle.
5. Paye la facture.
6. Va te servir de l'eau
7. Reste là, j'arrive.
8. Ne me parlez pas.
9. Écrivez votre nom.
10. Asseyons-nous.

EX. 4.20

1. Est-ce que tu **en** as pris ?
2. Nous **y** sommes depuis midi.
3. Je m'**en** occupe.
4. On **le** connaît bien.
5. Je vais **y** réfléchir.
6. Je **leur en** ai parlé.
7. Elle va **me la** prêter.
8. Elle **les y** a laissé.
9. J'**en** mange à tous les repas.
10. Tu **lui** as téléphoné ?

Solutions – Les Autres Pronoms

EX. 5.1

1. **Elles**
2. **Eux**
3. **Nous**
4. **Elle**

5. **Lui**
6. **Toi**
7. **Moi**

EX. 5.2

1. C'est pour **eux**.
2. Non, c'est à **moi**.
3. Non, je n'ai pas besoin d'**elles**.

4. Je suis perdue sans **toi**.
5. Nous sommes chez **nous**.

EX. 5.3

1. Elle ne pense qu'à **elle**.
2. **Lui**, il est arrivé premier cette année.
3. Elle a plus de succès que **toi**.
4. Je n'ai vu qu'**elles** à la réunion.

5. C'est mieux si tout le monde rentre chez **soi**.
6. Mon mari et **moi**, nous nous sommes mariés en 2018.

EX. 5.4

1. Il a écrit ce roman **lui-même**.
2. Elle a réalisé ce film **elle-même**.
3. Vous avez pris cette décision **vous-mêmes**.
4. Ils ont décidé cela d'**eux-mêmes**.

5. Je gère mon business **moi-même**.
6. Nous avons compris cela de **nous-mêmes**.
7. Tu as appris à conduire de **toi-même**.
8. Elles ont rénové cette maison **elles-mêmes**.

EX. 5.5

1. J'ai raté mon train, est-ce que tu as eu **le tien** ?
2. **Les siens** sont bien, mais **les nôtres** sont mieux.
3. Mes amis sont espagnols, **les vôtres** sont portugais.
4. Elle a perdu son téléphone, est-ce qu'elle peut emprunter **le leur** ?

EX. 5.6

1. Quel pantalon est-ce que tu veux ? **Celui-ci**.
2. Quelle pizza est-ce que tu veux manger ? **Celle-là**.
3. Quelles vacances est-ce que tu as réservées ? **Celles-ci**.
4. Quels champignons est-ce que tu manges ? **Ceux-là**.
5. Quelle écharpe est-ce que tu préfères ? **Celle-ci**.
6. Quel téléphone as-tu acheté ? **Celui-là**.
7. Quelles chaussures est-ce que tu as commandées ? **Celles-là**.

EX. 5.7

1. Ces-chaussures-**ci** sont plus confortables que **celles-là**.
2. Elle a vu **ce** manteau mais elle préfère **celui-ci**.

EX. 5.8

1. **Ceux** de Jules sont arrivés ce matin.
2. J'ai bien aimé **celle** de Lucie.
3. Tu te rappelles de mes cousins, **ceux** qui habitent en Louisiane ?
4. Elle a acheté **celui** en vitrine.
5. Mes réponses étaient fausses, mais **celles** de Luc étaient correctes.

EX. 5.9

1. Je pense que **cela** devrait fonctionner.
2. **Ce** n'est pas bizarre.
3. Il a prévu **ceci** et **cela**.
4. **Cela** en vaut la peine !
5. Comment **ça** va ?

EX. 5.10

1. Ça craint.
2. Ça suffit.
3. Ça ne me regarde pas.
4. Ça marche.
5. Ça me plaît.

EX. 5.11

1. **Certains** sont rentrés après le travail mais d'**autres** sont restés là-bas.
2. **Personne** n'est à l'abri d'un problème.
3. **Tout** s'est bien fini.
4. **Chacune** a eu son mot à dire.
5. **Plusieurs** ne sont pas venus, mais ce n'est pas grave.
6. **Quelque chose** me dit que ce n'est pas vrai.
7. **Quelqu'un** a téléphoné mais je ne sais pas qui.
8. **Quelques-uns** ont finalement réussi leurs examens.
9. **Quiconque** est allé à l'université sait que c'est difficile.

EX. 5.12

1. Je connais une histoire **qui** va te faire peur.
2. Les touristes **qui** étaient perdus, arrivent.
3. J'ai une tante **qui** est française.
4. C'est Marie **qui** a réussi son année.
5. Elle parle à une femme **qui** porte une robe rouge.

EX. 5.13

1. Le chat **avec qui** elle joue, s'appelle Miko. (**jouer avec**)
2. La personne **chez qui** ma fille passe le week-end est ma mère. (**passer chez**)
3. Les personnes **pour qui** je cuisine sont les clients. (**cuisiner pour**)
4. La personne **de qui** je tiens mon caractère est mon père. (**tenir de**)
5. Le chien **à qui** je pense est décédé il y a peu. (**penser à**)

EX. 5.14

1. Je connais un restaurant **que** tu vas adorer.
2. Voici le devoir **que** je viens de finir.
3. C'est pour ça **que** tu m'as fait venir ?
4. Le film **que** je regarde est horrible.
5. Tu n'as pas ouvert la lettre **que** je t'ai écrite.
6. La voiture **que** j'ai achetée est déjà en panne.
7. Le champagne **que** tu as acheté est bon ?
8. Le salon **qu'**on a installé est confortable.
9. Le chapeau **que** tu portais hier t'allait très bien.
10. Le couple **que** j'ai rencontré est un peu bizarre.

EX. 5.15

1. C'est quelque chose **dont** il est fier. (**être fier de**)
2. La juridiction **dont** je dépends va bientôt changer. (**dépendre de**)
3. C'est le résultat **dont** je suis heureuse. (**être heureuse de**)
4. Ce sont les photos **dont** je suis ravie. (**être ravie de**)
5. La glace **dont** j'ai envie est en rupture de stock. (**avoir envie de**)

EX. 5.16

1. L'endroit **où** je suis ne se trouve pas sur la carte.
2. La ville **où** nous cherchons à déménager est pleine de vie.
3. C'est le moment **où** j'ai su que c'était toi.
4. Elle ne sait pas **où** il va.
5. Le parc est un bon endroit **où** se reposer.

EX. 5.17

1. C'est la raison **pour laquelle** je ne suis pas venue.
2. La chaise **sur laquelle** elle est assise est cassée.
3. Les chemins **au bord desquels** il y a des arbres sont les plus agréables.
4. C'est ne pas le problème **auquel** je pensais.
5. C'est l'avion **au bord duquel** je vais passer mon test.
6. Ce n'est pas l'ambiance **à laquelle** je suis habitué.
7. Voici l'ordinateur **avec lequel** tu vas travailler.

EX. 5.18

1. Je ne peux pas lire **ce qui** est écrit.
2. Dis-moi **ce qui** s'est passé pendant le cours ?
3. Il n'a pas fini ses devoirs, **ce qui** n'est pas habituel.
4. Après tout **ce qui** est arrivé en 2021, j'espère que 2022 sera meilleur.

EX. 5.19

1. C'est **ce qu'**on a prévu.
2. Je ne sais pas encore **ce que** je vais chanter.
3. Pense à **ce que** tu as écrit.
4. **Ce que** je veux, c'est une semaine sans bruit.
5. Tu sais déjà **ce que** tu veux ?

EX. 5.20

1. Il m'a parlé de **ce dont** il se souvenait.
2. **Ce dont** je suis certain, c'est que demain je dois aller travailler.
3. C'est **ce dont** ils discutent.
4. C'est **ce dont** je suis responsable.
5. Ce voyage, c'est **ce dont** il a envie depuis longtemps.

EX. 5.21

1. C'est **ce à quoi** je m'attendais.
2. C'est **ce sur quoi** il travaille depuis l'année dernière.
3. C'est **ce en quoi** il croit.
4. C'est **ce pour quoi** il a acheté cet instrument.
5. C'est **ce sur quoi** il compte depuis quelques temps.

EX. 5.22

1. **Ce avec quoi** les coiffeuses travaillent peut être dangereux.
2. C'est **ce que** je pensais mais je ne voulais pas le dire.
3. C'est sa routine, c'est **ce à quoi** il est habitué.
4. **Ce qui** me dérange c'est qu'il ne prend jamais de nouvelles.
5. C'est **ce dont** les docteurs ont peur.

EX. 5.23

1. Chercher
   Je **chercherais**
   Tu **chercherais**
   On **chercherait**
   Nous **chercherions**
   Vous **chercheriez**
   Elles **chercheraient**

2. Réfléchir
   Je **réfléchirais**
   Tu **réfléchirais**
   Il **réfléchirait**
   Nous **réfléchirions**
   Vous **réfléchiriez**
   Ils **réfléchiraient**

3. Mordre
   Je **mordrais**
   Tu **mordrais**
   Il **mordrait**
   Nous **mordrions**
   Vous **mordriez**
   Ils **mordraient**

EX. 5.24

1. J'**aimerais** être en vacances !
2. Il m'a dit qu'il **serait** là à 15 heures.
3. Elle **dormirait** toute la journée si elle pouvait !
4. Il y **aurait** plus de monde s'il faisait moins froid.
5. On **voudrait** voyager plus.
6. Nous **pourrions** vous envoyer de l'argent.
7. Si tu marchais plus peut-être que tu **irais** mieux ?
8. Si elle avait plus de patience, elle **apprendrait** à cuisiner.
9. Nous **irions** au marché si nous avions plus de temps.
10. Qu'est-ce que tu **ferais** si tu gagnais un million ?

EX. 5.25

1. C'est le numéro de téléphone **que** je t'ai donné.
2. C'est **ce qui** m'intéresse.
3. Je préfère **le mien** mais je l'ai laissé à la maison.
4. **Ça** marche pour moi.
5. L'histoire **dont** je t'ai parlé est une histoire vraie.
6. **Ce** n'est pas ce que j'ai dit.
7. Tu as choisi **lequel** de ces appartements ?
8. C'est la raison **pour laquelle** j'ai introduit un dossier.
9. Est-ce que c'est **celle** de Marie ?
10. **Toi**, tu peux toujours y aller si tu veux.
11. **Plusieurs** des coureurs ont abandonné la course.
12. C'est la personne **à qui** je m'intéresse.
13. C'est **celui-ci** qu'elle veut.
14. Ne t'inquiète pas, je vais le faire **moi-même**.
15. Le restaurant **qui** a ouvert appartient à un ami.

Solutions – Les Adverbes et les Conjonctions

EX. 6.1

1. Légèrement
2. Malhonnêtement
3. Énormément
4. Couramment
5. Patiemment
6. Évidemment
7. Méchamment
8. Intensément
9. Sérieusement
10. Précisément
11. Timidement
12. Proprement
13. Gentiment
14. Profondément
15. Récemment
16. Amicalement
17. Bien
18. Premièrement
19. Mauvaisement
20. Peu

EX. 6.2

1. **Aussitôt** que la maison est vendue, nous partons au Mexique.
2. Le chien respire **bruyamment**.
3. **Pourtant** il est arrivé tôt.
4. Il a **faiblement** exprimé ses derniers vœux.
5. Il a **seulement** reçu une partie du remboursement.
6. Elle l'aime **aveuglément**.
7. Il est chanteur mais il est **aussi** auteur.
8. La tortue est arrivée tout **doucement**.
9. Nous avons **beaucoup** de choses en commun.
10. Il n'est **jamais** à l'heure !

EX. 6.3

1. Est-ce qu'il est **déjà** arrivé ?
2. Elle se plaint **moins** que d'habitude.
3. Il y a **trop** de mouches ici.
4. C'est **mieux** de partir maintenant.
5. Est-ce que tu as **assez** mangé ?
6. Ils avaient **tellement** à voir !
7. Est-ce qu'il est **là** ?
8. Il est **souvent** appelé chez le directeur.
9. **Heureusement** elle se plaît bien à son nouveau travail.
10. Je lis le journal **quotidiennement**.

EX. 6.4

1. Il **a enfin compris** comment opérer cette machine.
2. Après avoir découvert cela, nous **sommes vite partis**.
3. Elle **a souvent parlé** de cette possibilité.
4. On **a encore manqué** le train !
5. Il **est déjà parti** mais il va bientôt revenir.
6. Nous ne **sommes jamais tombés** en manque de riz.
7. Cette pièce de théâtre **a bien fini**.
8. Vous **avez beaucoup appris** durant l'année.
9. Il n'**a jamais dit** ça.
10. Est-ce que vous **avez assez mangé** ?

EX. 6.5

1. Ce n'est pas la **bonne** adresse.
2. Je te souhaite un **bon** rétablissement.
3. Il devrait faire **bon** ce week-end.
4. On a passé une **bonne** soirée avec nos amis.
5. C'est une **bonne** idée mais je ne sais pas si ça va marcher.
6. Est-ce que ce plat est **bon** ?
7. J'espère que nous aurons des **bonnes** notes.
8. On a reçu des **bons** d'achat pour ce magasin.
9. **Bon** appétit !
10. C'est vraiment **bon** marché !

EX. 6.6

1. Je ne sais pas encore, on verra **bien**.
2. **Bien** sûr que non !
3. Est-ce que tu te sens **bien** ?
4. Elle a **bien** étudié je pense.
5. Tu vas **bien** ?

EX. 6.7

1. C'est **bien** !
2. C'est **bon** !
3. C'est **bien** !
4. C'est **bien** !
5. C'est **bon** !

EX. 6.8

1. Tu n'es pas **toujours / encore** partie ?
2. Il a **toujours** cette couverture avec lui.
3. Vous jouez **toujours / encore** à ce jeu ?
4. Est-ce que tu en veux **encore** ?
5. Honnêtement, c'était **encore** mieux que sur la brochure.
6. Tu espères **toujours / encore** voir un koala ?
7. Nous sommes **toujours** ensemble.
8. Il reste **encore** du café ?
9. C'est **toujours** bon à savoir.
10. Est-ce qu'ils veulent **encore / toujours** faire une offre ?

EX. 6.9

1. Avez-vous **déjà** visité ce musée ?
2. Non, nous ne l'avons **jamais** visité.
3. C'est difficile à croire que tu n'as **jamais** vu ce film.
4. Je l'ai **déjà** vu mais je ne m'en souviens plus.
5. Est-ce que l'avion a **déjà** décollé ?

EX. 6.10

1. Visiter
   Que je **visite**
   Que tu **visites**
   Qu'il **visite**
   Que nous **visitions**
   Que vous **visitiez**
   Qu'elles **visitent**

2. Nourrir
   Que je **nourrisse**
   Que tu **nourrisses**
   Qu'il **nourrisse**
   Que nous **nourrissions**
   Que vous **nourrissiez**
   Qu'ils **nourrissent**

3. Descendre
   Que je **descende**
   Que tu **descendes**
   Qu'elle **descende**
   Que nous **descendions**
   Que vous **descendiez**
   Qu'elles **descendent**

EX. 6.11

1. Il faut que je **parte**.
2. Ce n'est pas normal qu'il **arrive** à cette heure !
3. On a cet appareil pour qu'il **puisse** se lever tout seul.
4. On joue aux cartes en attendant qu'il **se décide**.
5. Prends une décision avant qu'il ne **soit** trop tard.
6. C'est dommage qu'elle **travaille** autant.
7. Il faut que tu **mettes** ton manteau.
8. Il faut que je **boive** plus d'eau.
9. J'exige que tu **finisses** ton repas.
10. Il ne faut pas qu'ils **sachent** la vérité.

EX. 6.12

1. Ce sont mes frères **et** mes sœurs.
2. On n'a trouvé **ni** trésor **ni** indices.
3. Cela prendra du temps **mais** tu seras content quand tu auras fini.
4. Nous nous sommes disputés, **or** pour une fois j'avais raison.
5. Je vais pendre le canard **mais** pas trop cuit.
6. Il a accepté **car** il avait le temps.
7. Est-ce que tu prends du sucre **ou** du lait dans ton café ?
8. C'est **donc** lui dont tu me parlais ?
9. Je suis professeur **donc** je connais la réponse.
10. Je vais étudier ce matin **ou** cet après-midi.

EX. 6.13

1. **Puisque** c'est comme ça, autant ne pas y aller.
2. **Quand** tu arrives, nous en discuterons.
3. **Quoique** malade, il est tout de même venu.
4. Il est vrai **que** ce n'est pas facile.
5. **Lorsque** tu arrives, est-ce que tu peux commencer le ménage ?
6. **Si** je ne suis pas revenu dans une heure, appelle la police.
7. **Comme** je n'ai pas été choisie, je suis rentrée à la maison.
8. J'espère **que** tu vas bien.
9. Je me demande **toujours** si tu es sincère.
10. **Puisque** tu es là, est-ce que tu peux m'aider ?

EX. 6.14

1. **Si jamais** vous arrivez avant moi, appelez la réception pour ouvrir la porte.
2. Il peut rester **à condition qu'**il soit calme.
3. Elle a préparé assez à manger **pour que** tout le monde mange.
4. Reste ici **jusqu'à ce qu'**elle arrive.
5. **Même si** tu disais la vérité, ils ne te croiraient pas.
6. Il dort **tandis que** tout le monde travaille.
7. **Maintenant que** tu es là, est-ce que tu peux regarder à l'imprimante ?
8. **Au cas où** tu n'aurais pas compris, c'est non.
9. Il fouille son téléphone **de peur qu'**il ne le trompe.
10. **À moins que** tu le commandes maintenant, il ne sera pas livré.

EX. 6.15

1. Elle a étudié à New York **et** à Los Angeles.
2. Il était là **quand** tu as téléphoné.
3. **Puisque** tu le dis !
4. Il ne s'est pas arrêté après sa blessure, **si bien qu'**il a besoin de rééducation.
5. Tu es à l'hôtel **ou** à la plage ?
6. Je vais le jeter **à moins que** tu ne le veuilles ?
7. Ils sauront **lorsqu'**il sera prêt.
8. Elle est habituée à nager **vu qu'**elle a grandi près de la mer.
9. **Maintenant que** je l'ai vu, je ne vois plus que ça.
10. **Même si** j'avais le temps, je n'ai pas envie de venir.
11. Ils ne savent pas ce que c'est **mais** ils ont fait des tests.
12. On va rester ici **jusqu'à ce que** la tempête passe.
13. **Si** le client ne vient pas chercher sa commande, elle sera annulée.
14. Appelle-moi **dès que** tu arrives.
15. On est en retard **car** il y a des travaux.

EX. 7.1

1. Il est parti sans **bagages.**
2. **L'arbre** risque de tomber sur la maison.
3. Il a reçu **un avertissement** à son travail.
4. Est-ce que tu as vu **les nouvelles** ce matin ?
5. **La voiture** traverse **le pont** à toute vitesse.
6. Elle n'a pas besoin de **temps.**
7. Il est devenu **docteur** il y a quelques mois.
8. **L'agent immobilier** a arrangé un rendez-vous.
9. **Les jeunes mariés** ont fait le tour du monde.
10. J'ai acheté **une glace** et **un biscuit.**
11. **Le passager** est demandé à l'accueil.
12. **La tempête** s'approche rapidement.
13. **Le train** est encore en retard.
14. Est-ce que tu as fait **les courses** ?
15. C'est **une** incroyable **professeur.**

EX. 7.2

1. **Les oiseaux sont** sur la branche.
2. **Elles sont parties** ce matin avant le lever du soleil.
3. **Vous les avez** reçus ?
4. **Ils se sont mariés** il y a quelques mois.
5. **Vous êtes** au courant de **ces histoires** ?
6. **Ces pâtisseries coûtent** seulement 3 dollars.
7. **Ce sont les miens.**
8. **On s'est dépêchés** de partir.
9. **Les assistants regardent** l'opération de loin.
10. **Finissez vos** assiette**s.**

EX. 7.3

1. **Il est** parti de bonne heure
2. **C'est** mon petit frère, Jules.
3. **Il y a** 3 heures que je travaille sur ce projet.
4. **C'est** moi.
5. **C'est** une mauvaise idée !
6. **Il est** courageux de travailler autant.
7. Est-ce que **c'est** ton tour ?
8. **Ce sont** ses parents, Marc et Julie.
9. Tu penses que **c'est** bien comme ça ?
10. **Il y a** du fromage dans le frigo si tu veux.

EX. 7.4

1. J'ai reçu **son** courrier par erreur.
2. **Votre** voiture a été emboutie dans l'accident.
3. **Mes** parents ont déménagé en Espagne.
4. Tu as oublié **tes** affaires à la salle de sport.
5. **Sa** lettre est arrivée après quelques mois.
6. **Ton** portefeuille est tombé de **ta** poche.
7. **Leur** réception est prévue pour décembre.
8. **Mes** grands-parents viennent dîner ce week-end.
9. **Sa** maison a été détruite à cause des feux de forêt.
10. **Ses** symptômes se sont aggravés ces derniers jours.

EX. 7.5 Personnel

EX. 7.6

1. Je **ne** suis **pas encore** là.
2. Ma mère **ne** me laisse **pas** sortir tard le soir.
3. On **n'**a **pas** assez de nourriture pour la semaine.
4. Elle **ne** prend **pas** ses médicaments régulièrement.
5. Il **ne** travaillait **pas** ce jour-là.
6. Elle **ne** consomme **pas** trop de boissons sucrées.
7. Il **n'**a **pas** enfoncé le clou trop loin.
8. Il **ne** veut **pas** de vélo électrique pour son anniversaire.
9. Nous **n'**avons **pas** cueilli plus de 3 kilos de pommes.
10. Elle **n'**a **pas** trouvé son sac à main dans la poubelle.

EX. 7.7

1. Je suis **d'**accord avec toi.
2. Ce tableau vient **du** Maroc.
3. Tu as beaucoup **de** devoirs aujourd'hui ?
4. Nous sommes prêts **à** partir.
5. J'ai mal **à** la tête depuis ce matin.
6. L'avion décolle **de** Paris et sera là dans une heure ou deux.
7. Est-ce que tu as acheté un cadeau **à** tes parents ?
8. Le design **de** cette bouteille **de** vin est parfait.
9. Il faut boire 3 litres **d'**eau par jour.
10. C'est difficile **à** dire.

EX. 7.8

1. Hier, je suis allé(e) au magasin.
2. Demain, j'irai à la pharmacie.
3. Je viens de partir de la maison.
4. En 2015, j'allais à la piscine 3 fois par semaine.
5. En général, je vais chez ma sœur tous les lundis.

EX. 7.9

1. Je suis arrivée **à l'**heure.
2. Ils sont partis en week-end **sans / avec** les enfants.
3. Elle aime bien se regarder **dans** le miroir.
4. Tu as pris rendez-vous **chez** le dermatologue ?
5. Le voyage **aux** États-Unis semble incroyable !
6. Nous serons **à** Paris **jusqu'à** lundi.
7. Il est assis **à côté de** son père.
8. Je suis **devant** la gare mais je ne te vois pas.
9. Elle est arrivée **parmi** les 3 premières finalistes.
10. Il a été renvoyé **à cause de** son erreur.

EX. 7.10

1. Est-ce que tu as déchargé la voiture ?
2. Ça fait longtemps que tu fumes ?
3. Est-ce qu'il s'est déjà préparé pour aller au lit ?
4. La voiture ne s'est pas arrêtée ?
5. Est-ce que tu penses que ça va marcher ?
6. Sais-tu jouer aux cartes ?
7. Pouvez-vous répéter s'il vous plaît ?
8. Est-ce qu'il n'a jamais revu sa femme ?
9. Qui a vaincu le dernier niveau ?
10. Est-ce que tu as le temps ?

EX. 7.11

1. Un homme **gentil**
2. Une chanson **originale**
3. Des oiseaux **bleus**
4. Une **grande** communauté
5. Une **vieille** église
6. Une voiture **blanche**
7. Une idée **dangereuse**
8. Une route **étroite**
9. Un repas **chaud**
10. Une douche **froide**
11. Un chien **méchant**
12. Une voiture **rapide**
13. Un **gros** chien
14. Des friandises **délicieuses**
15. Une moto **bruyante**
16. Un terrain **énorme**
17. De l'eau **marron**
18. La peau **sèche**
19. Un chat **affamé**
20. Une jambe **cassée**

EX. 7.12

1. Elle **la lui** a offert**e**.
2. Tu ne **le** regardes pas ?
3. Le policier **lui** ordonne de s'arrêter.
4. Elle **lui** a fait mal en faisant la prise de sang.
5. Est-ce que cela **leur** convient ?
6. Je **l'**ai cassé**e** en vidant le lave-vaisselle.
7. Elle **les lui** a transmis.
8. Ils **la leur** ont promis**e**.
9. Tu me **l'**as donné.
10. Nous **lui** avons dit que le professeur est absent.

EX. 7.13

1. Il **en** est mort.
2. Est-ce que tu **y** restes ce week-end ?
3. Tu **en** prends dans ton café ?
4. Il **y** est toujours.
5. Vous **en** voulez ?
6. Est-ce que tu **y** es déjà allée ?
7. Nous **en** avons apporté **une**.
8. Le docteur **en** est satisfait.
9. La voiture **y** est.
10. Elle n'**y** est pas allée.

EX. 7.14

1. C'est le chien **que** j'ai adopté.
2. C'est le chien **qui** a été adopté.
3. C'est toi **qui** lui as dit ça ?
4. Je dois refaire le test **que** j'ai raté.
5. Les chaussures **que** tu as achetées sont magnifiques.
6. C'est une blague **que** je ne trouve pas drôle.
7. C'est une blague **qui** est drôle.
8. La dame **que** tu vois est célèbre.
9. Tu peux prendre le plat **qui** est dans le frigo.
10. C'est lui **qui** a demandé le divorce.

EX. 7.15

1. Elle ne comprend pas **ce qui** lui a pris.
2. Après tout **ce qu'**elle t'a fait !
3. Ce n'est pas **ce que** nous avons payé.
4. Je ne comprends pas **ce dont** tu parles.
5. **Ce dont** tu as besoin, c'est de plus de repos.

6. **Ce qui** est bizarre, c'est qu'elle a disparu sans une trace.
7. J'ignore **ce à quoi** elle pense.
8. **Ce pour quoi** il travaille c'est sa famille.
9. C'est **ce que** je t'ai dit !
10. Je ne sais pas **ce à quoi** tu joues mais je n'aime pas ça.

EX. 7.16

1. C'est arrivé **rapidement**.
2. Ils s'aiment **passionnément**.
3. Ils sont arrivés **vers** 15 heures mais ils sont **déjà** partis.
4. **Lentement** mais **sûrement**.
5. Cette route est fermée **depuis** des mois.
6. Il a trouvé une maison **facilement**.
7. Elle a annoncé **ouvertement** son divorce.
8. Je vais rester **ici** quelques semaines de plus.
9. Tu es **toujours** là ?
10. Il a **enfin** compris ce que j'essayais de lui expliquer.

EX. 7.17

1. Est-ce qu'il vit **toujours** en Espagne ?
2. Qu'est-ce que tu fais **déjà** là ?
3. C'est **bon** pour la santé.
4. Je vais reprendre **encore** un peu de café.
5. Est-ce que tu t'es **bien** reposé ?
6. Il fait du **bon** travail.
7. Les enfants ne sont pas **toujours** faciles.
8. Il a **déjà** 10 ans ?
9. Il a **bien** compris ce que je lui ai dit.
10. Je ne l'avais pas **encore** à ce moment-là.

EX. 7.18

1. Il a dit oui **puis** il a dit non.
2. Cela ne sert à rien **puisque** c'est fini.
3. Tu préfères le jaune **ou** l'orange ?
4. Je suis d'accord **à condition que** tu rentres tôt.
5. Allons au magasin et **ensuite** au garage.
6. Est-ce que ça va **si** je viens maintenant ?
7. **Comme** je t'ai dit, l'appartement est déjà loué.
8. Elle était en vacances **alors que** je travaillais.
9. Il est indécis **parce que** son budget est serré.
10. Ils pensaient pouvoir venir **mais** il a eu un empêchement.

EX. 7.19

1. J'espère que tu trouveras un travail.
2. Combien est-ce qu'il gagne ?
3. Je n'ai rien remarqué.
4. Nous avons peint les murs blancs.
5. Le professeur n'a pas toujours raison.
6. Quel film as-tu vu récemment ?
7. L'ascenseur est en panne.
8. Tu marches trop vite pour moi !
9. Cette famille a tout perdu.
10. Le lave-vaisselle utilise moins d'eau.

EX. 7.20

1. Tu te rappelles de **moi** ?
2. Est-ce que c'est **le** mien que tu as dans ton sac ?
3. Les fleurs que j'ai achet**ées** sont déjà mortes.
4. **Le** hamburger est fait de viande.
5. Ce sont des **nouveaux rideaux**.
6. Qu'est-ce que tu regardes **à la** télévision ?
7. Je ne sais pas **qui** est cette personne.
8. Nous **sommes** parti**s** tôt pour aller à l'aéroport.
9. Tu veux du café **ou** du thé ?
10. J'**en** ai besoin !

Made in the USA
Middletown, DE
02 September 2024

60244358R10205